LOUIS KAHN
DRAWING TO FIND OUT

The Dominican Motherhouse
and the Patient Search for Architecture

Michael Merrill

LOUIS KAHN
DRAWING TO FIND OUT
THE DOMINICAN MOTHERHOUSE
AND THE PATIENT SEARCH
FOR ARCHITECTURE

Lars Müller Publishers

"I don't want pictures. I just want to find things out." Piet Mondrian, 1957

CONTENTS

To make a plan is to determine and fix ideas. It is to have had ideas. It is to so order these ideas that they become intelligible, capable of execution and communicable. It is essential therefore to exhibit a precise intention, and to have had ideas in order to to furnish oneself with an intention. A plan is to some extent a summary like an analytical contents table. In a form so condensed that it seems as clear as crystal and like geometric figure, it contains an enormous quantity of ideas and the impulse of intention. Le Corbusier, *Vers une architecture*, 1923

Drawings and tracings are like the hands of the blind touching the surfaces of the face in order to understand the sense of volume, depth and penetration. John Hejduk, "Thoughts of an Architect," 1986

The journey of the following pages begins with curiosity and a plan. The plan is that of Louis Kahn's iconic and enigmatic Dominican Motherhouse (1965–69), that unbuilt convent conceived at the peak of Kahn's career for a site not far from his native Philadelphia. If we may rightly use the well-worn "iconic" for that project, this is not only because of its repeated publication over the past decades, but because it has so graphically epitomized this architect's mature thinking of space. Indeed, it's easy to see in that plan almost case-study demonstrations of some of the central themes in Kahn's late work: the discrete room as the beginning of architecture, the dialogue between individual and collective, the relationship between structure and light, the role of spatial archetypes, or the reciprocity of built and unbuilt space.

The Dominican Motherhouse belongs to—and is arguably the apotheosis of—Kahn's juxtapositional, "society of room" plans, those late-career compositions in which spaces "speak to each other" in search of a whole greater than the sum of their parts.[1] Previously described in terms of its debts to both Ecole des Beaux-Arts methodology and to modernist *bricolage,* there seems to be something still more elemental at work in this plan, something which transcends both of those sources and which has possessed the gravity to pull at more than a few architects' imaginations over the past four decades.[2]

1 "To other graphic representations of this type we might count: the First Unitarian Church (1959–62), the Meeting House for the Salk Institute (1959–65), the National Assembly of Bangladesh (1962–83), St. Andrew's Priory (1961–67), and the Indian Institute of Management (1962–73).

2 It's tempting to speculate on the architects who have lingered in the spaces of the Dominican Motherhouse over the past four decades: almost certainly, of earlier generations, James Stirling, Rafael Moneo, and Tadao Ando; and perhaps, more recently, Enric Miralles, David Chipperfield, and SANAA.

There are, of course, Kahn's mesmerizing, mandala-like plan geometries at work; here, though, apparently breaking open so that we might enter them with a little less awe than usual. Then there is that tenuous balance between the stasis of discrete rooms and a dynamism typically associated with the modernist free plan. In fact, after longer study the plan seems to be as much a means for setting up pairs of opposites as for ordering functions: teasing out tensions between part and whole, center and periphery, symmetry and disorder, figure and ground, the additive and the subtractive, etc. It's easy to sense in the parti a medieval monastery in the process of playing hide-and-seek; and even without instruction from Kahn's texts we may intuit an ambitious social program at work when we imagine the lives of the inhabitants unfolding within the plan.

If, in spite of its "iconic" status, the Dominican Motherhouse has remained enigmatic, this has been due to the sparse evidence available. In most of its publications a single ground-floor plan (more often than not of a not-quite-final scheme) and occasionally an elevation study or two illustrate the project: no upper floor or basement plans, no perspectives, rarely sections or models; little to explain the means of construction, the intricacies of interior space or the interaction between building and site.[3] Seeming to promise more than they prove, it is doubtless the suggestive power of these few drawings which, together with the willful energy of that plan, have inspired other architects to fulfill with their own designs the potentials suggested by the unrealized project.

And so, it was no minor revelation for this architect to encounter, and to slowly leaf through, the sixteen portfolios holding the over nine hundred sketches, drawings, and prints that make up this project.[4] Kahn's charcoal-clouded worksheets, his associates' meticulously drafted plans, messages in margins from master to assistant, area calculations, untold themes and variations: more than merely filling in the gaps of the final design, these drawings, together with a box of telling notes and correspondence, transport the patient viewer into the thicket of its three-year genesis.

3 See Michael Merrill, *Louis Kahn: On the Thoughtful Making of Spaces*, Baden, 2010, for a discussion of the project's publication history.

4 The following study was based on visits to the Architectural Archives of the University of Pennsylvania in fall 2004, spring 2006, and again in fall 2009.

The curiosity that spurred my visit to Kahn's archive at the University of Pennsylvania is that of a designing architect and teacher of architectural design, one of those who by profession oscillate between seeking and giving instruction. And so, my reasons for being there were slightly yet decidedly different than those of an architectural historian or scholar (those more accustomed archive-dwellers). These reasons had more to do with an interest in watching depth, coherence, and multivalence arise in a work than in questions of influence or context; they were more about the drawing of connections within a work than about situating that work from without. And while I was certain that there was nothing like a "process" to be found here (one word which Kahn particularly disliked), I was confident that lingering over these drawings would bring rewards beyond the pleasure of this particular project's story. If pressed to give a name to what I was there for, I would reply that more than attempting to discover a method or to describe a history, I was seeking to immerse myself in a specific *culture of making*.

To follow the still-tangible thoughts of Kahn and his associates over the three-year course of this project is to re-enact an engrossing journey, one complete with false starts, contradictions, slow accumulations, and hard-won insights. The plot thickens as the sheets are successively, carefully taken from the portfolios. A hypothesis is wagered and a next coherent step is sought. Why was one configuration found better than another? Why was an entire scheme redrawn in order to change a few lines? Why was an original detail abandoned in favor of a far less compelling one? From sheet to sheet the forms move, shift, evolve. Sometimes the whole will determine its parts; sometimes the part seems to lead the whole. Knowing the final outcome in advance does nothing to reduce the fascination of the story, for while leafing through the schemes it becomes apparent just how precarious the existence of that well-known design actually was, how near it often was to failure, and how ready to embark on alternative paths. Not everything emerging from the portfolios can freely be called "masterly"; in fact, much looks rather rough, even naive, with the architects' uncertainty or frustration at times almost palpable.

"A building is a struggle, not a miracle."[5] Anyone who has struggled to make architecture can likely empathize with Kahn and his associates in their strenuous search. With his drawings spread out on the archive's big table, Kahn feels much closer, more alive than that canonized, sage-on-the-mountaintop who inhabits so much of the literature on him.[6] "To make someone an icon is to make him an abstraction, and abstractions are incapable of vital communication with living people."[7] Indeed. The drawings presented here—a selection of approximately two hundred—are significant for, among other things, that empathetic moment, for offering an opportunity to see beyond that safely canonized Kahn to a colleague (admittedly, a considerably more accomplished one) wrestling with everyday problems of designing quite similar to our own. They offer us glimpses of his work from the *inside*. This is of course of great value in piecing together a more comprehensive picture of one of the past century's great architects, as well as in better understanding one of his most compelling unbuilt works. These are two good reasons for taking this excursion. Another reason, I suggest of at least equal interest, is what this might mean for us and for how we work as architects.

In a concrete architectural project, long-term ideals and ideas meet circumstantial conditions and attempt to become manifest through them. Design creates meaning out of intent through countless small everyday acts: of conjecturing and refuting; of (physically and meta-phorically) drawing connections between things; of enclosing, opening, shifting, finding distance. If the Dominican Motherhouse is typical of Kahn's work, then it is because it has come to life not through any simple act of representation—be it in a sweeping expressionist gesture or in illustration of a particular theory or procedure—but through its purposefully limited and elementary architectural means of accumulating and ordering a linked multitude of sensations and meanings.

If the "space" of designing is a timely place to reflect on Kahn's work—and by extension, our own—this is, among other reasons, because it has much to intimate about what discourse and theory have tended to leave out: things like skill, tacit knowledge, and the power of circumstance; about

5 Louis I. Kahn, "The Architect Speaks" [1953], interview by Henry F.S. Cooper, *Yale Daily News*, special supplement: "The New Art Gallery and Design Center Dedication Issue," November 6, 1953.

6 For a sample how rarified the air can get in Kahn's part of the Pantheon, see for example the titles of these essays in a publication celebrating Kahn's centennial: "Jehovah on Olympus: Louis Kahn and the End of Modernism" (Vincent Scully), "Cosmos and State" (William Curtis), and "The Emperor of Light" (Martin Filler), *Monografías de Arquitectura y Vivienda*, February 2001.

7 David Foster Wallace, "Joseph Frank's Dostoevsky," in *Consider the Lobster and Other Essays*, New York, 2005, p. 261.

experience and setting the known at risk; about collaboration; about moving forward with doubt and incomplete information. A drawing-board perspective of design as a means of architectural inquiry is not as materialistic or anti-intellectual as it might appear to some, nor does it offer a position-to-end-all-positions. What it does offer, among its other virtues, is a mild corrective to much of the theory and criticism of the last decades, which have tended toward the speculative, the hermeneutic; toward the positioning of architecture in ever-more-distant fields from which it has been ever-more difficult to credibly bridge the gap to making. If theory tends to analyze, contextualize, and compartmentalize, design is by nature synthetic, is its own way of knowledge-in-motion, of architectural research, and thus worthy of and waiting for our reflection.[8] The rare opportunity of Kahn's drawings—not only the results of thought, but in themselves a way of thinking—makes an excellent place to start.

While some might maintain that in the last forty years an unbridgeable gap has opened between Kahn and ourselves, making his thought and thus these drawings unlikely guides for us, I would propose otherwise. There *is* of course a tangible gap, and among its many causes has been the intellectual climate mentioned above. Another cause—one of crucial interest in our case—has been technological. For many architects born after the Dominican Motherhouse, Kahn's tools and drawing culture may seem to have more in common with those of Palladio than with those of our own digitalized practice. Our new tools have not only affected the conception and production of architecture, have not only restructured our profession's social and value systems, they have also changed our way of seeing. And while the richness and intelligence of the drawings on the following pages is self-evident, not all of their virtues are immediately accessible. This seems to make, if not an explanation, then some form of an introduction necessary. In the interest of thinking across that gap, I offer the following meditations on Kahn's drawings as a part of his culture of making; not as appraisals, critiques, or conclusions, but rather as questions to be taken along on the following narrative, and perhaps further, into our own, evolving cultures of making.

8 For a rare and provocative case study of architectural design as a form of knowledge-in-motion, see Albena Yeneva, *Made by the Office for Metropolitan Architecture,* Rotterdam, 2009.

DRAWING SPACE: TOWARD A CULTURE OF MEANS AND ENDS

9 Peter Lynch, "Architecture: An Overview," lecture at Cranbrook Academy, http://www.cranbrookart.edu/arch/ped3.html (accessed June 6, 2005, no longer available.)

Even a quick leaf through the drawings on the following pages makes obvious that traditional orthographic projections—sections, elevations and plans (especially plans!)—have been the architects' prime means of thinking spaces. What many will find astonishing is that in developing a project of such spatial complexity the architects built only one small model (apparently more for the benefit of their clients than for themselves), and other than an occasional thumbnail sketch, did not prepare a single axonometric or perspective drawing.

While this method of projecting spaces—a "plan-as-generator" culture—may have been self-evident for the Beaux-Arts heir Kahn (and for architects similarly raised since the Renaissance), the preeminence of this method of spatial projection has waned in recent decades. There have been reasons for this: an increased concern for architecture-as-representation (driven both by theory and media) has shifted many architects' attentions toward outer *shape* rather than toward a comprehensive Gestalt, while at the same time pragmatism and economics have run counter to the demanding discipline of a well-tempered plan. (A plan such as that of the Dominican Motherhouse isn't just *drawn,* but *emerges.*) At least as important as this, computer-aided, three-dimensional modeling and rendering have begun to challenge, even replace, classical orthographic projections as the privileged means of presenting, but also of projecting architectural space. Three-dimensional software has become ever easier, better, and more complex, leading to its use ever earlier in the design process (and ever earlier in the educational process), with things appearing ever more "realistic" from the very first drawings onward.[9]

One appeal of the drawings in this book for us as architects must be similar to that of partitas for musicians; for like musical notation, they are precise without being complete: they slow our vision, engage our imagination, and employ us in the making of the work, which in this case consists of forming spaces in our mind's (trained) eye. In this sense, the drawings presented here are not pictures for consumption, but objects of engagement, invitations to "collaborate" in the work before us. (If no three-dimensional renderings of the Dominican Motherhouse have been prepared for this publication, this is so as not to deny you, dear reader, the pleasure of making it "your own," and so, I submit, bring you that much closer to the architects who conceived its spaces.)

One of the questions these drawings seem to beg is, what qualities of space are foregrounded by the various means of its projection? Bound up with the advantages of abstraction, one way in which the well-tempered plan remains unexcelled is in its ability to represent all parts of an environment simultaneously, so that the architect may be everywhere at once. "Open before us is the architect's plan. Next to it a sheet of music. The architect fleetingly reads his composition as a structure of elements and spaces in their light. The musician reads with the same overallness." [10] Kahn participates in the drawing's conventions, understanding its distances to reality as helpful, using it as a tool for linking and interweaving small and large, part and whole, mass and void. A well-drawn floor plan/site plan will tend to unfold in the architect's mind more fully, into more dimensions, than a stationary perspective or a sequential 3D model, intimating not only elapsed time, but expansion, contraction, gravity, light, structure, etc. By making palpable the forces of interior and exterior at work, Kahn's "sculpted" charcoal drawings often remind us how the convention of a plan's cut walls may help foster an inside outside thinking of space. "Architecture as the wall between inside and outside becomes the spatial record of its reconciliation and its drama." [11] Look, for example, at the plans on pages 105, 117, and 173, and you may begin to sense that they consist of linked series of "insides," nestled in other "insides," in a reciprocal handling of built and natural space. By dwelling in the Dominican Motherhouse's "interiorist" plans we may begin to understand the "soft," receptive character of Kahn's spaces as an antidote to the relatively common, "exteriorist" way of seeing his work as consisting of "hard" volumes. And if you are, as Kahn was, urgently concerned with the social dimensions of space, the plan is a map of locales to be lived in, a choreography of choice, of probabilities, of human presence and absence.

10 Louis Kahn, "The Room, the Street, and Human Agreement" [1971], in *Louis I. Kahn: Writings, Lectures, Interviews*, ed. Alessandra Latour, New York, 1991. First published in the *AIA Journal* 56 (1971).

11 Robert Venturi, *Complexity and Contradiction in Architecture*, New York, 1966, pp. 88–89.

The Dominican Motherhouse is a compelling case of rich and multivalent spatial ends achieved through decidedly simple projective means. Those spaces are, of course, not inherent in the method itself, but rather in Kahn's cultivated and reflexive use of it. The drawings on these pages not only give occasion to reconsider the sense, sensuality, and strengths of their method, they pose, by extension, the question of how we might begin to organize our expanding repertoire into new, more reflexive, cultures of ends and means.

DRAWING A DIALOGUE: TOWARD A CULTURE OF COLLABORATION

Kahn has been aptly named a "gregarious loner," as stubbornly solitary as he was dependent upon others in his creative endeavours.[12] Although he never ceased to condemn design-by-committee and steadfastly held to the idea that he was a one-man practice, the entire spectrum of his creativity—from the gradual development of a philosophy to the final execution of building details—is in fact a case study in influence and reciprocity. This intertwining of interests and talents has been discussed elsewhere: in regard to his intellectual development and his profes-sional positioning (the influences of teacher Paul Cret, of colleagues and enablers such as George Howe, Oscar Stonerov, Anne Tyng, or Robert Venturi), in regard to the bridging of his technical deficits (the engineer August Komendant, associates such as Marshall Meyers), or in other felicitous give-and-takes (such as those with client Jonas Salk, with Isamu Noguchi, Luis Barragán, or Buckminster Fuller).[13] The drawings before you provide a glimpse of another, less public but no less important area of collaboration: that everyday drawing board exchange between Kahn and his associates.

We can see in these drawings a form of dialogue: Kahn's sometimes vague, sometimes certain leads; the associates' precisely drafted translations of Kahn's evocative sketches; his rough revisions of their fine plans; their variations of his themes—a pulsing between ambivalence and concreteness, opening and closing, which alternately drives the project forward and brakes

12 Michael J. Lewis, "The Gregarious Loner," book review of Carter Wiseman's *Louis I. Kahn: Beyond Time and Style: A Life in Architecture, Commentary Magazine Online* (July/August 2007), http://www.commentarymagazine.com/viewarticle.cfm/louis-i--kahn-by-carter-wiseman-10910?search=1 (accessed June 11, 2010).

13 See Sarah Williams Goldhagen, *Louis Kahn's Situated Modernism,* New Haven and London, 2001, for a valuable study of Kahn in discourse with his contemporaries.

its movement. (Touching in this back-and-forth play are the assistants' occasional attempts at second-guessing the master by doing what he might have done five years earlier.) While Kahn remains a drawing presence in this project—in all of his projects—from the initial mark to the final mortar joint, it's not always clear whether it is he or his assistant who is the initiator of a given move. What *is* clear is that both the quality of Kahn's work and the continuity of his decades-long explorations were grounded in his ability to find that difficult and delicate balance between leading and leaving space for his helpers. And so we see, for example, Kahn take up his assistant's early suggestion to turn it into his own lead (page 37), or later define parts in a very precise manner so that his assistants might better work on the whole (page 89), only to still later throw a cloud of doubt over the considerable work done thus far (page 146).

The drawings for the Dominican Motherhouse, while not offering any neat recipes for joint effort, do create an atmosphere, do project a sense of how the drawn part of this office's culture of collaboration looked and felt. Architecture is an art of synergy and mutual enabling, yet the complex histories of its collaborations remain largely untold. Besides helping to un-shroud the popular myth of the solitary genius, one benefit of such drawings is that they might awaken curiosity for the study of those collaborative cultures, giving cause for reflection on our own.[14]

14 See Guy Nordenson, "The Lineage of Structure and the Kimbell Art Museum," *Lotus International* 98 (1998), pp. 28–48, for an in-depth study of Kahn in collaboration with the structural engineer August Komendant.

DRAWN ON YELLOW PAPER: TOWARD A CULTURE OF LINGERING

American architects will occasionally be asked by colleagues from overseas—where architects' paper is almost universally white—whence our strange penchant for yellow sketching paper? One answer, one fitting to Kahn's drawings and to his preference for the thinnest of yellow paper, is that it is a sign—like a painter's flag—for work-in-progress; that however detailed and elaborate that which is drawn upon it may be, it is in fact still "wet," in flux, subject to change, criticism, rejection. (In Kahn's office, white vellum was generally reserved for the binding construction drawing phase.) And so, painstakingly drafted drawings such as the elevations on pages 197–199 become the curious inverses of computer prints, upon which even the most tentative thought can take on an unintended sense of finality. Of course, yellow paper will not make one a better designer, but in Kahn's case it does help to broach a question. In what way can the Dominican Motherhouse—with its nearly three-year gestation, and its failure due, in part, to its own slowness—serve as a model?

For the contemporary architect, equipped with a two-click, copy-paste command, the tedious redrawing of entire plans by Kahn's associates in order to change a few details or dimensions may seem hopelessly outmoded (see, for example, pages 158–163). Imagine spending days doing what can be executed in seconds! And while few of us would surrender our digital enablers for T-squares and triangles, longer looks at those older plans do intimate that something may have been left behind in the tempo change. For one: often those nearly-identical plans reveal, upon closer study, that a few changes made in one part have lead to subtle changes in other parts; that through its meticulous redrawing the plan is given the opportunity be treated as a Gestalt, as something organic, a living thing.

An architects' repeated tracing and retracing of lines amounts to more than a mere transfer of information, but is in and of itself a way of knowing, a meditative sinking into the plan, a kinesthetic grooving and reviewing of its information: its spaces, its details, the topography which it occupies. It is a recurrently reset search for opportunities for "stopping our pencils at the joints of pouring, erecting." [15] In this, a plan in the hands of an architect is not qualitatively different from wood in the hands of a sculptor or an instrument in the hands of a musician: to repeatedly "grasp" something is to slowly understand its nature. As anyone who has learned through repetition can attest, there can be something decidedly sensuous in this. So it is not surprising, in sifting through Kahn's drawings, to sense him yielding to the seduction and pure pleasure of repetition: watching raptly as those squares shift, turn, and interact in countless spatial-ornamental variations. In this way, his meditations are perhaps not so unlike those of Picasso's series-drawings: an art described by Rosalind Krauss as "a function of its *pulse.*" [16]

15 Louis Kahn, "How to Develop New Methods of Construction," talk at North Carolina State College, 1954, in *Louis I. Kahn: Writings, Lectures, Interviews,* ed. Alessandra Latour, New York, 1991, p. 57.

16 Rosalind Krauss, "The Im/Pulse to See," in *Vision and Visuality: Discussions in Contemporary Culture,* ed. Hal Foster, Seattle, 1988, p. 73.

The slowness that radiates from these drawings has something to do with tenacity, something to do with seeing design as a form of patient research, and something to do with Kahn's impressive mental strength and his ability to find inner peace amid the outward chaos of his life. There emerges from between the lines of the drawings a sense of a cultivated slowness and idling: a purposeful holding of material in flux, of keeping doors open for the slow-ripening, the serendipitous, the accidental; with not only a *tolerance* for gaps, errors, and repetition, but their actual *invitation.* (Evolution, which design appears to simulate, is of course, driven by repetition and accidents.[17]) Thus Kahn: "While drawing I'm always waiting for something to happen: I don't want it to happen too quickly, though."[18]

Kahn's culture of lingering may seem an unrealistic model for our market-driven times. (Or even for his own: Kahn's office was effectively bankrupt at the time of his death.) Yet its wonderful results do pose provocative questions. Should not the intended lifespan of an artifact have something to do with the length of its gestation? (And does not the quiet which Kahn's buildings emanate have something to do with the slowness of their conception?) To what degree has our capacity to reflect and conceptualize kept pace with the speed of our tools? How might new tools and methods of practice be organized to allow more, not less, time and space for conception?[19] "Architecture is the thoughtful making of spaces."[20] The architect is one who lingers to think about spaces.

IT DRAWS: TOWARD A CULTURE OF FINDING OUT

How might knowledge and theory best unfold into practice? Although guided by a set of ethical-architectural principles that had ripened over the length of his career in the form of texts and lectures, it is difficult to call Kahn's mature work "theory-driven" in the common, academic sense of the word. On the contrary, Kahn believed that a too-present or too-prescriptive theory might interrupt discovery, might harden the flux too early in the process, might color results too strongly.

17 See: Michael Benedikt, "God, Creativity, Evolution—The Argument from Design(ers)," in: *Center* 15 (January 2008).

18 Louis I. Kahn, in "Signature Against the Sky," documentary on Louis I. Kahn, WCAU-TV, 1967.

19 These and other questions regarding the transfer from "old" to "new" methodologies were asked by Peter Lynch in ibid. For an important study of this theme, see Sherry Turkle et al., *Simulation and Its Discontents,* Cambridge, Mass., 2009

20 Louis I. Kahn, "Architecture is the Thoughtful Making of Spaces, *Perspecta* 4, no. 2 (1957).

For Kahn, knowledge and theory stake out a fruitful field for the architect to get lost in; the goal being that the project draw itself *through* him.

We encounter this notion again and again in Kahn's familiar asking of things "what they want to be." His is a dual questioning: on the one hand, a consulting of tradition and convention (the search for deeper resonances and sources of common understanding, the understanding of a work of architecture as belonging to all of architecture); and on the other, it is an asking of the things of the present to reveal their true natures (the famous case of the brick that "wanted to be an arch"). Both sides of this dual allegiance—tradition and circumstance—are set up as productive antagonists by Kahn to heighten and transform each other as they drive the design forward. At the same time, in his asking, the architect's role is shifted from that of "creator" to that of "medium" or "midwife."

In reading the drawings for the Dominican Motherhouse, we may well sense Kahn at work to withdraw himself from the scene, with his personal mannerisms, expressionist tendencies, and regressions into repertoire being slowly purged by actions which grow out of a deepening understanding of both the institution and the circumstances at hand. In the development of the parti we can sense Kahn (at least partially) getting over his own romanticism of monastic life and slowly surrendering himself to a more dynamic, less antiquarian, view of that tradition. And then, those big Kahnian arches, direct imports from his projects in India and Bangladesh, soon disappear as the new materials and landscape are consulted. What is perhaps most instructive is how certain drawings are used to fix intent while leaving selected variables open in order to move forward, how things are left fragmentary in order to tease out "what they want to be."

Even more unfamiliar than Kahn's drawing method to our present architectural culture, with its system of stars and signature buildings, is his self-effacing wish to disappear behind the work, that wish that has imbued upon buildings such as the Salk Institute, the Kimbell Art Museum, or the

Library of the Phillips Exeter Academy that illusive, "just-so" authorlessness which critics have so struggled to name. T.S. Eliot maintained that the mature poet does not create great works by revealing the extraordinary, but by taking the ordinary and channeling it through the intensity of his métier, a process that, if successful, may allow his work to transcend the limits of the merely personal. "For it is not the 'greatness,' the intensity, of the emotions, the components, but the intensity of the artistic process, the pressure, so to speak, under which the fusion takes place, that counts." [21]

Perhaps, even more than those other "cultures" sketched out above, this is what makes these drawings so fascinating and so poignant. The transported sense of Kahn and his associates at work to establish a culture of fusion, "the pressure, so to speak," which might bring their work in touch with something universal and collective, something outside of self and a clockwork notion of time. "The greatest offering, the greatest work ... the most wonderful part of an artist's work does not really belong to him." [22]

21 T.S. Eliot, "Tradition and the Individual Talent" [1919], in: *Selected Prose of T.S. Eliot*, New York, 1975, p. 41.

22 Louis Kahn, interview with Patricia McLaughlin, *The Pennsylvania Gazette*, December 1972, quoted in: Richard Saul Wurman, *What Will Be Has Always Been: The Words of Louis I. Kahn*, New York, 1986.

"Constantly the question, What is a Monastery?
What inspired the first Monastery? You needn't know the truth
of the circumstantial fact because that is not a guide at all.
Anything in history which happens circumstantially is of little
worth. What in history is a sign of the inevitable is of
tremendous worth." Louis I. Kahn, "The Institutions of Man," 1968

PRELUDE: CLIENTS, SITE, AND PROGRAM

The drawings that tell their story over the following pages are to be found in Kahn's archive under the rather formidable title of "The Mary, Queen of All Saints Motherhouse, Dominican Congregation of Saint Catherine de Ricci."[23] The commissioning congregation was founded in 1880 near Albany, New York, as a convent and laywomen's retreat house, the first of its kind in America. The congregation flourished in its first decades, and by 1900 had established new foundations in Philadelphia and Cuba.[24] In 1964, after over eighty years in upstate New York, the Albany sisters were forced to leave their aging wooden home after it failed to meet the fire department's new regulations for communal buildings. A plan to move in with the second foundation in the Philadelphia suburb of Elkins Park was short-lived: there the sisters had operated the former William L. Elkins estate as a convent and retreat house since 1932, but a renewed interest in spiritual life at the time meant that the estate was simply too full to take in the Albany sisters. Opportunity presented itself thirty miles to the south, though, near Media, Pennsylvania, in the form of a country estate named Windy Hill. Figs.1–4, 7–9 Not long after the sisters had bought and settled into their new home, the spiritual groundswell also reached Media, and brought with it a growing number of new postulants and the need for more space.

Deciding to build a new motherhouse on their property, the congregation, under the leadership of its Prioress General, Mother Mary Emmanuel, began its search for an architect. Mother Emmanuel's good friend, the Reverend Thomas Phelan, chaplain at Rensselaer Polytechnic Institute and specialist on liturgical art, was quick to suggest Kahn. Although Jewish, Kahn was not an unlikely candidate for the Dominicans, his freewheeling religiousness seemingly at home in all faiths and in none: "I can't speak about religious sects. I just know about the Catholics, the Jews, and the Moslems—I have a vague idea of the various sects. But I don't have a vague idea about religion itself. I feel conversed with religion as a very sacred part of the intimate. But as far as people practicing their philosophies of religion, I can frankly say I don't know anything about them. None of them seem to be of the quality of religion itself."[25]

At the end of March 1965, Kahn's office received Mother Emmanuel's inquiry in the form of a letter. Fig.5 Kahn was away in Pakistan, at work on the twin capitals at Islamabad and Dhaka, but his senior associate David Wisdom responded immediately. Fig.6 After this brief exchange it would take a full year before Kahn and the sisters would finally meet. The project was by no means a small undertaking for the congregation, and before embarking the sisters needed to reassess their needs and to arrange funding. After much deliberation, they agreed on a schematic program and calculated a budget of $1,500,000 before again taking up contact with the architects.[26]

23 Unless otherwise noted, the source of the original drawings of the Dominican Motherhouse used in this text is the Louis I. Kahn Collection, Kroiz Gallery, University of Pennsylvania (hereafter referred to as "Kahn Collection"): Project File 700, Folders LIK 030.I.A.700.1–LIK 030.I.A.700.4 and Folders LIK 030.I.C.700.001–LIK 030.I.C.700.012, as well as correspondence and project files in Box LIK 10. A second source was the archive of the Dominican Motherhouse in Elkin's Park, PA.

24 Sources of information on the congregation: website of the Dominican Motherhouse of Saint Catherine de Ricci, http://www.elkinsparkop.org (accessed January 2005); interview, author with Sister Mary Irene Lolli, O.P., and Sister Eileen Priscilla Primrose, O.P., Dominican Motherhouse, Elkins Park, PA, April 15, 2006; correspondence, author with Sister Mary Irene Lolli, October 2007.

25 Kahn, in conversation with Richard Saul Wurman, October 1973, in *What Will Be Has Always Been: The Words of Louis I. Kahn,* ed. Richard Saul Wurman, New York, 1986, p. 231.

26 The budget of $1,500,000 appears several times in the correspondence for the Dominican Motherhouse. See Box LIK 10, Kahn Collection.

1–4 Photos of Motherhouse property, Spring 1966
5 Letter from Mother Mary Emmanuel to Louis Kahn, March 26, 1965
6 Letter from David Wisdom to Mother Mary Emmanuel, April 2, 1965

mary, queen of all saints

motherhouse ~ dominican congregation of st. catherine de ricci

10-6- 5 218

2850 NORTH PROVIDENCE ROAD
MEDIA, PENNSYLVANIA

Mr. Louis Kahn, Architect
158 South 20th Street
Philadelphia, Penna.

Dear Sir:

Shortly, we hope to begin the development of our
55-acre tract on Providence Road midway between Media and
Newtown Square by building a Motherhouse for our religious
Congregation.

You have been suggested to us by the Catholic
Chaplain at Rensselaer Polytechnic Institute in Troy, N.Y.
as someone well qualified to plan a very fine building. As
we value the opinion of Rev. Thomas Phelan we are writing
to inquire if you would be interested in this project and
to ask where we might see work you have done.

Father Phelan, I believe, has visited and greatly
admires a Unitarian Church you built in Rochester, New York.

May we hear from you?

Sincerely yours,

Mother Mary Emmanuel OP

Prioress General

March 26, 1965

April 2, 1965

Mother Mary Emmanuel, O.P.
Prioress General
Dominican Congregation of
 St. Catherine de Ricci
2850 North Providence Road
Media, Pennsylvania

My dear Reverend Mother:

We have your kind inquiry about Mr. Kahn's possible interest in the design
of a Motherhouse on a tract of land near Media.

Mr. Kahn is presently in Pakistan on matters pertaining to the design of
the Second Capital in Dacca and the President's Estate in Rawalpindi. He will
return about April 12th.

I am sure that he would be pleased to help you. He is looking forward to
working on a development of buildings and site for St. Andrew's Priory in
Valyermo, California. He has had several conversations with Father Vincent
Martin, although no actual planning work has been started.

In addition to the Rochester Church mentioned by the Reverend Thomas Phelan
as a work that would interest you, we would like to have you know about the
Richards Medical Research Building and the adjoining Biology Building on the
University of Pennsylvania campus, the Eleanor Donnelley Erdman Dormitory on
the Bryn Mawr campus, the Yale Art Gallery on the campus in New Haven, Conn.,
and the Tribune-Review Publishing Company building in Greensburg, Pennsylvania.

Two years ago, Father Frederic Debuyst, Director of "Art d'Eglise", Abbaye de
Saint Andre, Bruges, Belgium, visited our drafting rooms to see some works in
progress in various stages of study in drawings and models. You would be most
welcome to make a similar visit here.

Respectfully,

David Wisdom
DW:lmb

The congregation's property consisted of fifty-five acres (22 hectares) of wooded land with a handsome manor house and outbuildings embedded in a rural landscape. Given that the existing house was to be used for guests and older sisters, and the topography and extent of the woods, the natural site for the new monastery presented itself immediately: a hillock on the edge of a meadow. Deep within the property and surrounded by deciduous forest on its south, east, and west sides, the hill could be accessed either from the northeast over North Providence Road or from the northwest over Bishop Hollow Drive. The site—dubbed "Daffodil Hill" by the sisters for the lush blanket of flowers that covered it each spring—had the virtues of good drainage, solar exposure, and being relatively free of trees. The forest edge, meadow, and mild terrain joined in an idyllic setting, with the reciprocal qualities of openness and closure, the twin promises of prospect and refuge.

On April 26, 1966, Kahn and his assistant Galen Schlosser finally met with the congregation's building committee in Media. Figs.11–14 Schlosser took notes as Kahn led the discussion, questioning the sisters on the traditions and rules of the order while sifting through their schematic program. This was the beginning of a project-long process of self-education through questioning in which Kahn would gradually refine his—more than mildly romantic—understanding of monastic life. The program Kahn and the sisters discussed in their first meetings was more qualitative than quantitative in nature. While types of use and approximate numbers of users were specified, exact room sizes, adjacencies, and means of mediation were left for the architects to develop in dialogue with the sisters through the architects' designs.

7–8 Auction poster, Windy Hill, 1964
9 Surveyor's plan, April 16, 1966

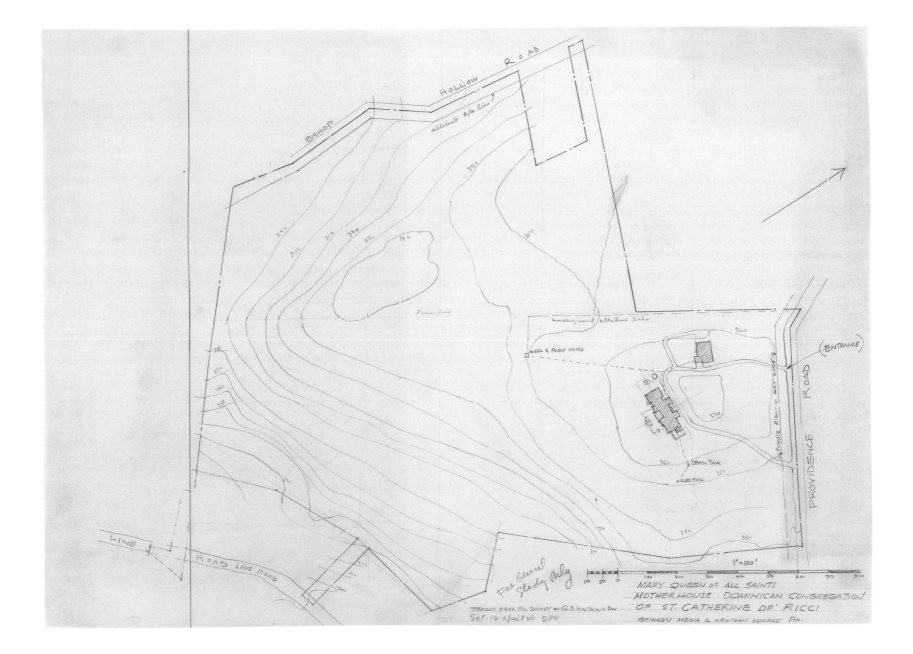

MARY QUEEN OF ALL SAINTS
MOTHER HOUSE · DOMINICAN CONGREGATION
OF ST. CATHERINE DE' RICCI
BETWEEN MEDIA & NEWTOWN SQUARE PA.

For General
Study Only

1" = 100'

FROM PROGRAMMING TO REPROGRAMMING

This programming as an open-ended dialogue between client and architect well-suited Kahn's holistic ideal of the design process, one that stands at odds with conventional prescriptive practice in which the architect is presented with a comprehensive written document at the beginning of a project. For Kahn, architecture can never result from the simple translation of predefined "functions" into spatial diagrams and further into buildings. The role of the architect in programming is to be active rather than passive: thanks to an (ideally) enlightened education and experience, it is the architect rather than the client who is best equipped to plumb the deeper cultural nature of the institution at hand, who has the insight to see beyond circumstantial "needs" to the deeply seated "desires" from which all institutions spring. "There are few clients who can understand philosophically the institution they are creating.... Few clients have it or even sense the lack of it. Usually a written program is handed to you and you must assume the role of the philosopher for the client."[27] Given a program consisting of functions, areas, and relationships, it is the architect's duty to "reprogram": to reshape that program in light of a transcendent image of man, liberating it from the narrow paths laid out by functionalism or modern behavioral science. "Our profession is shabby only because we do not change the programming. If you change that programming, you release wonderful forces because the individual then never makes the mistake of making something which just pleases himself. You please society in your programming, not in the way you do your lousy building. The architect trains himself in expression which is true."[28] A remarkable statement from an architect often judged for his formal and technical skill! In this statement and others like it, Kahn effectively shifts the creative focus of designing away from the aesthetic making of an object ("the way you do your lousy building") toward its social grounding and toward the often-overlooked creative potential inherent in the initial framing of the project.[29]

THEORY INTO PRACTICE

Not surprisingly, then, that at the first meeting Kahn spontaneously proposed an element not previously considered by the sisters: a gatehouse, tower, or ceremonial place of arrival to mark a threshold between convent and outer world. Within this threshold building could be an entry hall, administrative offices, and guest rooms. Kahn suggested the entry hall be decorated with symbols of all world religions, assembled as reminders of the universality of belief. The position at the building's threshold, rather than inside the monastery, was to celebrate the Dominicans' particular form of belief. The sisters were immediately enthusiastic about these suggestions. As Kahn later elaborated, "I have a gateway building. This gateway is the transition between the inside and the outside—I mean—is the center of the Ecumenical Council. It is not in the program. It comes from the spirit and nature of the problem. This is why I think it is so important that the architect does not follow the program but simply uses it as a point of departure of quantity and not of quality.... The program that you get and the translation you make architecturally must come from the spirit of man, not the program. The program is not architecture—it is merely instruction, it is like a prescription by a druggist. Because in the program there is a lobby which the architect must turn into a place of entrance. Corridors must be changed into galleries. Budgets must be changed to economy and areas must be changed to spaces."[30]

Kahn and the sisters soon assembled a schematic program as a point of departure. The program divided itself according to the "double life" of the Dominicans into two distinct and equal halves: the nuns' private quarters, which included dormitories for 120 sisters; and the communal spaces, which consisted of a chapel, an auditorium, classrooms, a library, and a refectory. The sisters were ordered according to a four-tiered hierarchy: newly arrived postulants, novices who had taken their first vows, younger professed sisters who had entered the order, and, finally, older professed sisters. Each rank of sisters was to be housed separately, each group with its own living room. The cells of the professed sisters would be larger and contain private bathrooms; those of the postulants and novices would be smaller and have access to shared bathing and toilet rooms. In addition to ancillary spaces such as kitchen, housekeeping, storage, and administration, gardens might be included for contemplative work and recreational facilities were to be considered. As to the material of construction, Kahn was certain: stone would be the most sympathetic to the existing buildings on the site.

With budget, site, and schematic program in place, the architects were ready to put first thoughts on paper.

27 Kahn, quoted in *What Will Be Has Always Been: The Words of Louis I. Kahn*, ed. Richard Saul Wurman, New York, 1986, p. 120.

28 Kahn, talk with students at Rice University, Spring 1968, in Louis I. Kahn, *Conversations with Students*, ed. Dung Ngo, 2nd. ed., Houston, 1998, p. 54.

29 On this theme, see Jeremy Till, *Architecture Depends*, Cambridge, Mass., 2009, p. 168.

30 Kahn, quoted in Heinz Ronner and Sharad Jhaveri, *Louis I. Kahn: Complete Work*, 1935–1974, 2nd ed., Basel et al., 1987, p. 303.

10 Sisters' program with notes from July 22, 1966

GENERAL ADMINISTRATION

7-8 OFFICES - Records Filing Archive

MEETING RM

Office (rather large) Prioress General
"   Secretary to the Prioress General
                  (space for files, office machines, etc.)
"   Bursar General
                  (adjacent space for records, reports, etc.)
"   Secretary General
                  (archives, files, records, etc.)
3 or 4 other offices for Councillors or others incharge of each section of
              our apostolate. - in ~~offer towns~~ - concerning sisters
Meeting Room - usually to accommodate 5 or 6, but sometimes 10 or 12 people.
2 (not large, but more than closets) reception rooms ;or parlors

LOCAL ADMINISTRATION

Chapel

Superior's Office
Bursar's Office. - storage space, etc.   *Loc "Presence" not convenience*
                                            filling part of ritual
Apostolate Work Room - Office machines, etc.
2 reception rooms
                                            Sacristy - need room for
2 suites for Chaplains - Bedroom, Bath, Study *6 or 7 priests on certain days*
6 guest rooms with baths   *Liturgical information*

FOR ALL

Kitchen, pantries, etc.
Sisters' refectory
✓ Priests' dining room
✓ Guests' dining room
  ~~3~~ large reception rooms capable of being divided into smaller sections *suite of 6*
  Visiting rooms - in main section of Bldge (for older sisters)
Laundry - *large*

Auditorium   Library   Indoor swimming pool?

Chapel - monastic choir withstalls - some space for lay visitors
              2 areas

For Community Sisters

Community room
Recreation room - ~~exixxxxxxxxx~~ kitchenette?
Sewing room   Utility room with wash tub and ironing board and iron
Project room   on each dormitory floor. -
Cells for 40 Sisters - Showers rooms - toilet rooms - supply closets, etc.
     About 20 of these to have individual toilet and lavatory for older and sick
     Here also, pharmacy and treatment room, small kitchen and dining room, social
              room and porch.

For Postulants (And pretty much the same for Novices and Young professed)
     Individual rooms with running water.
School 2 class rooms   *6 class Rms*
School 1 large class room that can be divided. —— *2 large class Rms*
School 2 sound proof music rooms   *6 music Rms (sound proof)*
         1 common room
         1 recreation room - kitchenette
         1 sewing room
         Office for Mistress - real privacy
         Parlors for visiting, capable of being divided. - *lavatories*
              (Perhaps postulants and novices could share these - different days)

"I believe that the architect's first act is to take the program that comes to him and change it. Not to satisfy it, but to put it into the realm of architecture, which is to put it into the realm of spaces." Louis I. Kahn, "Wanting to Be: The Philadelphia School," 1961

26 April 1966

DOMINICAN SISTERS - MOTHERHOUSE - MEDIA, PENNA.

Notes from meeting with Sisters Jane and Monte, April 26, 1966
Galen Schlosser/L. I. Kahn

Novices - class together   Novices - postulants

Classes near people who use them:

    Classrooms - Novices
    Recreation space

School close - Novices have intense training - Spiritual

    Postulants - college classes

      Mingle - classrooms

LIK thoughts:

    School - related
    Postulants and young professes

    Novices - 2 classrooms

    Novices by themselves

Postulants and young sisters close to younger and older sisters.

  Larger garden

  Rooms - large rooms for older sisters
      the rest similar 11' - 10'   12x15 big
                    10x8   small

                         Measure the servitude
                         more square

Built-in closet

Desk - chairs and bed

11-14 Program, April 26, 1966, Galen Schlosser

School:

Service to outside?

College education

Extension section - 1st and 2nd year

Come with at least high school education.

Classes: Spiritual

Brother & Father - teachers

Priest or Chaplain: Accommodation for two priests to be considered.

Mother General - Administrator - plus: 4 Counsellors (Bursars)

LIK thoughts:

Locate administration near gate   (Sisters agree and like this idea)

No more than two or three stories

Infirmary - 1st flr. - away from all movement.

Retreat - associated - more or less workshop

Vatican council

Own dining room

Own domain

Monastery

Right of cell

Chapel

Refectory

Corridor free

Elevator for three stories

Novices & Postulants:

Recreation - land use

Social room - library - kitchen
Noisy & quiet

Crafts: Painting - Sculpture
Live to express
Religion and art

Sewing

Laundry in each group

Large for community

Kitchen

Employees

Grounds

Orchard - farm - gardens

14   7   4

Large common library (with the school)

Garden of mind - Search for truth

Auditorium - could be part of school

Total community in domain of older sisters

Auditorium:

Performances (Yes)

Feast days

Environments different - social rooms
P; N; YS; OS

Mother General - Office not near room

Counselors

Guest - the towers or gatehouse

Chaplain - outside the gates!!!

Need dining

Two

Keep tradition in refectory

In keeping with double life:

a. Silence

b. Communication, conversation

Tennis court

Swimming Pool

Springs - water

Materials: LIK: Stone and concrete

Arches - structure

TENTATIVE BEGINNINGS

There are no shortcuts in architecture—something Kahn's first sketches remind us of. A sixty-four-year-old architect with over forty years of experience, Kahn, as does any student, needs to grasp the quantities of the program before he can begin to translate its raw square feet into any sort of meaningful spatial arrangement. Fig. 15 He starts with the sisters' cells—the raison d'être of the program—drawing them freehand and to scale: thirty newly-arrived postulants, forty-five novices, thirty junior professed sisters who have taken their vows and entered the order, and thirty older professed sisters. The cells are dimensioned: smaller cells (10 × 15 ft. [3 × 4.5 m]) for the younger sisters, larger (10 × 20 ft. [3 × 6 m]) for the elder sisters. In the first meeting, Kahn had already proposed, conflating geometry and behavior, that a squarish geometry for the younger sisters' cells would in some way serve to "measure the[ir] servitude."

Below, this linear graphic summary begets linear plan diagrams. The chapel is blocked out on a square-feet-per-person basis in a conventional rectangular plan. Further below, probing toward a first disposition of main spaces, Kahn demonstrates to himself that by stacking the four groups of cells around a court or the chapel, this portion of the program could take on a form similar to that of his First Unitarian Church. Still further below and now thinking in terms of the whole program, he draws a tiny linear scheme with the elements of the program strung along a shifting, street-like spine.

15 Elements of the plan, Spring 1966, Louis Kahn

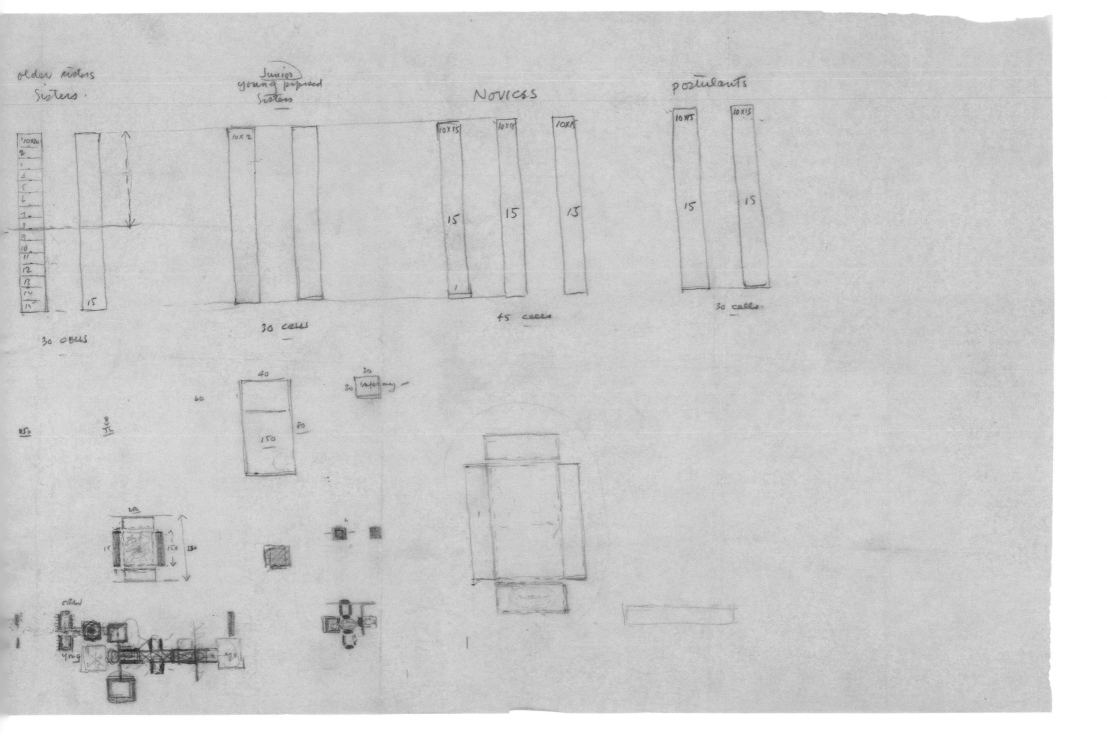

older sisters
Sisters.

Junior
young professed
Sisters

NOVICES

postulants

30 cells

30 cells

45 cells

30 cells

Kahn soon blocks out a traditional monastic chapel while asking himself how a "new relationship" between members of the convent and laypeople might be achieved. Fig. 16 The linear program elements are regrouped in second and third sketches. Figs. 17–18 An ambulatory forms the thick outer edge of a nave, circumscribing the chapel, the adjacent refectory, and a large court at the center of the plan. Minor axes are made of the four groups of cells and their respective sub-courts, which open, in turn, to the main court. The schemes resemble rudimentary Beaux-Arts plans: symmetrical, processional, and tightly ordered within their tartan grids; their secondary bays dedicated—in somewhat schoolbookish Beaux-Arts manner—to galleries and minor spaces. In spite of their spare hieroglyphics, we can glean much from these little drawings. All elements of a traditional Western monastic type are here—ambulatories, inner and outer cloisters, etc.—though assembled in a configuration with no obvious antecedent. Although it is not exactly clear how this plan relates to its site, a tuft of forest and an arrow pointing toward what must be North Providence Road (the "R" in plan) seem to indicate that the major axis runs in an east-west direction. (Which would be the correct orientation for the chapel.) The main entry is indicated on the western end of this axis by a second arrow.

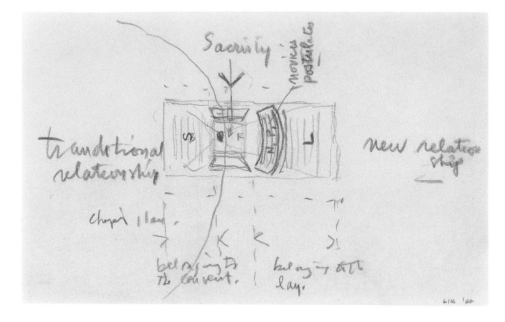

16 Chapel, Spring 1966, Louis Kahn
17 Plan, Spring 1966, Louis Kahn
18 Plan, Spring 1966, Louis Kahn

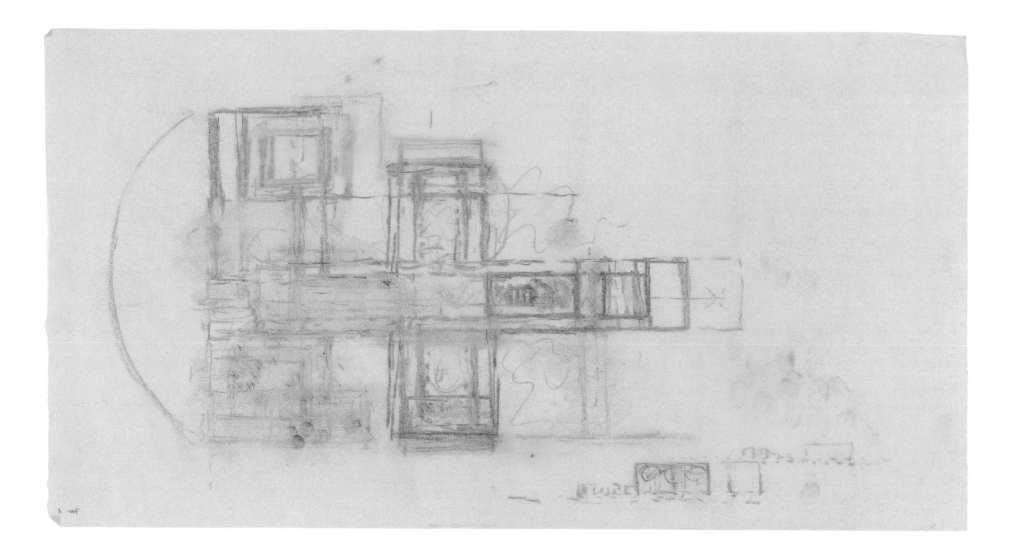

"FORM AND DESIGN"

It is easy to see in Kahn's first drawings more a means of engaging hand, paper, and program than attempts at fitting a building to this particular site. More architectural stick figures than comprehensive diagrams, the evidence from this phase deals exclusively with the inner world of the program: shifting its components in search of resolution while leaving the context unaddressed. But this was not atypical for the mature Kahn; by then he had come to see the act of building first and foremost as a social act, "an offering to an institution of man." When confronted with a program, the search for that configuration of parts that spoke most profoundly of the institution in question became his first priority, transcending the contingencies of material, construction, or site.

Kahn's mature description of how architectural artifacts might come into being emerged in 1960 in what he identified to be a process of "Form and Design." Worth repeating here is his description of what he found to be the twofold nature of the architectural act:

"Form encompasses a harmony of systems, a sense of Order and that which characterizes one existence from another. Form has no shape or dimension. For example, in the differentiation of a spoon from Spoon, Spoon characterizes a form having two inseparable parts, the handle and the bowl. A spoon implies a specific design made of silver or wood, big or little, shallow or deep. Form is 'what,' Design is 'how.' Form is impersonal. Design belongs to the designer. Design is a circumstantial act, how much money there is available, the site, the client, the extent of knowledge. Form has nothing to do with circumstantial conditions. In architecture, it characterizes a harmony of spaces good for a certain activity of man.

"Reflect then on what characterizes House, a house and home. House is the abstract characteristic of spaces good to live in. House is the Form, in the mind of wonder it should be there without shape or dimension. A house is a conditional interpretation of these spaces. This is Design. In my opinion the greatness of an architect depends on his powers of realization of that which is House, rather than the design of a house, which is a circumstantial act."[31]

For Kahn, our institutions—of home, learning, government, etc.—were all "on trial," their meanings clouded by layers of cultural detritus and circumstance: "When we think of the simple beginnings which inspired our present institutions, it is evident that some drastic changes must be made which will inspire the re-creation of [their] meaning."[32] The search for "Form" is a metaphorical search for these "simple beginnings." Here lies for Kahn the deeper purpose of architecture: not in the expression of "program," personal whim, or other conditions of circumstance, but in providing access to the root human inspirations behind that program, beyond personal taste, beyond circumstance. The grasp of Form, grounded in man's "sense of appropriateness" or "sense of commonality," belongs, according to Kahn, to his intuition and embodied knowledge of human history; the understanding of Design, as a means of questioning Order, belongs to his reason.

The Form-Design hierarchy structures the work of the architect. In practice, presented with a project, the architect searches the mind for the most suitable among the archetypical forms which it has stored away: this becomes the hypothetical "Form" of the building at hand, be it "House," "School," "Library," etc.[33] These archetypes are not abstract forms which exist in some distant realm, but rather represent basic modes of being-in-the-world. For Kahn, the "Form" of a project defined the hierarchical and reciprocal relationships between its activities and was thus the architect's insight into the unchanging essence of the institution in question. This spatial order is, then, an intuition to which all further decisions must be referred. Once implemented, the educated guess of "Form" is to be proved or refuted by confronting it with the contingencies of reality during the "Design" phase: budget, site, materials, building codes, etc. If the "Form," however deformed by "Design" holds true against these tests, it is the "true" Form, if not, a new "Form" diagram must be conceived and the process begins anew.

Kahn's insight into the architectural process as one uniting intuition and reason, Platonic idealism and realism, cultural heritage and empiricism, representation and its transcendence—provocative against the background of modernism's empiricist tabula rasa methodology, and equally so in the context of contemporary formalist tendencies—remains one of his most helpful thoughts. For whether we share Kahn's depth-giving paradigm of architecture's common "simple beginnings" or not, most of us would agree upon architecture's dual, ideal-real, nature. Kahn's "space" of designing not only addresses this nature but provides a structure for its unfolding.

31 Louis I. Kahn, radio lecture for "Voice of America," November 1960. First published as "A Statement from Louis I. Kahn," *Arts and Architecture* (February 1961), and later as "Form and Design," *Architectural Design* 31 (April 1961).

32 Kahn, quoted in William Jordy, "The Span of Kahn," *Architectural Review* (June 1974).

33 See also Vincent Scully, "Introduction," *Kahn Libraries*, Barcelona, 1989, pp. 16–44.

"Form is what. Design is how. Form is impersonal, but design belongs to the designer. Design is prescribed by circumstances: How much money there is available, the site, the client, the extent of skill and knowledge. Form has nothing to do with such conditions. In architecture, it is a harmony of spaces good enough for a certain activity of man." Louis I. Kahn, "Not for the Faint-Hearted," 1971

A GENTLE NUDGE, A SENSE OF "FORM"

After his initial probing, Kahn awarded his assistant David Polk the position of project architect, giving him his tentative sketches to develop into a first, scaled study. Soon after visiting the site, Polk suggested to Kahn that the forest might be used as a natural edge against which the elements of the convent could be positioned. The sisters' cells could engage in an intimate relationship with the woods while defining a place for the communal rooms.[34] To Polk's delight, Kahn approved of his proposal for development during his upcoming absence from the office and continued to consider the idea himself while away. A series of tiny sketches on the back of an invitation to lecture in Stockholm may have been drawn while en route to that very appointment: four variations in which the elements of the program—the four bars of cells (one for each group of sisters) and a more or less solid block of common spaces—are juxtaposed across a large open space. Figs. 19–20 Regardless of where Kahn sketched these diagrams, Polk's reading of the site seems to have helped him focus his thoughts on the program: in contrast to his earliest sketches, the spatial intention of this simple two-part parti—which holds monastic seclusion in equipoise with communal life—is now abundantly clear.

If the resulting diagram overlays neatly with plans of medieval Carthusian charterhouses, this is less a case of historicist or academic quotation than a result of Kahn's essentialist method. Expressed in his own terms, both the Carthusians and himself, working some seven hundred years apart, had sought and found the appropriate "Form" for "Monastery." A spatial archetype—according to Kahn—does not belong to anyone, any more than "the waltz belongs to any musician or oxygen to the discoverer of that element," it is simply that "one finds a certain nature, and as a professional we must find that certain nature."[35]

Fitting sketches to site, we can see that the cells are arranged in an arc corresponding roughly to the natural topography and to the course of the sun, leaving the crest of the hill unbuilt. Rudimentary as they may be, already laid out in these diagrams are the inherent dichotomies of the problem: on one hand, the private world of the sisters, on the other, the communal areas and the interface with the public world; on the one hand, the wish for a comprehensive form, on the other hand, the wish to articulate the program's constituent parts; on the one hand, the particulars of topography and site, on the other, the will of geometry to assert itself. The sum of these frictions and reciprocities would equal Kahn's first serious translation of this monastery's "Form."

34 Interview, author with David Polk, Polk Residence, Chestnut Hill, PA, October 20, 2004; see also Polk interviewed by Kazumi Kawasaki in *Architecture and Urbanism*, extra edition (November 1983), p. 234: "He wasn't too much aware of the site when working on the original schemes, and when I went to look at the site and I found the woods in relation to a clearing to be a certain way and proposed the idea of the cells sort of related to the woods in a kind of inter-edge to the woods and making a place within which the other things could sit."

35 Louis I. Kahn, *Conversations with Students,* ed. Dung Ngo, 2nd. ed., Houston, 1998, p. 54.

19–20 Letter with plan sketch (verso), March 28, 1966, Louis Kahn

SVENSKA TEKNOLOGFÖRENINGEN
AVDELNINGEN SVENSKA ARKITEKTFÖRENINGEN

STOCKHOLM
BRUNKEBERGSTORG 20
TELEFON: 22 08 90 (VÄXEL)
POSTGIRO: 540
BANKFÖRBINDELSE:
AB GÖTEBORGS BANK

Louis I. Kahn, Architect F.A.I.A.
1501, Walnut Street
Philadelphia
Pennsylvania
USA.

EDER BETECKNING	EDERT BREV	VÅR BETECKNING	STOCKHOLM 16
		CN/am	28.3.1966

Dear Mr Louis Kahn.

We have got your program in Scandinavia from Akademisk Arkitektforening
København and together with Sven Silow I will meet you at Arlanda air-
port thursday 21.4.

As your time in Stockholm is very short, we have invited the School of
Architecture to the Architect Association in the evening, and it will be
only one lecture.

This will take place at the Museum of Modern Art where our students at
that time just have a Town planning exhibition.

We have booked a room for you at Grand Hotel, St. Blasieh.hamnen 8.

We are looking forward very much to see you in Stockholm

Yours faithfully

Carl Nyrén

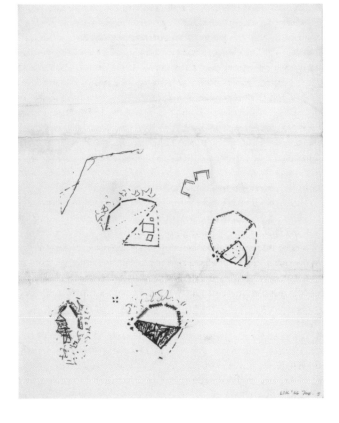

A DIALOGUE IN DRAWINGS BEGINS

Project architect David Polk soon took up his pencil. Like Kahn, he seems to have first dirtied his sketch paper by laying out the elements of the program as scaled building blocks. Figs. 23–24 Unlike Kahn, who began with the cells, he apparently first directed his attention toward the communal spaces. Attempts to grow Kahn's "Form" using some kind of serialism generated by the interlocking parts were quickly abandoned. Figs. 21–22 With Kahn apparently taking the initiative, the whole would begin to lead the parts rather than letting a system generate the whole. Figs. 25–27

Working together over May and June, Kahn and Polk would soon develop a first scheme to present to the sisters.

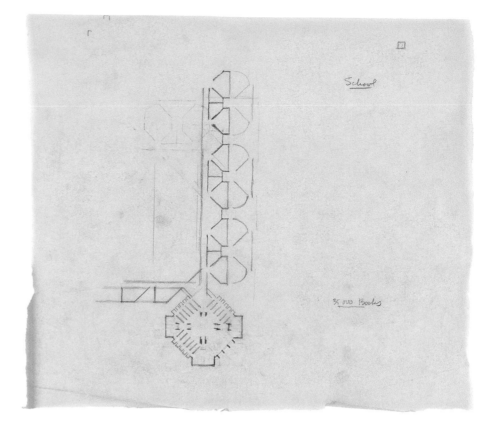

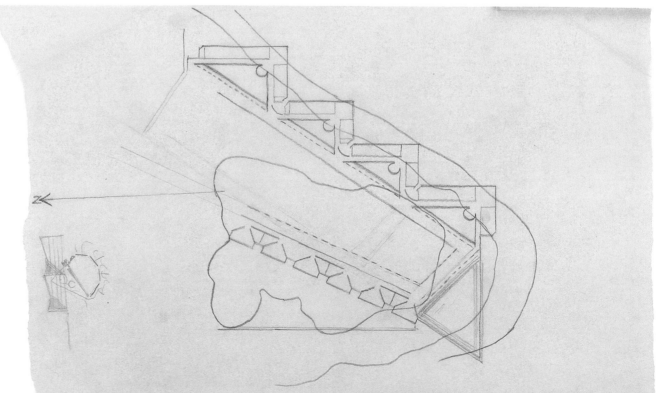

21–24 Elements of the plan, May/June 1966, David Polk

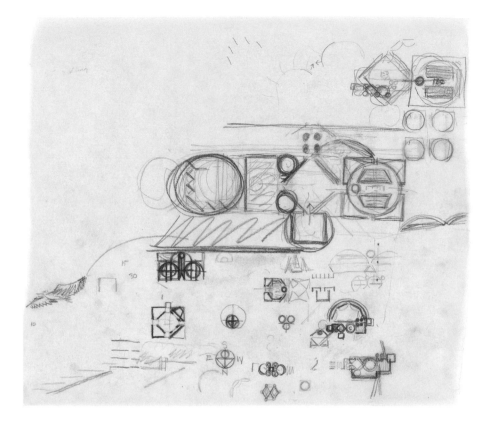

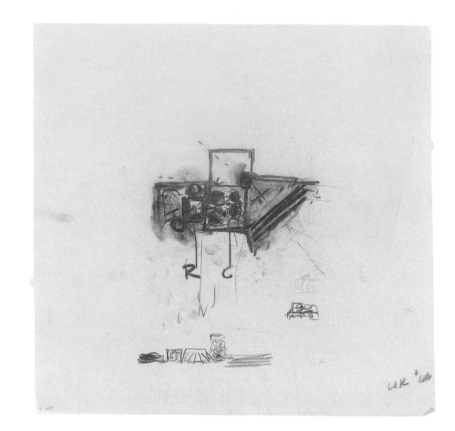

25 Plan, fragments, May/June 1966, Louis Kahn (attributed)

26 Plan, elevation, May/June 1966, Louis Kahn

27 Plan, May/June 1966, Louis Kahn

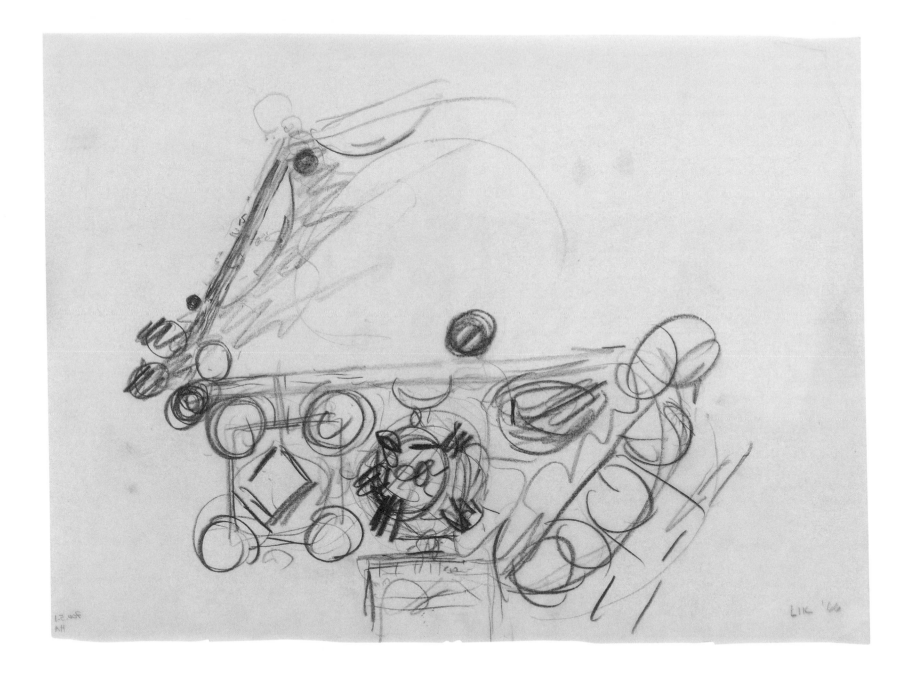

A FIRST SCHEME

A comprehensive plan in 1 in. = 50 ft. (1:600) scale showing the new monastery in relation to topography, forest, and existing buildings was submitted to the sisters along with a succinct description from David Wisdom on June 22, while Kahn was once again away in Asia. Figs. 28-32 Immediately clear is to what great degree Polk's drafted scheme has remained true to the miniature "Form" diagrams on the back of Kahn's letter. But the drafted plan reveals more than just a tame translation of a type: further study shows that—in contrast to Kahn's first attempts—program and site are beginning to engage in a relationship which is based on something more than mutual negation. In the new scheme, the "double life" of the congregation is spatially accentuated by the way in which private and public halves of the program are divided along the edge between forest and meadow. To the north of this edge are the communal buildings, to the south, the cells submerging into the forest.[36] Fitting the four cell tracts to the topography and adding the counter-arcs of retaining walls and sunken gardens strengthens the centrifugal movement of the plan, fortifying the cells' reclusive gesture.

This said, further consideration of the site plan reveals that things are somewhat more complex than at first glance, for in most Western monasteries the cloister/courtyard makes a strong figure, anchoring the whole. But here, the figure inscribed within the cloisters is overgrown with the forest, challenging its focal clarity. What in the first reading of the plan is a strong "figure," has in a second become a part of the "ground" of the forest. Our reading of the plan oscillates: a traditional cloister type has been both implied by the plan's geometry and "crossed out" by the growth of the forest across that plan. If it is Kahn's goal to reveal the monastery's "Form," or type, this is to be a veiled revealing, not a blunt quotation.

36 See Appendix (pp. 228–31) for plan legends for this and the following schemes.

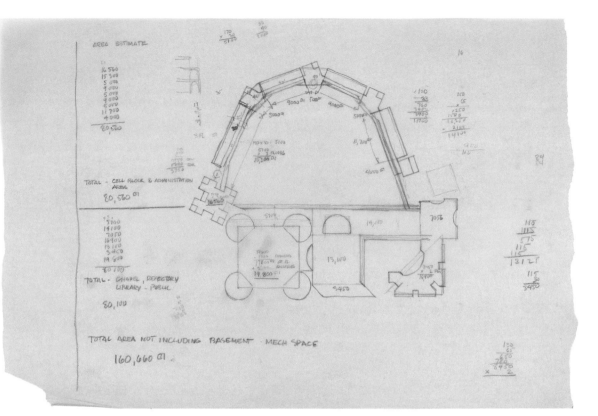

28 Plan with area calculations, June 1966
29 Site plan, June 22, 1966, David Polk (attributed)

LOUIS I KAHN ARCHITECT FAIA

David Polk

June 22, 1966

Mother Mary Emmanuel, O.P.
Prioress General
St. Catherine de' Ricci
Dominican Congregation of
2650 North Providence Road
Media, Pennsylvania

My dear Reverend Mother:

We respectfully submit for consideration the Site Development Plan showing proposed new buildings and surroundings for the Motherhouse, and the general character of the buildings.

The approach is obliquely through an orchard replanted where the old orchard grew, arriving at a paved entrance platform, the Gateway and Administration Building lying ahead, and the Chapel, Refectory, School and related courts stretching away to the right.

The individual cells are organized in an arc facing south along the brow of the hill in the woods beyond the main platform. They are placed so that each room has its own private relationship with the woods - the serenity of the woods being felt to be in harmony with the nature of the cell.

The rooms are arranged in three tiers with access being from the middle level which is also the main ground level of all buildings. Thus one descends one flight of stairs to the first level and ascends one flight to the third level. All the rooms are connected by an interior gallery and open cloister which looks across one of four sunken gardens to that portion of the woods encircled by the arc of rooms. The sunken gardens are at the first level giving light and outlook to the galleries and cloisters at that level.

The Chapel, Refectory and School are organized linearly along the main platform forming, with their courts, a community of buildings, each being accessible from the principal gallery which widens to form a generous hall at the entrances to the major spaces. These buildings begin to become a realm of spaces appropriate to their purpose.

1501 WALNUT STREET PHILADELPHIA 2 PENNSYLVANIA LOCUST 3-9844

LOUIS I KAHN ARCHITECT FAIA

To: Mother Mary Emmanuel, O.P.   June 22, 1966

Re: Mother House   -2-

As shown the number of cells is 135 consisting of:

        45 novices
        30 postulants
        30 younger professed sisters
        30 older professed sisters

The cells for novices, postulants and younger sisters are 9 feet 4 inches wide and 12 feet long. Those of the older professed sisters are 11 feet 4 inches wide and 15 feet long.

The Chapel will accommodate 164 persons with the possibility of expansion to 200 for special occasions.

The Refectory will accommodate 160 persons at the four long tables indicated on the plan.

The Auditorium will accommodate 180 - 200 persons.

Please let us know when another meeting may be held to discuss further development of your program.

Very truly yours,

David Wisdom
DW:kml

2 copies Site Plan Development
under separate cover

1501 WALNUT STREET PHILADELPHIA 2 PENNSYLVANIA LOCUST 3-9844

30–31 Letter from David Wisdom to Mother Mary Emmanuel, June 22, 1966
32 First floor: plan, June 22, 1966, David Polk (attributed)

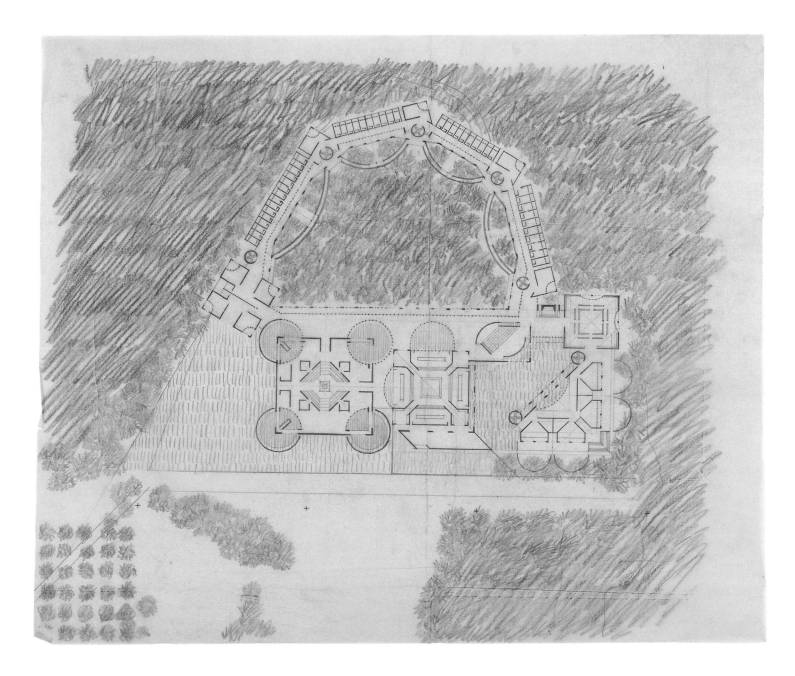

"AN ARCHITECTURE OF CONNECTION"

Kahn and Polk have devised a lavish "architecture of connection": an arcaded cloister that rings the wooded center combined with a series of galleries, courts, and sub-courts that mediate between the elements of the program. Judging from the generosity of these spaces—they account for a good half of the scheme's total area—we might assume that the cloisters are the main reason for building. We might imagine how Kahn imagined the sisters in these spaces: silently walking the galleries, lost in meditation, or perhaps spontaneously engaged in philosophical discourse. It is an elaborate architecture of that which has no instrumental function: contemplation and chance encounter.

Arrival, movement, encounter: for Kahn, each deserving of its own architecture, a more or less autonomous space within which to unfold. Indeed, these spaces—in themselves and as spacings between programmed uses—were for Kahn a primary means of interpreting the institution at hand. Tellingly, they most often fail in the client's program: "The places of entrance, the galleries that radiate from them, the intimate entrances spaces of the institution form an independent architecture of connection. This architecture is of equal importance to the major spaces, though these spaces are designed only for movement and must before be bathed in natural light. This Architecture of Connection cannot appear in the program of areas, it is that which the architect offers the client in his search for architectural balance and direction."[37]

Considering the two-part parti as given, a series of variations worked out during the weeks before presentation explore the communal areas of the plan. Figs. 33–35 What is at issue here are minor variations of the individual parts, their relationship to each other, and their degree of autonomy or submission to a larger whole. The architects additionally test the consequences of rotating the communal spaces eastward in order to establish frontal, rather than oblique, access.

Reading in the meeting minutes that only the first of these variations Figs. 29, 32 was presented to the sisters, one may ask why this solution was deemed better than the others. In this case, Kahn himself might help still our speculation. Speaking to students at Rice University, he explained:

"Suppose you had a great kind of alley, or gallery, and walked through this gallery, and connected to this gallery are the schools which are associated in the fine arts, be it history, sculpture, architecture, or painting, and you saw people at work, in all these classes. It was designed so that you always felt that you were walking through a place where people were at work. Then I present another way of looking at it, say as a court, and you enter this court. You see buildings in this court, and one is designated as painting, one as sculpture, another as architecture, as history. In one, you rub against the presence of the classes. In the other, you can choose to go in if you want to. Now, without asking you which is better, which is a very unfair question, let me tell you what I think is better. I think the latter is greater by far. In the halls that you go through, you will absorb by some osmosis … you will see things. If you can choose to go in there, even if you never do, you can get more out of that arrangement than you can of the other. There is something which has to do with the feeling of association which is remote, rather than direct, and more remote association has a longer life and love."[38]

This preference for a combination of free choice and "remote" contact with what Kahn called "the Availabilities" provides a means for deciphering virtually all of Kahn's mature plans, "be they at the scale of a house, an institutional building, or an entire city."[39] Accordingly, all variations drawn here share a porous combination of courtyards and galleries in order to increase both the number of interfaces and the types of possible relationships between spaces. If the version chosen to show to the sisters was judged superior to the others, one likely reason is how it fulfills the Kahnian imperative of choice, of remote rather than direct association. In the presented version, for example, the school rooms huddle together as if in dialogue, forming their own sub-court that in turn gives on to a larger court—a situation richer in possibilities of association than the linear disposition of those spaces as shown in the other variations. In the preferred version, the dependence on conventional single-loaded galleries has been held to a minimum. The position of the library in plan makes it a mediator between the school and the rest of the convent. In addition to its promising frictions and gaps between uses, this version

seems to find the best balance between the solitary realm of the cells and the communal forum. As in the original "Form" drawings, each half of the program is given equal weight in the plan.

37 Louis I. Kahn, quoted in *What Will Be Has Always Been: The Words of Louis I. Kahn*, ed. Richard Saul Wurman, New York, 1986, p. 257.

38 Louis I. Kahn, *Conversations with Students*, ed. Dung Ngo, 2nd. ed., Houston, 1998, p. 57.

39 See David B. Brownlee, "The Houses of the Inspirations," in *Louis I. Kahn: In the Realm of Architecture*, ed. idem. and David G. De Long, New York, 1991, p. 110.

33 Plan variation, June 1966, Louis Kahn (attributed)

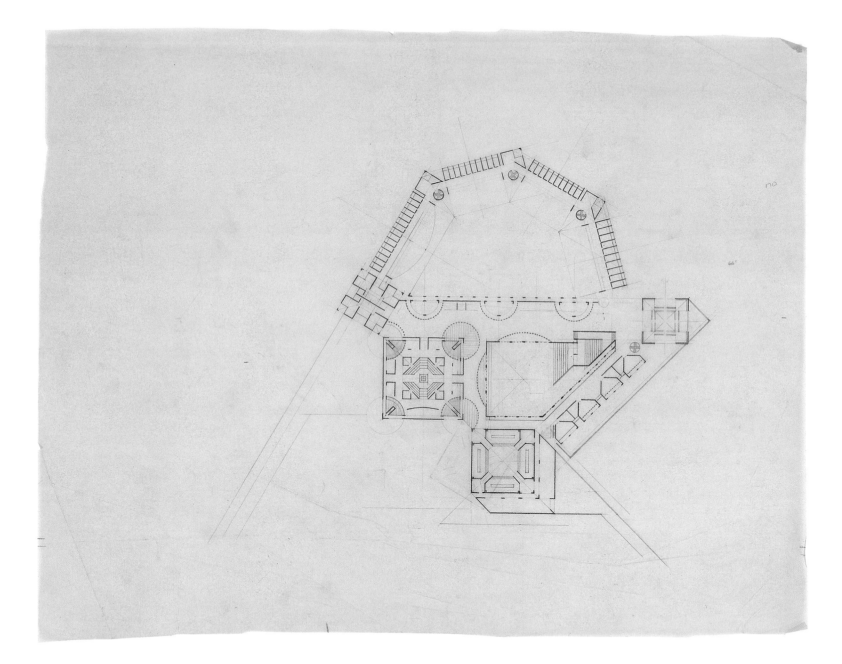

34 Plan variation, June 1966
35 Plan variation, June 1966

ON LEADING AND FOLLOWING: THE CHAPEL

Both the quality and the continuity of an architect's explorations are grounded in his or her ability to find that delicate balance between leading and leaving space for helpers and collaborators. It is a balancing act suggested by David Polk and another of Kahn's associates, Duncan Buell. Said Polk, "You never had the feeling that if you had been thinking about something that it wouldn't get absolute full consideration.... You really felt that you were working on those buildings with him and not just a tool."[40] And Buell, "It was understood that we were never allowed to get too far ahead of Lou."[41]

Evidence of this oscillation between leading and executing is manifest throughout the Motherhouse portfolios, and a fascinating subplot in the monastery's development becomes the development of its chapel. Certainly it must be the most expressive part of the monastery? When Kahn holds back, his associates venture forward, second-guessing the master in generating a small portfolio of schemes in his most expressionist mode. Figs. 36–40

40 Interview, author with David Polk, Polk Residence, Chestnut Hill, PA, October 20, 2004.

41 Interview, author with Duncan Buell, April 14, 2006, office of Buell, Kratzer, Powell, 1501 Walnut St., Philadelphia.

THE PLAN RISES: A FIRST SEARCH FOR A "BRICK ORDER"

Four elevation studies were prepared for the first scheme, three in Kahn's hand and one in Polk's. Figs. 42–45 Showing the north facade only, the drawings reveal the communal buildings as a bulky wall against the forest, each figure scaled to announce itself from a distance. If in his first discussion with the sisters Kahn seemed set on stone, the buildings were now conceived of in brick. Of a similar "brick order" to that of the contemporary Indian Institute of Management and the hostels at Dhaka, their flat arches and great circular voids lend the monastery an expressive and imposing face.

Aside from his long-term preoccupation with the material, Kahn's decision to use brick is understandable in this case: prevalent and indigenous, it can expressively accommodate both the small- and large-scale spaces of the program within its constructive order. This said, the resulting elevations do raise some questions. Can Kahn's monumentally scaled Indian architecture—developed, among other things, in response to the extreme sun, heat, and scale of the Indian subcontinent—be so literally transplanted to the mild climate and delicate scale of this wooded Pennsylvanian landscape? As with his very first attempts with the floor plan, it is difficult not to sense that Kahn is dipping into repertoire or purging himself of something. Accusations of formalism would be—at least for the moment—difficult to defend. The brick may, as Kahn claimed, "want to be an arch," but these elevations, with their huge openings and shadowy depths, do seem to express more for expression's sake than would a truly lucid response to the particulars of *this* context, climate, and program.

41 Entry tower, June 1966, Louis Kahn (attributed)
42 North elevation, June 1966, David Polk

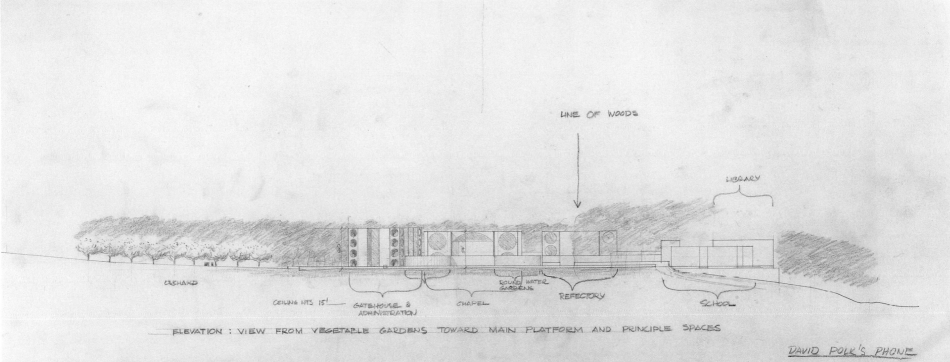

LINE OF WOODS

LIBRARY

ORCHARD

CEILING HTS 15' GATEHOUSE & ADMINISTRATION   CHAPEL   ROUND WATER GARDENS   REFECTORY   SCHOOL

ELEVATION : VIEW FROM VEGETABLE GARDENS TOWARD MAIN PLATFORM AND PRINCIPLE SPACES

DAVID POLK'S PHONE
LA 5 1089

43 North elevation, June 1966, Louis Kahn

Gatehouse   Chapel   Refectory   School, library
behind

44–45 North elevation, June 1966, Louis Kahn

Gateway   Chapel   Refectory

PRESENTING THE FIRST SCHEME

On July 22, 1966, Kahn and Polk met with the congregation's building committee to present their drawings. Figs. 46–49 An atmosphere of friendly affirmation colored with subtle undertones of resolve shines through Polk's extensive meeting notes and the other project documents; the sisters would prove to be agreeable, yet by no means submissive partners for Kahn in the following months. They were generally appreciative of Kahn's interpretation of their program, approving of the disposition of the building on the site and of the individual parts to each other. They responded positively to the architects' suggestions regarding the relationship of the cells to the forest ("The cell should express the dignity of the individual"), the strong connection between chapel and refectory, and the idea of the tower as a threshold and "special place" of entry. Kahn was off to a good start.

The clients were less enthusiastic, though, about the distance between school and cells, feeling that each rank of sisters should have its own schoolroom as a part of their living quarters, more strongly segregating the groups and making the woods a more active part of the convent. Although he suggested how the schoolrooms might be integrated into the cloisters, Kahn would fail to follow up on this, most certainly as it opposed his bi-polar "Form" diagram. Brick was acceptable as a building material, but the proposed balconies for the cells were considered too expensive. Regarding the refectory, the sisters maintained that "meals were now a social as well as a religious experience" and that many small tables would be more appropriate than the four great slabs that had been drawn in the plan. Kahn protested, saying that the smaller tables would "make the place feel like a restaurant rather than a dining hall." Sensing, perhaps, that the sisters' sense of ritual might not live up to his own idealized images of convent life (there had already been requests for recreational facilities with swimming, badminton, basketball, and tennis, soon to be followed by wishes for further comforts such as air conditioning and intercoms), Kahn expounded on "the presence of the Chapel—the sense of ritual, not convenience, a feeling of exaltation." He must have harbored the greatest of expectations for the nuns: who, if not they, would be willing to trade comfort for architecture? In the following months the sisters would not always live up to his romantic visions, though, and the cleft between his medievalist visions of monastic ritual and theirs of a modern religious life would reopen more than once.

Agreeing on a follow-up meeting at the end of August, the architects left the sisters with a copy of the standard AIA contract and a fee schedule. Although Polk had already prepared a summary of the areas, Kahn hedged when asked by the sisters about the costs of his plan, stating that it would be more profitable to discuss costs after they had "brought the project closer to a true expression of their needs." Polk laconically concluded his notes, "The sisters do not seem overawed by the size of the project." Perhaps he was thinking what the sisters should have been: that a bit of awe would have been particularly appropriate in their case. The project on the table measured a proud 160,660 square feet (14,456 m²), excluding basement. Fig. 28

There must be stalls for 135 nuns with space for visitors up to about 80-90 maximum (45 postulants taking vows with parents, family present. Would 45 postulants take vows together?). DCSP's feeling at the meeting was that guest space for 45 or total seating 180 would suit the sisters.

LIK spoke of the presence of the Chapel - the sense of ritual, not convenience, a feeling of exultation. The Parterre as exterior Chapel.

Chapel connected to Refectory is good.

Sacristy a pretty large room - space for 6 or 7 priests on certain days and storage of all materials needed to conduct services; all hymn books, prayer books, robes, vessels, etc.

An organ should be provided.

Refectory and Dining rooms: A priests' dining room and guest's dining room to be added to the program.

The Sisters' Refectory seen as a cheerful room related directly to a garden in which the sisters may eat when the weather is good. Meals are now a social as well as religious experience. Therefore the sisters felt small tables would be alright instead of great tables. LIK pointed out that small tables make the place feel like a restaurant rather than a dining hall.

The hall should be cheerful.

The diner should be permitted the luxury of conversation but not deprived of the sense of the hall as a religious room intimately associated with the Chapel.

An indoor connection must be provided between the kitchen and the rest of the monastery by-passing the Dining room.

Reception rooms to be provided near Refectory and entrance. Must provide for 6 or 8 rooms of different sizes which can be simultaneously occupied.

Views from the Refectory are desirable.

Cells: The porches were seen as being probably too expensive. LIK suggested, alternatively, deeply revealed windows - window walls of wood and glass with some panels fixed and some operating so that the pattern of light in the room might vary with use - some panels of glass and some of wood. The sisters thought the idea interesting. They do not like window seats.

-2-

Utilities for the cells should be on each floor: broom closets, ironing room, wash tubs, etc.

Pharmacy and treatment room near older sisters' quarters.

(See Notes from Dominican Sisters - July 22, 1966, for specific requirements).

Brick was generally accepted as the building material, used in conjunction with concrete where necessary. The sisters hate efflorescence.

Masonry divisions between cells are desirable for sound insulation.

The cell should express the dignity of the individual.

In cell communities, classrooms are private; novices go only to their classrooms, postulants only to theirs.

Cell	Chapel	Refectory
Porch	Parterre	Garden

A ceiling height of 9' was thought to be good.

Recreation: Tennis, badminton, croquet, possibly an indoor swimming pool, basketball?

Outdoor recreation areas should be private on the site away from the eyes of undesired spectators.

Parking: Provision for 20 cars.

Providing a main entrance from Bishop Hollow Road was discussed. The sisters liked the idea of not coming past the old building to reach the convent. In the event of the main entrance coming from Bishop Hollow Road (as the present service entrance does), the public room portion of the plan would be flipped so that the room relationships would remain much as they are now.

LIK left Mother Mary Emmanuel a copy of the Standard A.I.A. (B-131) contract (percentage of cost fee type) and a copy of the fee schedule.

We said that we would have revised plans ready for further discussion by around the end of August.

It was requested that we send a copy of these revised plans to:

Reverend Thomas Phelan
2156 N. 13th Street
Troy, N. Y.

-3-

The sisters asked about the cost of the project but LIK said it would be more profitable to discuss the costs after we had made some further study and brought the building closer to a true expression of their needs - cost was not further discussed.

The sisters do not seem to be over-awed by the size of the project.

The possibility of expansion was discussed and the most promising idea was to build new quarters for postulants when necessary and allow the professed sisters to take over all 135 cells in the currently proposed building.

David C. S. Polk
3 August 1966

-4-

ECONOMY AND INCONSISTENCIES: A SECOND SCHEME

It did not take long for the first harbingers of trouble to cloud the optimistic beginning. In September, Mother Emmanuel, developing a sense for the project's dimensions, wrote Kahn to express her worries and to remind him of the congregation's limited budget. Fig. 50

Kahn and Polk immediately began to reconsider their design. Attempting to press the parti into a more compact package, they developed a second scheme. Figs. 51–53 The monastery's position on the site remains, but responded to the sisters' wish that the entrance drive lead in from Bishop Hollow Road. The entry tower—now octagonal in plan—shifts accordingly from west to east. In an attempt to tighten up the plan, a narrower main gallery skewers the tower, connecting the communal spaces and terminating in the school and living quarters. The generous system of cloisters has been compacted by pressing the building blocks tightly against each other; gone as well are the figure-ground-interlocking "hollow columns" and "water gardens" of June's plan. The direct relationship between chapel and refectory—favored by both architect and the sisters—remains. Whereas in the previous version the governing geometry may be derived from both program and relationship to topography, here an "irrational" order takes over in which both internal parti and external relationships are considerably less lucid than before.

While this squeezing has wrung almost 35,000 square feet (3,252 m²) out of the plan—now measuring 131,600 square feet (12,226 m²) and estimated to cost roughly $4,000,000 Fig. 52—it is difficult not to sense more probing than progress. Reading the plan as a "Forum of Availabilities," it is apparent that, in contrast to the previous scheme, associations tend to be "direct rather than remote," unfolding along a mostly linear circulation system. Also troubling is how the ring of cells now includes a guest wing, the schoolrooms, a kitchen, and secondary rooms—an extension that considerably muddles the formal clarity of the parti. Accordingly, the architects seem to be at a loss when it comes to integrating the school, leaving it unfinished in plan. This scheme would apparently find its way quickly into the drawer without being shown to the clients.

50 Letter from Mother Mary Emmanuel to Louis Kahn, September 6, 1966
51 Plan, September 1966, Louis Kahn

mary, queen of all saints
motherhouse ~ dominican congregation of st. catherine de ricci

2850 NORTH PROVIDENCE ROAD
MEDIA, PENNSYLVANIA

September 7, 1966.

Mr. Louis I. Kahn,
1501 Walnut Street
Philadelphia, Pa.

RECEIVED
LOUIS L KAHN   ARCHITECT
SEP 8   1966
1501 WALNUT ST.
PHILADELPHIA 2. PA.

My dear Mr. Kahn,

Since our last meeting with you, we have given much thought to our new building. Also, we have had the opportunity of inspecting the First Unitarian Church you designed in Rochester. We are happy to have had this experience to see another way in which you develop your theories. The building seems uniquely adapted to its purposes.

The present economic picture, however, makes us pause before committing ourselves to proceeding with our project right now. The inflationary period and the current high interest rate make immediate building seem impossible.

The copy of the A.I.A contract you left for us to consider differs from others we have signed previously; perhaps this is a later version. There are a few provisions I would like to ask you about sometime.

We are not giving up the thought of our new building, and we hope you will keep it in mind, too, but we do feel we cannot take positive steps at the moment.

Perhaps if we had some concrete notion of what our project would cost we would be in a better position to know what we can do.

I would appreciate hearing from you, Mr. Kahn, with any suggestions you may have to offer.

Sincerely in J.C.
Mother Mary Emmanuel OP

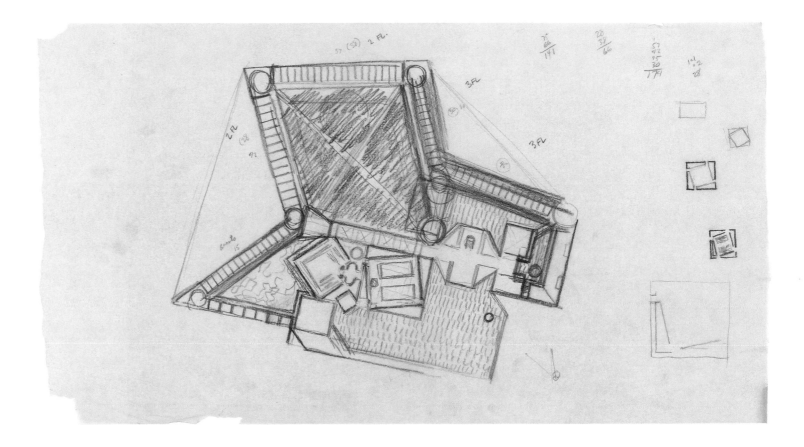

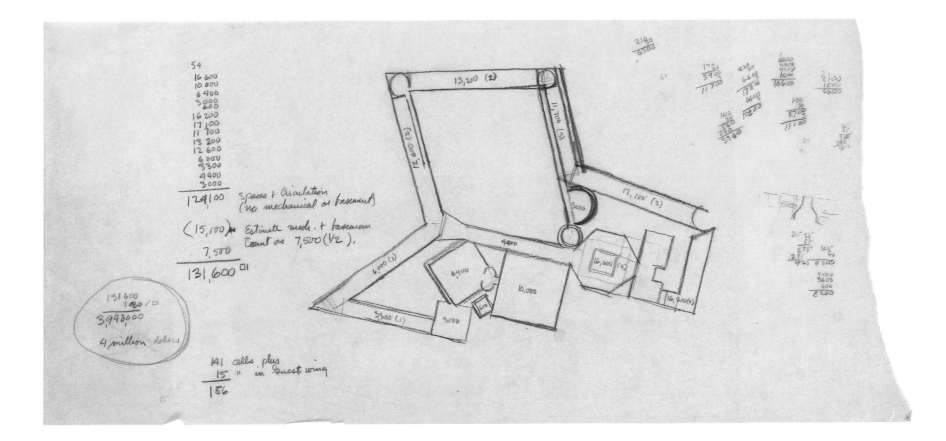

54
16 600
10 800
6 400
3 000
600
16 200
17 100
11 700
13 200
12 600
6 000
3 300
4 400
3 000

129,100   Spaces + Circulation
(no mechanical or basement)

(15,000) Estimate mech. + basement
Count as 7,500 (½).

7,500

131,600

151 600
3,948 000

4 million dollars

141 cells plus
15 " in Guest wing
156

52 Plan with area calculations, September 1966, Louis Kahn
53 Plan with notes, September 1966, Louis Kahn

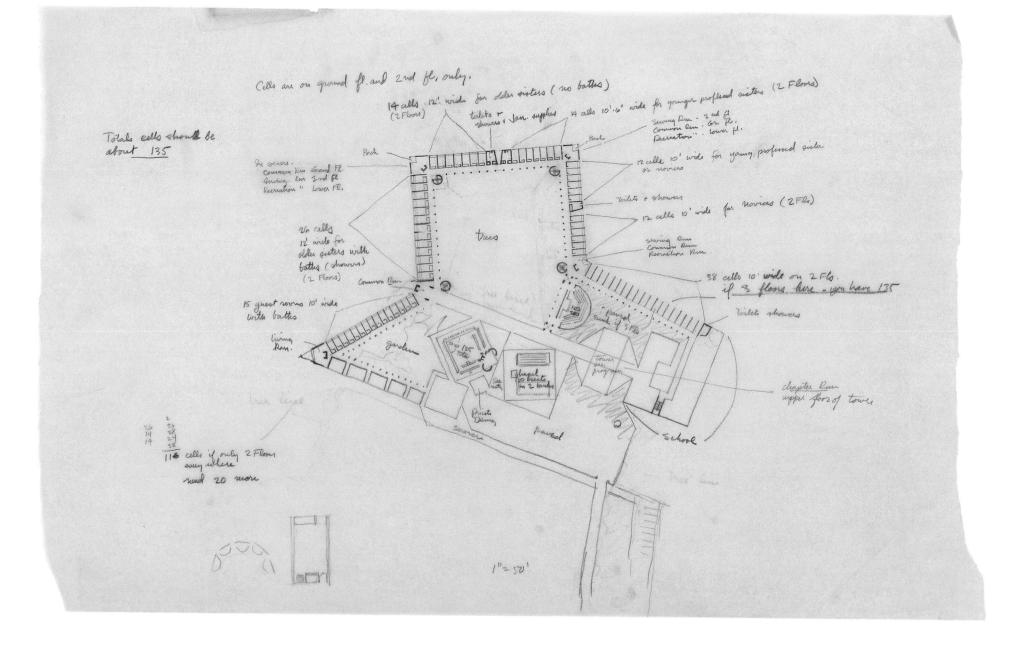

Cells are on ground fl. and 2nd fl. only.

14 cells, 12' wide for older sisters (no baths)
(2 Floors)

toilets + showers + Jan. supplies

14 cells 10'·6" wide for younger professed sisters (2 Floors)

Sewing Rm - 2nd fl.
Common Rm - Gr. Fl.
Recreation " - Lower fl.

Totals cells should be about 135

In corners -
Common Rm Ground Fl.
Sewing Rm 2nd fl.
Recreation " Lower Fl.

Porch

Porch

12 cells 10' wide for young, professed sisters or novices

toilets + showers

12 cells 10' wide for novices (2 Flrs)

trees

26 cells 12' wide for older sisters with baths (showers) (2 Floors)

Sewing Rm
Common Rm
Recreation Rm

Common Rm

38 cells 10' wide on 2 Fls.
if 3 floors here - you have 135

Toilets showers

15 guest rooms 10' wide with baths

Living Rm.

garden

See nuns

Priests Dining

Servers

paved

Chapel 20 priests in 2 banks

tower see program

School

chapter Rm
upper floor of tower

26
14
14

2
22
38
24
58
116 cells if only 2 Floors every where
need 20 more

1" = 50'

A NEW SCHEME: ROOMS FINDING THEIR OWN CONNECTIONS

Moving forward, Kahn and Polk continued to develop their plan. A new, third scheme is the first that questions the important, but expensive, main circulation gallery. Figs. 54–57 Instead of being able to reach the individual communal rooms by moving along that spine, the buildings themselves now begin to *become* the spine. This collision of bodies, the corners of which give way to allow movement within the plan, had been "discovered" by Kahn in Erdman Hall at Bryn Mawr College (1959–64) and the Fisher House (1961–67). Here, though, the collisions are handled with a casualness hitherto unknown in Kahn's larger projects. A collaged plan gives insight into a method that may have encouraged this freedom. The shapes of the various spaces have not been called into question, but rather the connections between them and how they are to be grouped. By cutting the rooms from a blueprint and repositioning them on paper, Kahn was able to shift, butt, and adjust the bodies until—as if through the alternating pulls of attraction and repulsion—they had "found" their desired resting places, where they could finally be pasted into place. This method was both a means to expedite variation, and a manner to encourage groupings at those odd angles, which would not necessarily be generated if drawing freehand or working with T-square and triangle.

It is difficult not to be drawn into speculation by Kahn's compelling collage. What, beyond the quickness of its method, motivated him to this new technique? And what was behind the quirky geometry that had slowly taken over the schemes? It is tempting to look at Kahn's contemporary work with Isamu Noguchi for the Levy Playground in New York (1961–66), in which Noguchi's earthforms and sculptural objects played against Kahn's architectural fragments in a collaged landscape—a collaboration which may have encouraged more free play in his work.[42] Then there were the profession's recent rediscoveries of planning-meeting-accident which lay heavy in the air: Delphi, the Athenian Acropolis, or the Villa Hadriana. We know, too, from Vincent Scully that a reproduction of Piranesi's etching of the Campus Martius in Rome, with its tumbled collage of monuments, hung at this time on the wall above Kahn's desk.[43] Certainly, all these—and a myriad of other—images were present in Kahn's well-stocked visual treasury. Still, simple source hunting will not bring us very far with Kahn: the lessons of the past may have revealed essence and given guidance, but were not there to be mined as academic quarries.

42 Interview, author with Harriet Pattison, October 21, 2004, Architectural Archives, University of Pennsylvania.

43 Vincent Scully, *Louis I. Kahn*, New York, 1962, p. 37.

"The rooms talk to each other and they make up their minds where their positions are. And they must aspire, each room, to be as all comprising, as all rapport, with its nature. If you name a room before it becomes a room, it dies; because it becomes just another item." Louis I. Kahn, *Architecture: The John William Lawrence Memorial Lectures,* 1972

54 Collaged plan, October 9, 1966, Louis Kahn

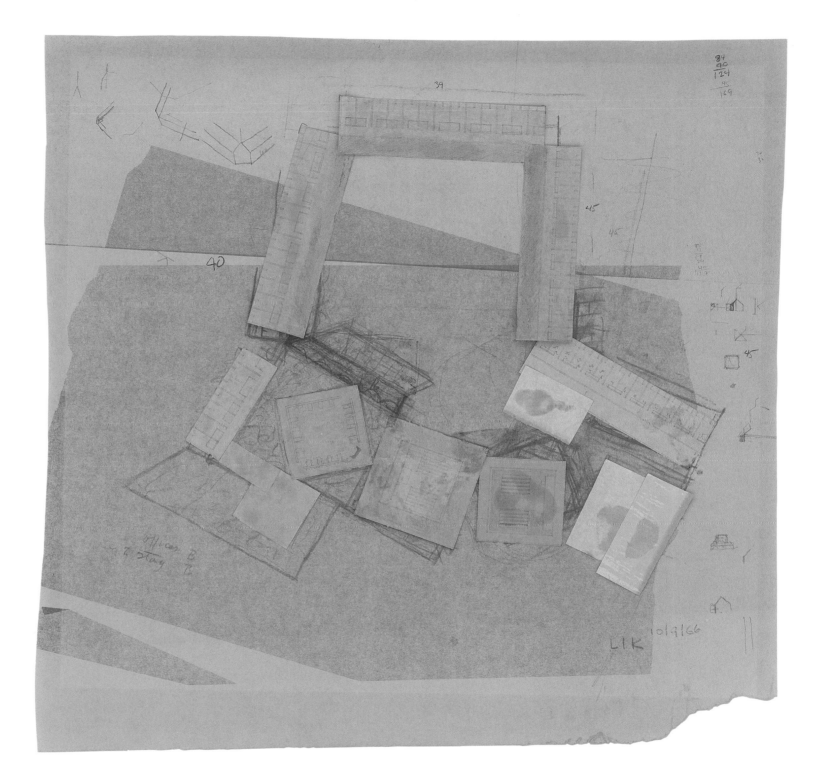

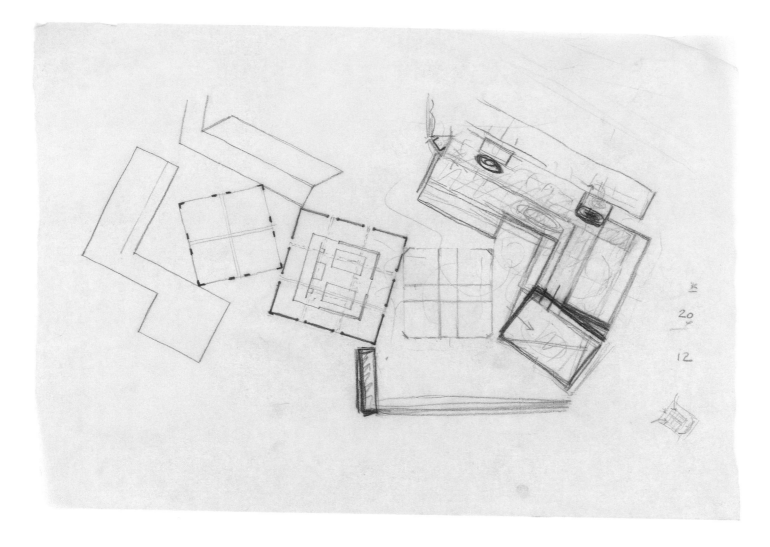

"Make the building find its own connections."

Louis I. Kahn

55 Plan fragment, October 1966, Louis Kahn
56 Floor plan, October 1966, Louis Kahn

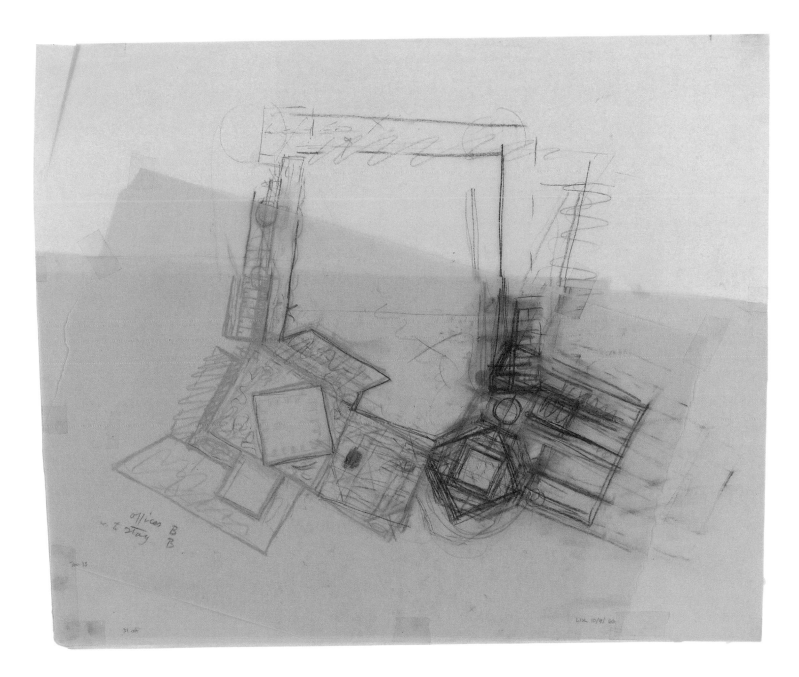

INTERNAL MOTIVATIONS

Rather than scouring history for precedents, a more fruitful way to continue our questioning would be on a project-immanent level. Earlier, speaking of the DeVore House (1954), Kahn had remarked, "In searching for the nature of the spaces of a house, might they not be separated by a distance from each other theoretically before they are brought together? A predetermined total form might inhibit what the spaces want to be."[44] In this method there can be no preconceived total shape, as the planning consists of first establishing the individual spaces required by the institution; the rooms are then assembled as to make apparent the nature and strength of their relationships. By establishing their relative powers of attraction or repulsion, they make visible their roles in the whole and thus show what the institution really "wants to be."[45]

While this may explain Kahn's understanding of a plan as a series of discrete "locales" and their respective "spacings," it does nothing to explain this particular plan's irregular geometry. One may ask if there is a project-immanent logic that exempts this plan from Kahn's "Euclidian imperative," that regular and quite rigorous geometric order which had informed his larger projects up to this point. One impetus for the irregular, as opposed to regular, diagonal collisions in "letting the rooms find their own connections" may lie in the program's varied "grain," in the varied sizes of its individual rooms: from small to large (with the exception of the cells) with little repetition. In contrast to, for example, Erdman Hall or the Indian Institute of Management, the program for the Dominican Motherhouse does not allow for a meaningful serialism generated by repeatable, regularly sized elements. Polk seems to have come up against this fact in his earliest sketches. Figs. 21–22 An irregular geometry was one way of allowing multiple collisions to occur between the different pieces without drawing them into a too-rigid geometrical corset: the Achilles' heel of many of Kahn's earlier plans.

An irregular geometry additionally underscores the *independence* of each fragment: a move away from serialism toward an individual character of parts. If until now Kahn had been employing ordering devices such as symmetry, serialism, or organic-growth metaphors to unify the elements of his plans, he begins to consistently employ here what Robert Venturi called in his contemporary *Complexity and Contradiction in Architecture* the principle of "independence and inflection," in which discrete parts gesture beyond themselves toward a "difficult" whole.

Kahn's bipolar "Form" is still fundamentally intact: the desired equipoise between the sisters' cells and the communal rooms remains. The number of pieces in the composition remains likewise largely the same. The four bars of cells still dig into the mild slope of the hill, connected by a new version of the cloisters and sunken courts with doubled corridors and generous (and costly) arcades. A fifth bar of guest cells has been added, forming a small court together with the refectory and service rooms. At the request of the sisters, a small guest dining room has been added. The bundle of communal rooms wedges upward into the cloister, prying apart its arch in an effort to densify the plan while maintaining its two discrete realms. This variation shares the formal inconsistencies of its predecessor, as schoolrooms, kitchen, and service rooms merge in formal dissonance with the outer ring. As in the previous scheme, the school and auditorium are the most non-committal moments in the drawings.

44 Kahn, quoted in Heinz Ronner and Sharad Jhaveri, *Louis I. Kahn: Complete Work*, 2nd ed. Basel et al., 1987, p. 70.

45 See Christian Devillers, "The Indian Institute of Management," *Casabella* 54 (September 1990), p. 60.

57 Floor plan, October 1966

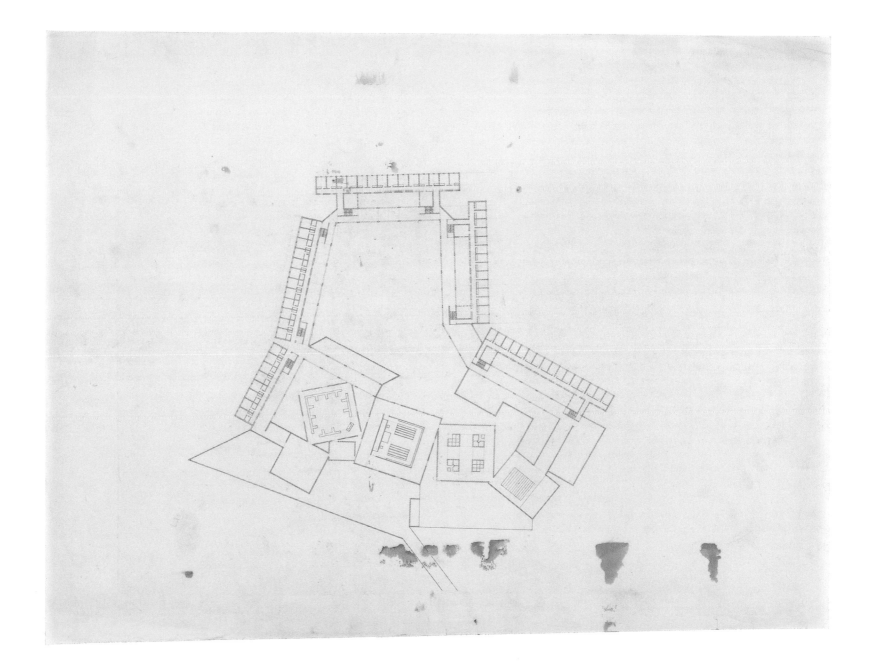

BETWEEN REPRESENTATION AND ABSTRACTION: THE ELEVATIONS

Kahn now blocked out elevations in iconically child-like drawings, abandoning the cubic, Ahmedabad-inspired forms of the first scheme for a more figurative language. Figs. 58–64 The roofs—thin folded plates in the form of multiple gables—seem to repeat "house" over and over again, or to evoke some kind of elementary gothic architecture. Large, circular cutouts still perforate the walls, now inviting us to see in them colossal rose windows. Each "house" is formally related to yet distinct from its neighbors. The entry tower is perhaps the most striking, tapering as it rises from its broad base to reach the same height as the chapel. It is at once squat and vertical, as much ziggurat as tower. In a whimsical visual pun, its silhouette echoes the bells drawn in its belfry. The section through the monastery Fig. 65 intimates how the thin walls, folded and perforated to the point of fragility, make a light-and-shadow box of the chapel and how the chapel and the wings of the cells embrace the top of the hillock.

58 Entry tower, October 1966 (est.), Louis Kahn
59 Chapel, tower, school (elev.), October 1966, Louis Kahn

60 Entry tower, October 1966, Louis Kahn
61 Tower, chapel, cloister, October 1966, Louis Kahn

62 Tower, chapel, refectory, October 1966, Louis Kahn

63 North elevation, October 1966, Louis Kahn

64 North elevation, October 1966, Louis Kahn

Refectory   Church   Entrance Tower   Auditorium   School

"I draw a building from the bottom up because that's the way it is constructed. It depends on gravity. You begin with the way the weights can be distributed on the land, and then you build up. If you do that, then you draw like an architect." Louis I. Kahn, in conversation with Richard Wermischner, 1971

65 Section looking east, October 1966, Louis Kahn

Section Thru chapel   Arcaded Rooms   Section Thru Rooms

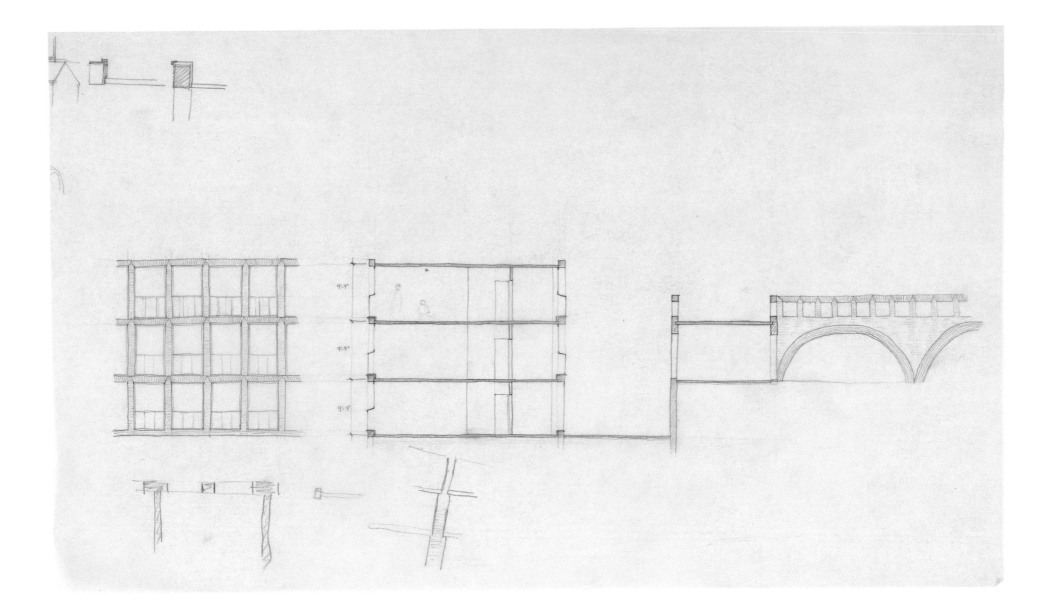

66 Section: cell and cloister, October 1966
67 Section: cell and cloister, October 1966, Louis Kahn

THE CELL AS PRIME UNIT, THE WALL AS BORDER-SPACE

Kahn now returns to address the cells in a series of detailed drawings, seeking to define the monastery's basic unit for his associates' plans. Figs. 68–73 If he had first considered stone, and then brick, for the building's main material, economy has now moved him to concrete block. The drawings show him at work on the cell as a constructed space, exploring the tectonic repercussions for the exterior wall and the atmosphere within. Small didactic notes (for himself as well as for his associates?) show him stacking and layering blocks, counting rows and joints, and attempting to determine the morphological rules of the material in question. A room height of thirteen blocks plus joint, or 8 ft. 8⅜ in. (2.65 m), is set. Tapering piers and concrete lintels structure the facade, while concrete floors complete a spartan interior.

If the sisters had vetoed the inside-outside mediating balconies at the meeting in June, Kahn is now at work to make the wall into a habitable "border space." A first attempt shows a (costly) arched double-wall solution, which is followed by an atmospheric drawing which shows a nun by her built-in desk/window seat/alcove. Fig. 71 The wall has been virtually thickened to a room-in-room, with the rough masonry space turned smooth and wooden where the habitants come into contact with the building. The section, with its human-scaled, light-regulating layer straddling inside and outside, has a precedent in Kahn's First Unitarian Church (1959–62) and will return to be built as the study carrels in Kahn's library for the Phillips Exeter Academy (1965–72).

By the mid-fifties both Kahn and his intellectual sounding board, Robert Venturi, had realized that the wall was the locus of architecture's appearance, and one of modernism's greatest mistakes was to have reduced it to the smallest necessary climatic barrier. According to Venturi, "I would say that architecture occurs at the meeting of particular interior forces of use and space, and particular and general forces of environment. Architecture as the wall between inside and outside becomes the spatial record of this reconciliation and its drama."[46]

The cells are a further case of Kahn's long-term attempt to reinvent the thin modernist membrane as a shaper of a thick spatial layer: folding it, capsizing it, doubling it, "wrapping ruins around buildings," and gradually devising a uniquely modern, mediating architectural space.

46 Robert Venturi, "Ideas of Reconciliation in Architectural Composition," proposal sent to John Entenza of the Graham Foundation, February 15, 1962, p. 10. Architectural Archives of the University of Pennsylvania.

68 Cell: details, interior, October 1966, Louis Kahn

Parapet?

1) element
2) detail
3) shadow
4) light
} → one

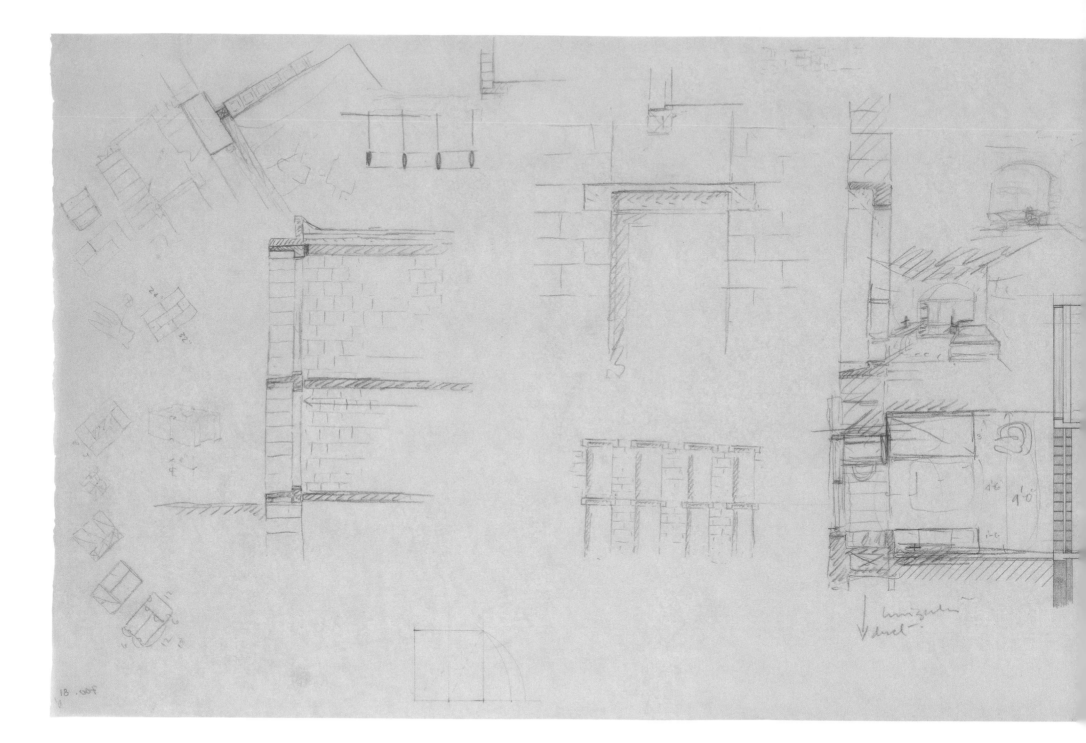

69 Cell: details, interior, October 1966, Louis Kahn

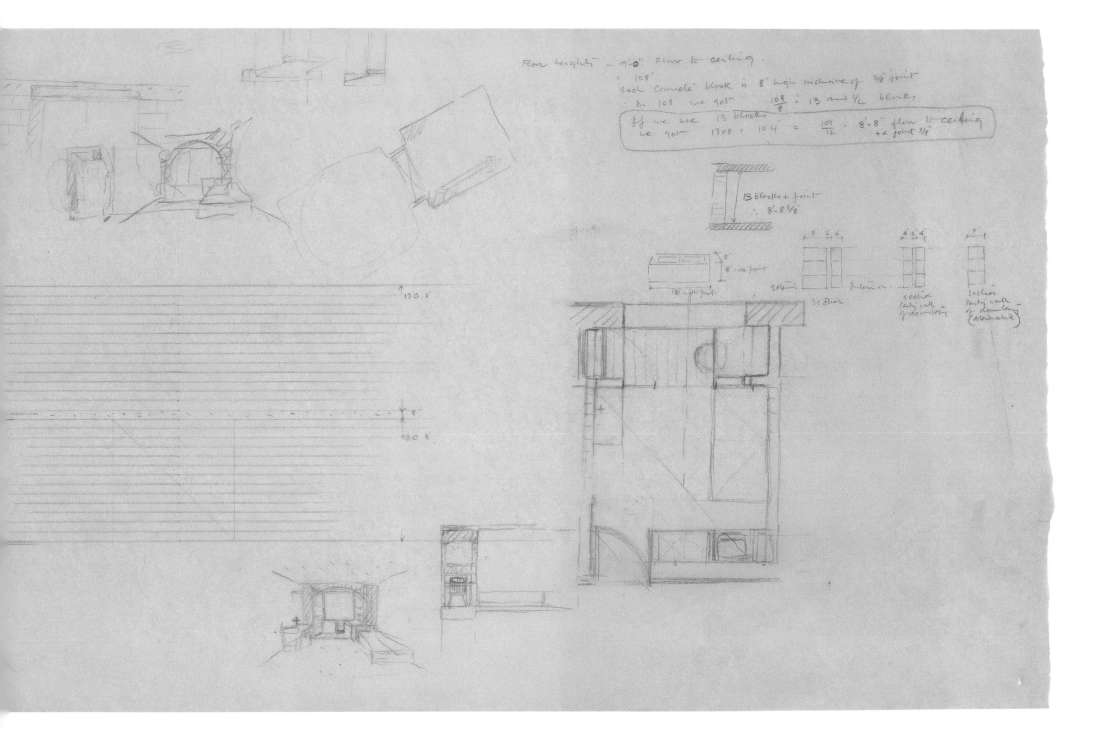

Floor heights — 9'-0" Floor to ceiling.
= 108"

Each "concrete" block is 8" high inclusive of 3/8" joint
∴ In 108" we get $\frac{108}{8}$ = 13 and 1/2 blocks.

If we use 13 blocks
we get — 13×8 = 104" = $\frac{104}{12}$ = 8'-8" floor to ceiling
                                              + a joint 3/8"

13 blocks + joint
∴ 8'-8 3/8"

13 0 8

8

13 0 8

"The window wants to be a little room."

Louis I. Kahn, "The Room, the Street, and Human Agreement," 1971

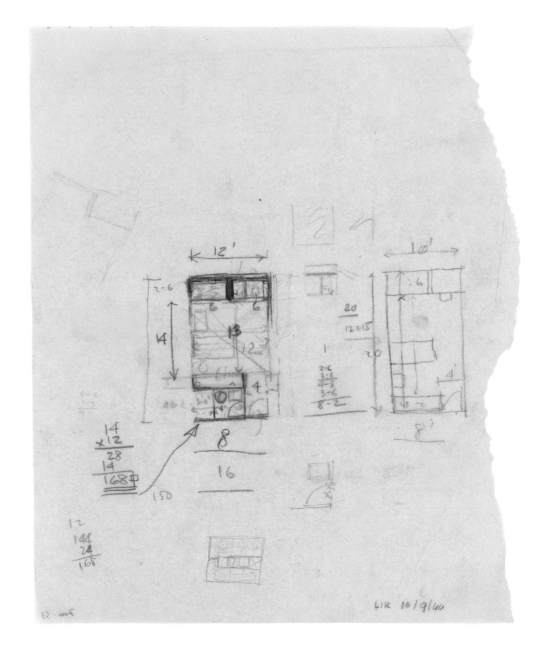

70 Cell: plan, October 1966, Louis Kahn
71 Cell: details, interior, October 1966, Louis Kahn

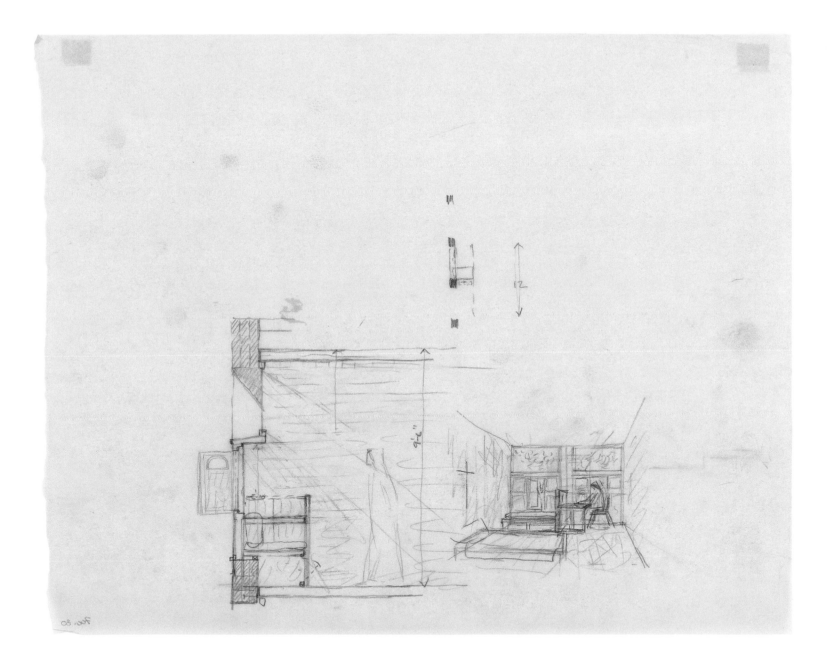

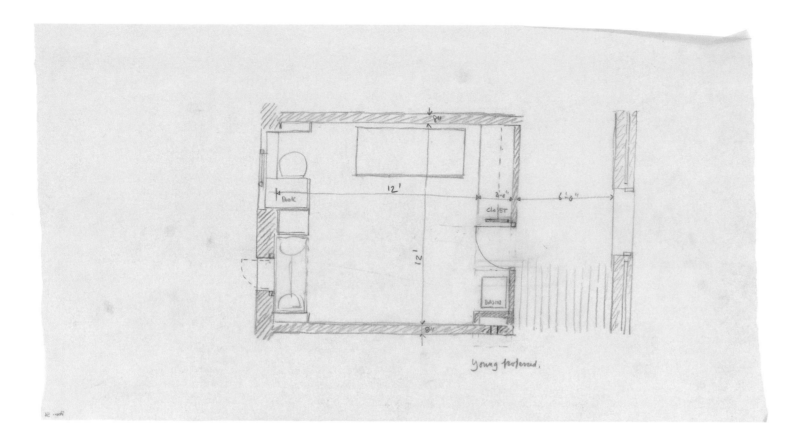

young professed.

"Each room has its own private relationship with the woods—
the serenity of the woods being felt to be in harmony with the
nature of the cell." David Wisdom, letter to Mother Mary Emmanuel, June 22, 1966

72 Cell (young professed): plan, October 1966, Louis Kahn
73 Cell (professed): plan, October 1966, Louis Kahn

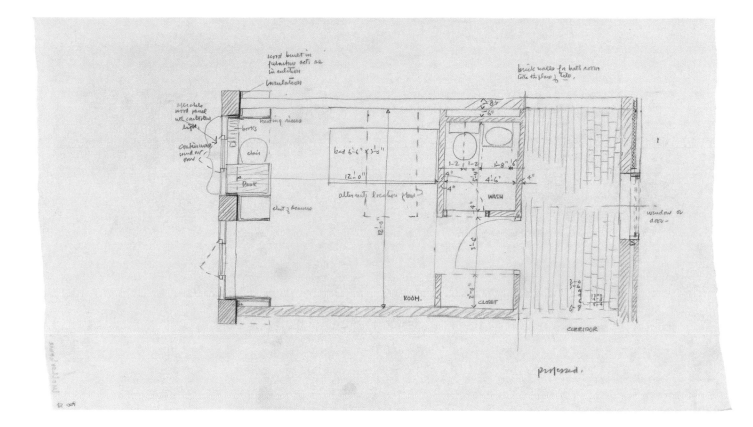

PRESENTING THE THIRD SCHEME: FORM AND BUDGET, PARTS AND WHOLE

On October 10, 1966—six months after beginning the project—Kahn and Polk presented drawings of this third version together with a model in Media. Figs. 74–75 From Polk's notes we read that the sisters approved of the architects' means of reduction, including the elimination of the main gallery: "The Sisters liked the easy but strong relationship between the major elements themselves and between those elements and the cells."[47] While the architects apparently had little difficulty gaining approval for their specific design decisions, the sisters again aired concern over the cost of the project. (Astonishingly, the architects had still not outed themselves on this ticklish theme.) Even without an architect's estimate, by now it was clear to the sisters that the project on the table was beyond their means. Taking matters into their own hands, they suggested that the monastery be realized in stages. Kahn, obviously not keen at the prospect of having to realize the project piecemeal, but certainly aware of the discrepancy between the size of his design and that of the congregation's budget, spoke of "the need for that which is built to invite construction of the whole. The beauty of the whole must be in the part. Thus the inclusion of the tower and possibly the auditorium, which might also be used temporarily as the Chapel, in the first stage of development should be considered."[48] In this first admission that his design was not buildable for the sisters' budget, Kahn suggested the possibility of indicating future construction in the form of gardens: a sort of topiary plan which could be filled in with the real buildings as funds became available.

But—crutch of a topiary plan aside—just how *does* one design an artifact so that the "the beauty of the [unfinished] whole be in the part"? At this point we—and Kahn—are faced with a fundamental question of method. If architectural design is manifestly a "top-down" operation of conceiving of "wholes," then to what degree can this wholeness be achieved through the apparently "bottom-up" procedure of accumulating parts? In spite of statements that might lead us to think otherwise, the evidence of his oeuvre shows that in the end Kahn never surrendered his allegiance to the whole. And in the case of the Motherhouse, his reservations were not only of a formal order: for him the institution envisioned gained its full meaning only with the presence and interplay of all its constituent parts.

He must have feared that, like the only partially realized designs for the Salk Institute or the Fort Wayne Fine Arts Center, an unfinished monastery would remain forever a fragment of the intended social vision. "Form is that which deals with inseparable parts. If you take one thing away, you can't have the whole thing. Nothing is ever fully answerable to that which man wants to accept as a part of his way of life unless all its parts are together."[49] Perhaps in an effort to convince the sisters of this necessity (perhaps, in a worst-case scenario, to at least end up with an attractive presentation for future publication), Kahn requested that the sisters invest in a "fine model" of the complete scheme.

This tension between "top-down" and "bottom-up" methods of design—manifest throughout the modern movement as the tension between "rationalist" and "functionalist" morphologies and explicitly installed as the twin poles of the creative act by Kahn in his "Form-Design" dichotomy—is neither a question of budget, nor is it peculiar to the Dominican Motherhouse, rather, it is a principle source of the characteristic charge in all of Kahn's mature work. At this uncomfortable impasse the meeting ended, with the next meeting scheduled for the 25th of October.

47 Meeting minutes, October 10, 1966, David Polk, Kahn Collection, Box LIK 10.

48 Ibid.

49 Kahn at Yale (undated) on the Fort Wayne Fine Arts Center, quoted in *What Will Be Has Always Been: The Words of Louis I. Kahn,* ed. Richard Saul Wurman, New York, 1986, p. 13.

74–75 Meeting notes, October 10, 1966, David Polk

DOMINICAN SISTERS - MOTHERHOUSE

Meeting Notes of October 10, 1966

Present: Mother Mary Emmanuel
                Sister Monte
                Sister James

                Louis I. Kahn
                David C. S. Polk

Site model, plan, elevation and section were presented to the Sisters.

The new general layout was approved. The Sisters liked the easy
but strong relationship between the major elements themselves and
between those elements and the cells. The grouping of classrooms
together was questioned at first but we believe accepted at the
end.

After the presentation and lunch, the Sisters commented as follows:

1. Their concern over the possible cost of the project was voiced.

2. They, therefore, felt that the project might be built in
    stages. The first stage of building consisting of the
    following elements:

          Cells for the Postulants and Novices
          (74 as shown on plan 10/10/66)

          Visiting Parlors

          Common Rooms

          Recreation Rooms

          Small Laundries

          Kitchen

          Refectory

3. LIK spoke of the need for that which is built to invite construction
    of the whole. The promise of the beauty of the whole must be in the
    part. Thus the inclusion of the tower and possibly the Auditorium,
    which might also be used temporarily as Chapel, in the first stage
    of development should be considered.

Dominican Sisters - Motherhouse
Meeting Notes of 10/10/66

4. The possibility of indicating future construction in the
    form of gardens was mentioned. Also, a fine model of
    the whole.

5. A study of the rooms themselves at larger scale would
    now be undertaken.

6. The Sisters expressed a desire for air conditioning in
    the Refectory and Chapel. (The Auditorium would need
    it as well).

7. The date of the next meeting was set for 10:00 a.m.,
    Tuesday, October 25th.

David C. S. Polk
DCSP:lmb

A LETTER AND ITS ANSWER

Within a few weeks of October's meeting, in a letter dated November 18, 1966, the sisters received the long-awaited cost estimate together with a fee proposal from Kahn. Figs. 76–77 The new scheme, now measuring 147,061 square feet (13,662 m²), was estimated to cost approximately $3,500,000. Kahn tellingly spoke no longer of a "building," but of a "master plan," indicating the possibility—which for the sisters would have been a necessity—of realizing the monastery in stages. Whether in parts or as a whole this sum was worlds away from the $1,500,000 the congregation had imagined they would spend for their new home. Mother Emmanuel answered Kahn with a letter dated December 16, letting him know in friendly but no uncertain terms that the design was, both in terms of means and cost, far beyond the pale. Fig. 78

If Kahn had beguiled the sisters into joining his "Trappist dream" over the previous months, planning an ideal monastery within a financial vacuum, this dreaming would suffer a cold awakening with Mother Emmanuel's letter. In retrospect, one might question Kahn's wisdom (and professionalism): he knew months earlier of the project's costs, yet apparently failed to reveal them to the sisters, in spite of their regular queries. Was he confident that that they could secure funds for their project after realizing what was possible? (This had been the case before, and didn't the church have its share of sponsors and secret coffers?) Was he as yet incapable or unwilling to let the modest budget steer his thoughts on "Monastery"? Did he need to develop an ideal version of his "Form" diagram before distilling it into its more affordable essence? Just how much bluffing, how much necessity, and how much wishful thinking were at play here is impossible to ascertain from our distance. Kahn had often attempted to explain what he considered to be the difference between "economy" and "financing," and an excerpt from his address at the 1959 CIAM Congress in Otterlo might provide insight into his thinking on budgets and institutions: "A school or a specific design is what the institution expects of us. But School, the spirit school, the essence of the existence will, is what the architect should convey in his design. And I say he must, even if the design does not conform to the budget." [50] But this kind of lectured idealism does have its limits for an architect passionate about building; and one thing must have by now been abundantly clear: although the sisters had been the most patient of clients, there was now a real danger of either losing the project entirely or of only realizing a fragment of the desired scheme if he did not soon bring costs within their means.

In an effort to rein in her architect, Mother Emmanuel followed with a reduced program, now naming a budget of $1,000,000. She, too, had by now understood the difficulty of designing so much monastery for so little money. In her revised program of December 27, she sacrificed forty-five cells—reducing the required total to seventy-five—in addition to making various other reductions in order to cut costs.

50 Louis I. Kahn, "Talk at the Conclusion of the Otterlo Congress" [1959], in *Louis I. Kahn: Essential Texts,* ed. Robert Twombly, New York, 2003, p. 42.

76–77 Letter from Louis Kahn to Mother Mary Emmanuel, November 18, 1966
78 Letter from Mother Mary Emmanuel to Louis Kahn, December 16, 1966

November 18, 1966

Mother Mary Emmanuel, O.P.
Dominican Sisters Congregation
3850 North Providence Road
Media, Penna.

Dear Mother Mary Emmanuel:

We are glad to have presented an initial architectural expression of
your program at the several meetings we held. Our speculations on
the cost, based on these studies, will serve as a guide toward a
budget and the decision on the quantity of work now to be built.
Naturally, the undeveloped state of the drawings cannot set this
budget accurately, but the cost sheets and drawings we submitted to
you on November 10, 1966, show that the costs should range between
$3,000,000 and $3,500,000.

At our last meeting, I outlined the major stages of architectural
service. The development of the Master Plan will indicate diagrammatic
plans, the positioning and, in general, the architecture of buildings
and their connecting architecture of porticos, arcades and ambulatories,
and the entire site development of roads, paths, and landscaping features.
It is good to feel the whole aesthetic order from which individual designs
are derived. Then the architecture of the buildings chosen for the
initial stage will be in sympathy with all the buildings of the future.

The Master Plan should be accompanied by a detailed model, preferably in
wood, to present an articulated, three-dimensional image of the site and
building features. I propose that you approve the making of such a model.
This finished model will remain in your possession. It is estimated that
its cost should not exceed $3,500. This will not take the place of study
models for our work, such as the ones you have already seen.

You will see in the yellow folder enclosed (Pennsylvania Society of
Architects Schedule of Minimum Fees) that religious buildings are listed
under Schedule "A", and dormitories and other buildings on our site are
listed under Schedule "B". (Libraries are also listed under "A", but in
this case, the Library should have no more complications than the other
buildings under "B").

To: Mother Mary Emmanuel   18 November 1966
                                        -2-

Accordingly, the fees would be determined by interpolation as follows:

Chapel & Refectory	$ 800,000 x 8.30% =	$ 66,400.
Other Buildings and Site	$2,200,000 x 6.60% =	145,200.
Approx. fee if built at one time:		$211,600.
First stage Master Plan Schematics 15% of $211,600.		= $ 30,000 approx.
Schedule "A", Est. Cost Refectory - $265,000		
Est. Fee: 9.22% x 265,000 x 85%		= 20,000 "
Schedule "B", Est. cost other Bldgs.- $700,000		
Est. Fee: 7.20% x 700,000 x 85%		= 42,000 "
First stage approximate total fee:		92,000
Initial payment 5% of $92,000:		4,600
Remainder to be made in Progress Payments:		$ 88,400.

Since 15% of the total fee will have been paid on the Master Plan, in the
future when other sections are authorized for construction, the architectural
fee for completion will be only 85% of the appropriate fee for the work.

Please let us know if you have any questions or suggestions.

Sincerely,

Louis I. Kahn
LIK:hb

Extra copies for distribution by Mother Mary Emmanuel to those concerned.

December 16, 1966.

Mr. Louis I. Kahn, Architect FIAI
1501 Walnut Street
Philadelphia, Penna.

My dear Mr. Kahn:

Since our last meeting in Media our little
group has discussed frequently our building
program and the suggestions that you have
made. Much as we admire the plan we are
agreed that it is not practical for several reasons.

1) Our funds are limited (though our
desires are not) and we do not have the
money that the series of buildings would
require. Perhaps we asked for more than
we could afford or may need in the immediate future. At any rate we do not wish to
be involved in such an extended program.

2) Even if the necessary money were
available, we would hesitate long before
committing ourselves to spend so much in
wide, exterior covered, cloister walks with
high brick walls and numerous arches. This
seems utterly inconsistent with a life
dedicated to voluntary poverty.

3) What made us actually reconsider the
plan was the realization that the cost of
the refectory alone would be in the neighborhood of $275,000.

4) The Dominican Order is an apostolic order.
Its spirit is one of action flowing from
contemplation. The plan as you have developed it is geared more to a Trappist or
Carmelite spirituality, where contemplation
and solitude are their own end.

Could a single building be planned that
would include all our basic necessities that
would cost in the neighborhood of one million
dollars? We need housing for about 50 Sisters
now. Can we provide for them and permit
future expansion to remain a possibility?

We deeply appreciate all the time and ability
you have given to our problem, Mr. Kahn.
If we have permitted ourselves to be carried
along by your plans it is because they appeal
to us very much. But we are sure now that
such expensive building does not suit our needs
nor our funds.

I realize that my message must be a disap-
pointment to you as it is to me. However, I
would appreciate hearing from about further
possibilities.

Respectfully yours

Mother Mary Emmanuel OP

THE THINKING HAND: DRAWINGS BEGET DRAWINGS

Mother Emmanuel's critique of November's scheme, together with her reduced program and budget, would quickly push the project on a new trajectory. Acting directly on the communiqués from December, Kahn and Polk would, by February 1967, dramatically distill and densify the project. A series of sketches from these weeks are compelling evidence of the architects' struggle to compact the plan. Although undated, it is possible—without delving too deeply into speculation—to reconstruct an "operational" order for the sketches based on the context of the design thus far.[51]

In what we might assume to be the first of these sketches Fig. 79, October's scheme has been streamlined into a regular pentagon, with two of its sides given to communal spaces and three to cells. Kahn must have realized immediately, though, that the long periphery of the building meant no significant savings in terms of area; in addition, the linear circulation can have hardly appealed to him. (See "remote" vs. "direct" association.) Elaborations of this scheme (by Polk?) Fig. 80 are no more convincing, the strong geometric figure anathema to both the topography and to the architects' previous attempts at a loosely informal "society of rooms." In further variations Figs. 81–82, cells and communal spaces flatten to press up against each other on either side of a narrow crescent-shaped court in attempts to minimize the circulation space. While the parts remain largely the same, any sense of a balanced Gestalt is lost while the relationship between topography plan becomes increasingly uncertain. It is more than a little tempting to read in the hasty charcoal strokes Kahn's impatience with his efforts.

Drawings have a life of their own and an observer may find it difficult to judge to what degree the drawing tool has been led and to what degree it has done the leading. With the series of sketches at hand we seem to have reached one of those passages where strokes of the charcoal stick play quickly back upon themselves to generate further and still further drawings. As a result of this self-propelled pulse, something unexpected falls into place. Fig. 83 In this variation, the communal rooms are no longer held in equipoise with the cells across a court, but have been neatly assembled—like pralines in a box—within the rectangular space formed by those cells. The entry tower—until

now a constant—has been abandoned in favor of an entry court. While the reward for this change of tack is a promising take on a vexing problem, the diagram is still mute in regard to its (undrawn) context. Apparently sensing potential in this variation, Kahn now proceeds to adapt it to the specifics of the site in successive attempts. Figs. 84–85 The figure is pressed tightly together, rotated ninety degrees counterclockwise, and fitted into a forest clearing across from some sort of place of arrival. Several tiny diagrams on these sheets show Kahn's concern for fitting the plan both to the topography and to a space "excavated" from the arboreal mass. In further developments, he continues to explore the interaction between figure, site, and program. Figs. 86–87 Finally, the regularly shaped pocket in the forest is now almost equally filled with the monastery to the west and a clearing to the east. The threshold/tower has now returned to the composition, straddling the border between these two realms. Fig. 88

51 It is at this point of the narrative that reconstructing the path becomes most difficult. Whereas virtually all other steps may be chronologically verified either by dated plans, project files, and/or by the context of other drawings, in terms of both attribution and chronology, these undated and unsigned sketches represent the most speculative passage. On attribution: although none of these sketches have been filed among those eighty-five project drawings which have been "definitively" identified as Kahn's, the "handwriting" of most of them does seem to indicate that they belong to him. We have, then, either a case of Kahn's drawings having been filed in the office drawing portfolios, or of Polk sketching in a Kahnian manner, leaving us to find contentment with a picture of both Kahn and Polk pushing the project forward together. On the drawings' chronology: while in their *Complete Work,* Ronner and Jhaveri have placed figures 79 and 82 as intermediate steps between the schemes of June and September, 1966, I propose that at least three facts speak for the chronology presented here: first, the unity of handwriting and medium in all the sketches in question; second, that the proposed chronology best matches the architects' and sisters' goal of compacting the project (figs. 79 and 82 indicate considerably fewer cells [a maximum of sixty: see Kahn's note on fig. 82, "60 cells on 3 floors"] than the schemes of September and October 1966, indicating that they were almost certainly drawn after Mother Emmanuel's reduced program with seventy-four cells from December 27, 1966); and third, the fact that the proposed chronology describes a plausible development within the scope of the project. Because the tendencies illustrated by the sketches are long-term, I propose that the general argument presented here in form of a narrative remains feasible even with allowance for certain deviations from the presented chronology.

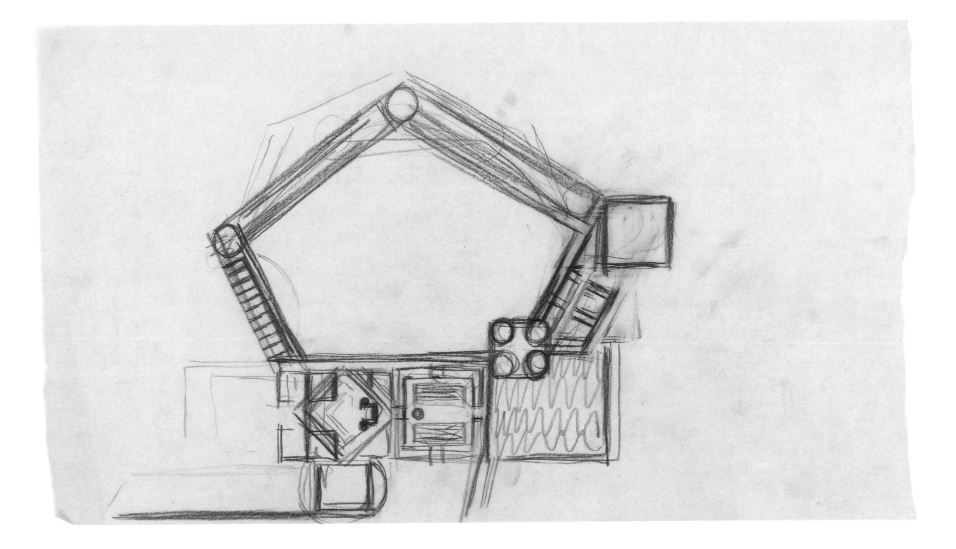

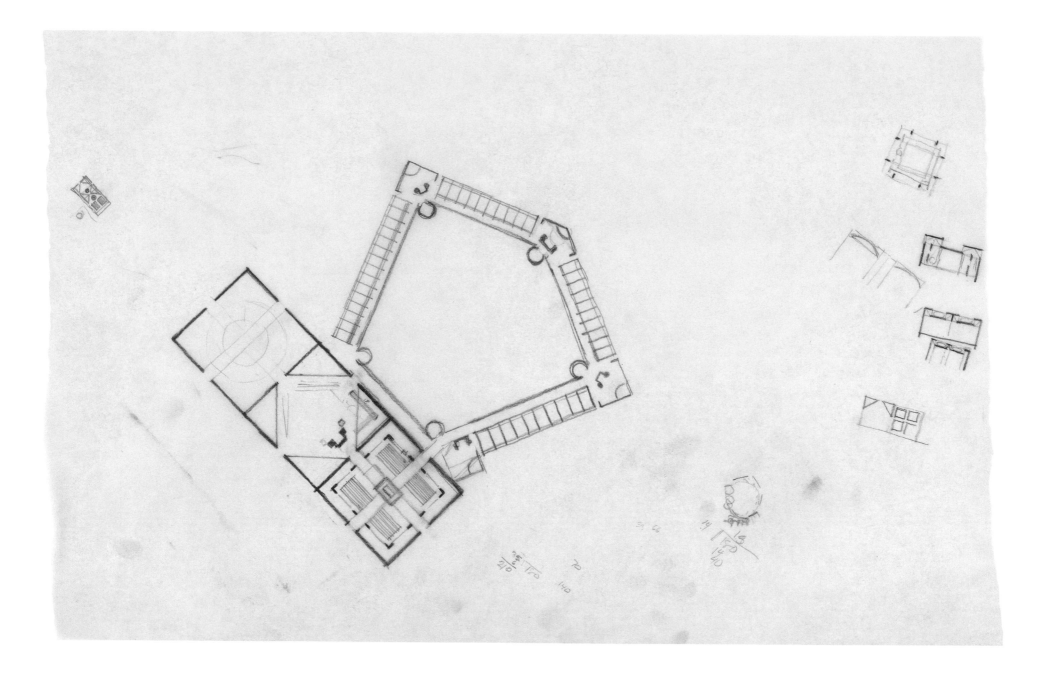

80 Plan, January/February 1967, David Polk (attributed)
81 Plan, January/February 1967, Louis Kahn (attributed)

82 Plan, January/February 1967, Louis Kahn
83 Plan, January/February 1967, Louis Kahn

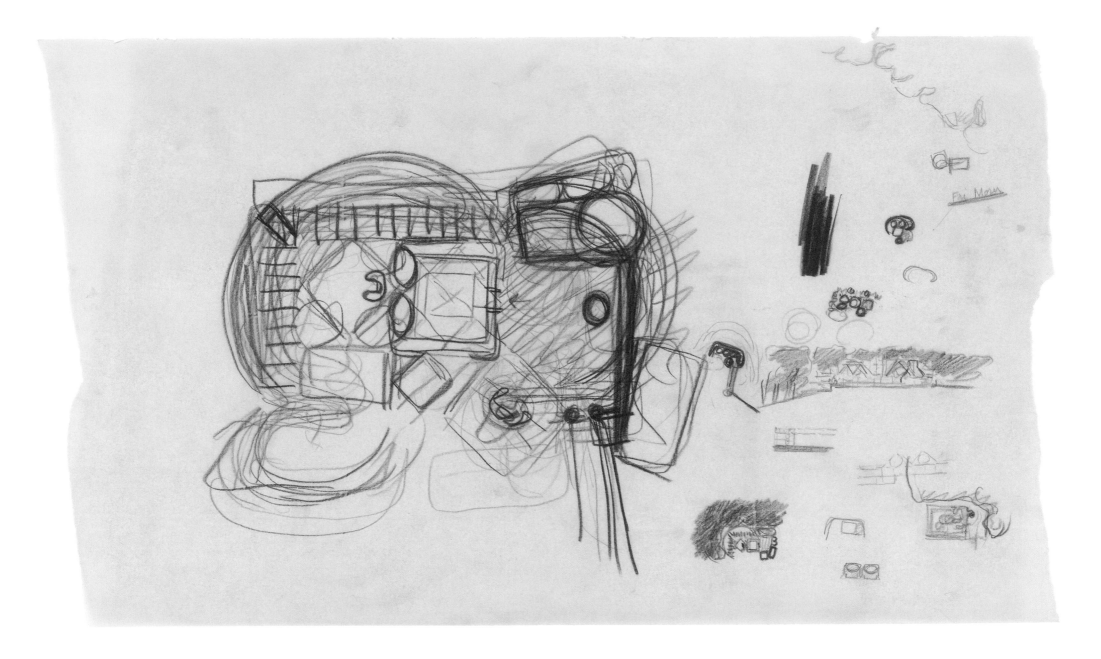

84 Plan, January/February 1967, Louis Kahn
85 Plan, January/February 1967, Louis Kahn

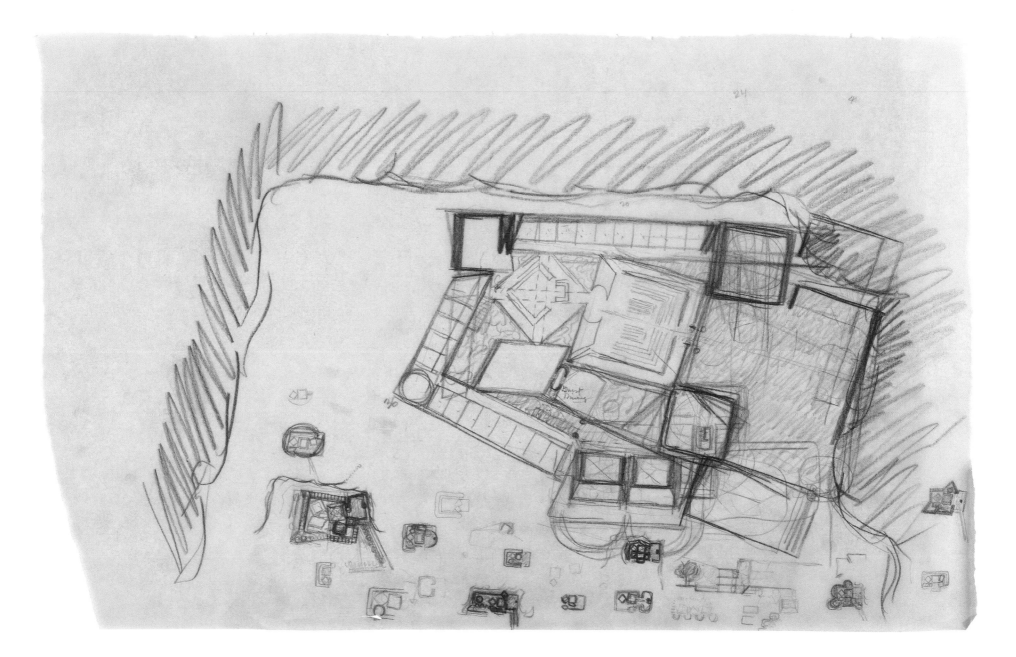

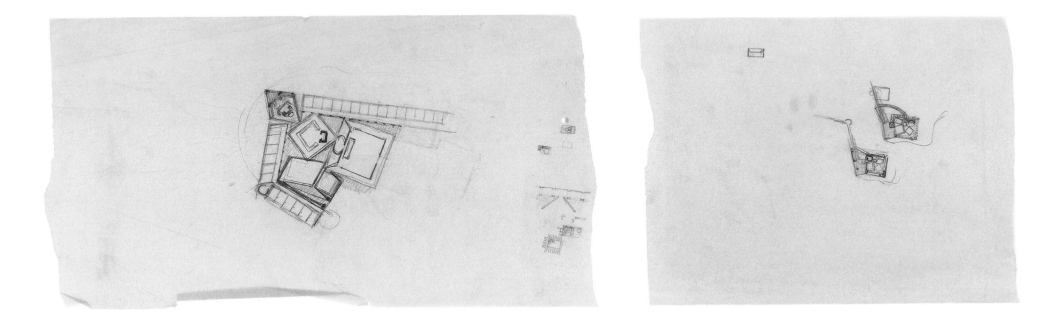

"Making architecture is not a process." Louis I. Kahn

86–87 Plan fragment, January/February 1967, Louis Kahn (attributed)
88 Plan with site, January/February 1967, Louis Kahn

102

A NEW PLAN, A NEW CHANCE

Out of the previous weeks' struggle, a drawing presented to the sisters in Media on February 16 emerges as a significant breakthrough. Figs. 89, 91 The emphatically dualist interpretation of the program, with its two realms held in equipoise across an open center—a constant of all previous schemes—has been called into question after nine months of work. The cells, until then divided according to the sisters' four-tiered hierarchy, now form a three-sided, rectangular frame that is staked out at its four corners by the living rooms. Into the open arms of this frame the plan now implodes, the communal rooms being drawn as if by force into what had previously been the cloister. It is remarkable how the contrast between the simple shapes and their seemingly spontaneous collisions within the orthogonal frame gives the plan a hitherto unknown internal tension, as if the several buildings of the previous plans were striving—without quite succeeding—to become the "single building" Mother Emmanuel had envisioned. The elaborate system of arcades and galleries that had been so unmistakably criticized in her letter has now all but disappeared, the building blocks straining, as Kahn would describe, "to find their own connections."

If the previous schemes represent a series of variations based on a group of constant premises, the new scheme may in many respects be seen as a series of inversions of those premises. For example, the relationship of the plan's figure to the forest and to the site's topography has changed. Whereas the earlier schemes had used the edge between woods and meadow as a line of demarcation between the monastery's private and communal realms, the new configuration forms concentric rings moving out from the center of the clearing to the forest's edge. The orientation of the ensemble has changed as well: by rotating the whole ninety degrees counterclockwise, a wing of cells now closes the figure to the north, strengthening the impression of a man-made clearing in the forest. (The previously unchallenged parameter of direct sunlight for all cells was sacrificed in the process.) Instead of first experiencing the monastery in its frontality, one now approaches the tower obliquely, slipping in along the edge of the clearing in order to find oneself at its center. A crescent-shaped pond brackets the clearing to the north. Where the previous schemes had held the top of the hillock open, nestling the cells into the brow of the hill with a series of (expensive) retaining walls and sunken gardens, the new scheme exaggerates the existing topography, building up from ground level and placing the tallest buildings—the tower and the chapel—on the crest of the hill. Geometrically as well, the new scheme is an inversion of the first scheme, in which the freely floating cells were juxtaposed to the orthogonal communal spaces; now it is the cells that form the orthogonal counterpart to the informally ordered communal spaces.

On March 2, 1967, shortly after submitting the new plan, David Polk sent Mother Emmanuel a summary of areas together with an estimate of construction costs.[52] The complex had been dramatically reduced to 50,171 square feet (4,660 m²), including basement and mechanical spaces, and was now estimated to cost $1,593,000, with landscaping. In his accompanying letter, Polk assured the prioress that the project could be built for $1,500,000. Relieved that the architects had so dramatically reduced area and cost—cutting both by well over half—the sisters reinstalled the original budget of $1,500,000. The architects could breath deeply again: their project could continue.

52 Letter with cost estimate, David Polk to Mother Mary Emmanuel, March 2, 1967, Box LIK 10, Kahn Collection.

89 Plan with site, February 1967

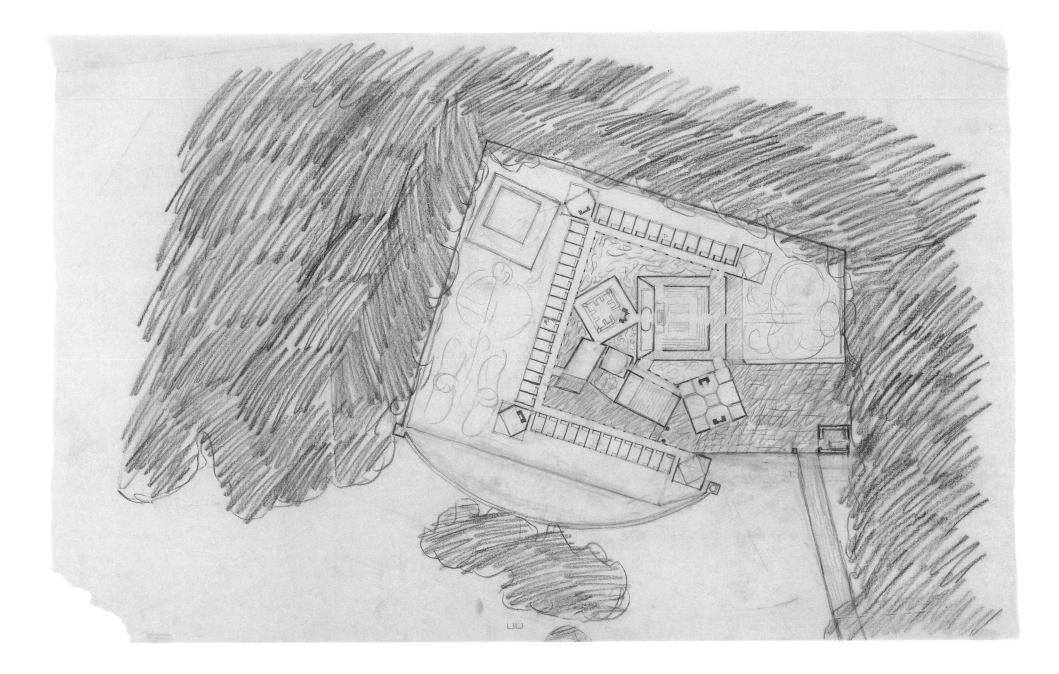

REACTION

The game leap to this new, fourth scheme was undoubtedly the boldest in the process to date, shaking the very root of the "Form" diagram. At the plan's presentation the sisters praised their architects, not only for their new-found economy, but moreover for discovering a scheme more appropriate to their institution.[53] By superimposing public and private realms, by eliminating halls and galleries and forcing spaces to meet in severely unmediated fashion, the new plan suggests a substantially different environment than the previous schemes, one in which the monastery's various activities—contemplation, worship, learning, assembly, even cooking—are given nearly equal significance and bound together in a vision of community in which the distinction between private and communal lives has begun to erode. It's surprising to read no opposition to this unorthodox plan in Polk's meeting minutes. Was the sisters' trust in Kahn that great? Did they really understand the drawing on the table? Perhaps they did indeed understand the plan, and saw its boldly unmediated spaces to be in accord with the Dominican rule of voluntary poverty, in harmony with a vision of community that is, in spite of its hierarchies, fundamentally egalitarian. Whatever the case, the sisters must be credited for their insight and courage in approving such an unconventional—and as of yet schematic and unresolved—plan.

In retrospect, they may have sensed in the germinating plan an attempt to make spatially manifest the equilibrium called for by their order's ideal of spiritual life: "That which characterizes the Dominican Brother [Sister] is the concord, the harmonious synthesis, of virtues, apparently the most contrary: gentleness with energy, love of study with love of action, genius for contemplation with the spirit of organization.... An apostolic message that has not been shaped in the sanctuary, the choir, and the cloister is never complete."[54] More than the previous versions, this new scheme—with its multiple juxtapositions and diminished hierarchies—may be read as an attempt to make palpable the delicate balances and desired synergies between the constituents of Dominican life.

53 Meeting minutes from February 13, 1967, Box LIK 10, Kahn Collection.

54 William A. Hinnebusch, O.P., *Dominican Spirituality: Principles and Practice,* Washington, D.C., 1965, p. 123.

90 Meeting notes, February 16, 1967, David Polk
91 Plan with site, February 16, 1967

DESIGN AS RE-SEARCH

That Kahn would spend several months working through the consequences of his first "Form" diagram before modifying his stance may seem extreme, yet is emblematic for his development of an idea. Seen within the scale of his entire career or that of a single project, Kahn's moving forward was a methodical and purposeful searching, a building upon that which came before, rather than an introduction of a plethora of new impulses or themes. In this economy of ideas, a hypothesis or theme—once introduced—will be explored in all of its consequences before it is abandoned or modified. What appears to the outsider as stubbornness or a paucity of ideas may instead be seen as the hidden strength of the work. For it is precisely this quality of sustained attention to a limited number of themes, of holding an idea firmly while working upon it, which lends the activity of designing a character approaching that of "re-search" in the original meaning of the word.

Ten months had passed since beginning the project. The plan's new hypothesis—that established monastic ritual and modern informal religious life might both be done justice in a unified spatial gesture, in a single "big house," as it were—is a challenging one. The unorthodox plan brings, coupled with its promise of becoming a "society" of equally significant spaces, its share of functional, spatial, and formal difficulties. Kahn's proposal largely attempts to do without that helpful repertoire of mediating architecture—corridors, galleries, halls, and courts—which he knew so well from his neo-Beaux-Arts training. To renounce

this "architecture of connection" raises first of all functional questions. How, for example, does one move through the plan without disturbing the sanctity of the chapel, the concentration of the classrooms, a gathering in the auditorium? How to mediate between spaces if not with corridors? If there is no longer a "back door" to the complex, how to separate access to the valorized public spaces and the profane service spaces? Furthermore, if—as we have heard Kahn declare—it is precisely this "architecture of connection" which "gives the man walking through the building a feeling for the entire sense of the institution," how to reach a sense of coherence without it? Can the subtle hierarchies in the program be done justice by a plan in which the distances have collapsed? And then, formally and spatially: To what degree are the individual parts autonomous, to what degree do they consolidate within a single whole? These questions are by no means trivial, and will occupy Kahn and his assistants for months to come.

Inherent to this method of functional bricolage is that each element may be developed independently—the potential being, in Kahnian terms, that the "existence will" of each space may develop freely into what it "wants to be," uninhibited by a totalizing form or structural unit. Taken to its extreme, this method of "growing" and then assembling individual spaces might produce works that would transcend the designer's existing preferences or prejudices. A suspension of judgment is required of the architect, who to a certain degree becomes a spectator

of his own work, the potential reward being results that surprise their maker by transcending the limits of his will and imagination. The craftsman is never cleverer than his craft; or, according to Kahn, "Order is not what you want it to be."[55] In this sense, the Motherhouse must be the most literal and extreme illustration of Kahn's setting a process of discovery into play toward a house that is a "society" of quasi-independent rooms, each engaged in finding out "what it wants to be" while it at the same time "talking together and making up their minds where their positions are."

55 Kahn, in *What Will Be Has Always Been: The Words of Louis I. Kahn,* ed. Richard Saul Wurman, New York, 1986, p. 235.

"From what the space wants to be the unfamiliar may be revealed to the architect. From order he will derive creative force and power of self-criticism to give form to this unfamiliar." Louis I. Kahn, "Order Is," 1955

92 Plan, February 1967

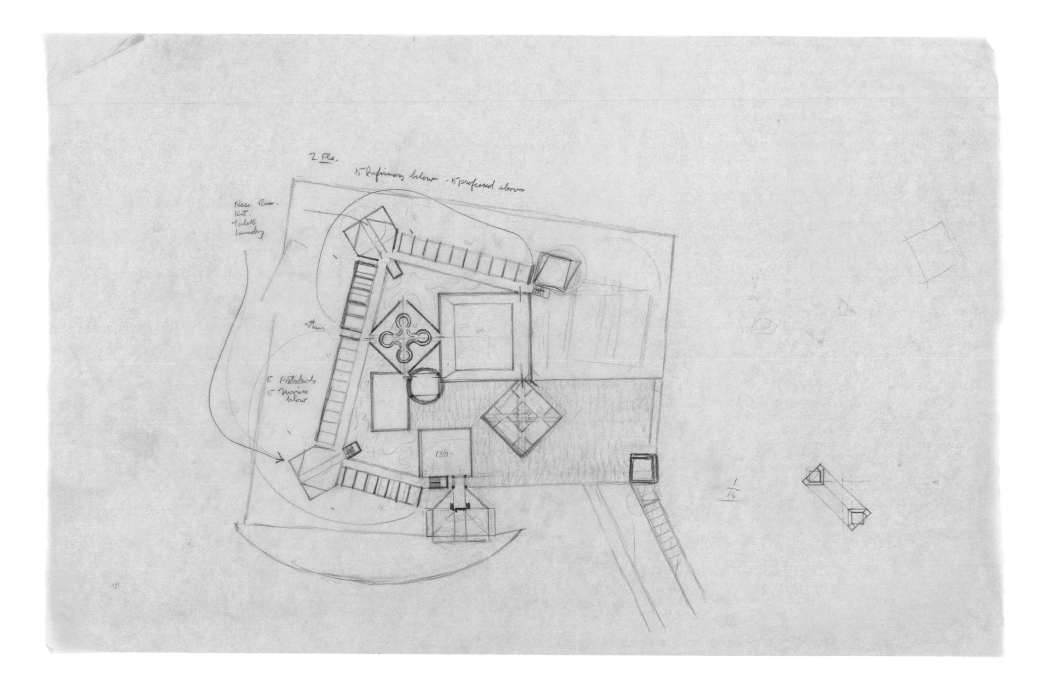

A DIFFICULT PROPOSITION

Closer study of the plan of February 16, compelling as it may be within the context of the project's development, offers more promises to what it might become than convincing answers to how its self-imposed conflicts are to be resolved. The plan has been drawn in a manner that fixes intent while leaving much open: functionally, formally, and spatially. Functionally, circulation and adjacencies are difficult to imagine in several instances. The axial link between chapel and refectory directly behind the altar undermines the sanctity of the holiest of holies, the passage to the cells via the auditorium means a compromise in both the usability of that space and the accessibility of the cells, the use of an institutional kitchen as a connective space between private and communal rooms would certainly stretch even the most liberal of clients' sense of decorum, while the adjacency of the main entrance and the service court entrance— the crossing of garbage cans and visitors in plan—is a banality over which even an architect of Kahn's stature may stumble. For the time being, the question of vertical circulation has been left completely open: not a single stair has been drawn.

Formally, too, the architectural consequences of "letting the rooms find their own connections" are as yet unresolved. Whereas certain rooms naturally "find their connections" through direct collision with their neighbors, others need "adapters" in order to make those connections work—an additional, superfluous, architectural order is thus called into play. Spatially, the oblique entry approach toward the tower tends to direct movement either toward the chapel, or to unintentionally deflect it toward the service court.

A multitude of drawings exist from the phase that begins here, testimony to the difficulty of the topological puzzle Kahn proposed for himself. Figures 93 to 100 have been chosen from these sketches to illustrate some of the architects' many attempts to organize and connect the core spaces during the weeks of spring and summer.

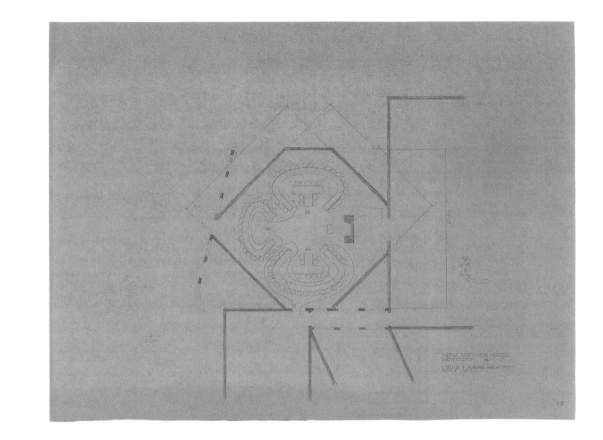

93 Refectory: plan, May 1967
94 Chapel: plan detail, for June 28, 1967, Louis Kahn

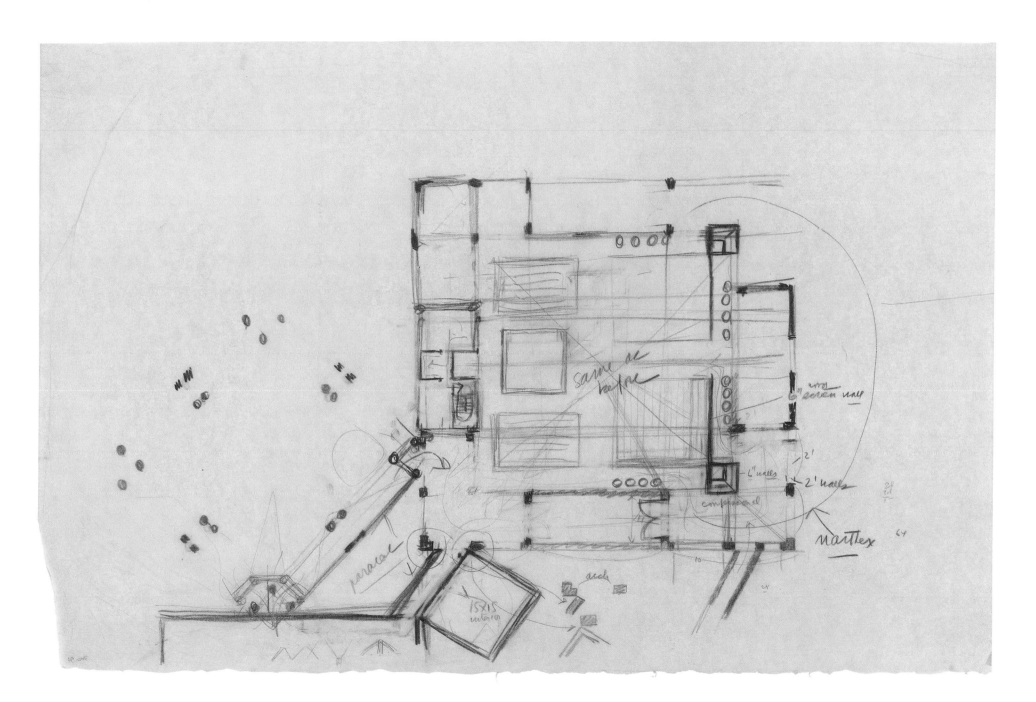

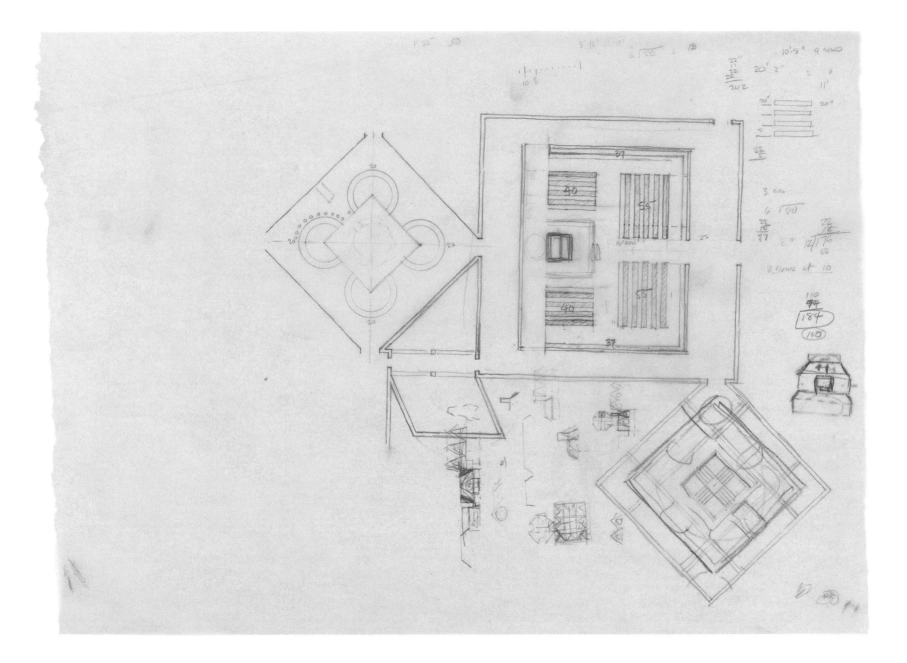

95 Core: plan, Spring 1967
96 Core: plan, Spring 1967, Louis Kahn

TOWARD FORMAL RESOLUTION

The entrance to the tower has been displaced ninety degrees, now greeting visitors more graciously than February's plan. Fig. 97 This has the added advantage of pushing the service entrance into a secondary position, out of sight and traffic flow. Unfortunately, this comes at the cost of transforming the central court—in the last version a small *hortus conclusus*—into a service court. Kahn must have been uneasy with this; even in a "non-hierarchical" plan, a service court occupying the geometric center—and sharing a wall with the chapel at that— would have certainly violated his sense of propriety. In addition, the schoolrooms, auditorium, and north wing of cells are now cut off from direct access from the main entrance, resulting in either "open-air" circulation or extremely long routes through the building. The octagonal shape of the refectory—a recurring motif in classicist and Beaux-Arts plans—is a device that permits this space to elegantly turn the corner in plan. The schoolrooms have consolidated to form a hammerhead block at the head of the northern wing. As with the schemes of September and October 1966, a question of "order" or syntax is raised: the larger, communal room-type in discord with a periphery formed by smaller cell-types. Again, Kahn seems aware of this contradiction and hesitant to commit to it—the schoolrooms are left unfinished in plan.

A subtle, yet important change in the geometry of the plan: whereas in February's version the core spaces float freely within the frame of the cells, apparently unbound by geometrical rule, they have now—with the exception of the tower, which is tilted approximately thirty degrees away—locked into the same grid. It is instructive to note that this geometric cleansing has at the same time increased the tension in the plan, the volumes of the communal spaces rotating now in unison to "pull" against the orthogonal frame that contains them. Kahn knows that meaningful dissonance exists only in the context of order. As if aided by the simplified geometry, the core spaces no longer need "adapters" to find their connections. Although still functionally flawed, formally, at least, the plan has taken a step toward possible resolution.

"The chapel has a central space which for the moment we won't describe; around it is an ambulatory for those who don't want to enter. Outside the ambulatory is an arcade for those not in the ambulatory; the arcade overlooks a garden for those not in the arcade. The garden has a wall for those who don't enter and merely wink at the chapel." Louis I. Kahn, "Not for the Fainthearted," 1971

97 Plan with site, May 19, 1967, Louis Kahn

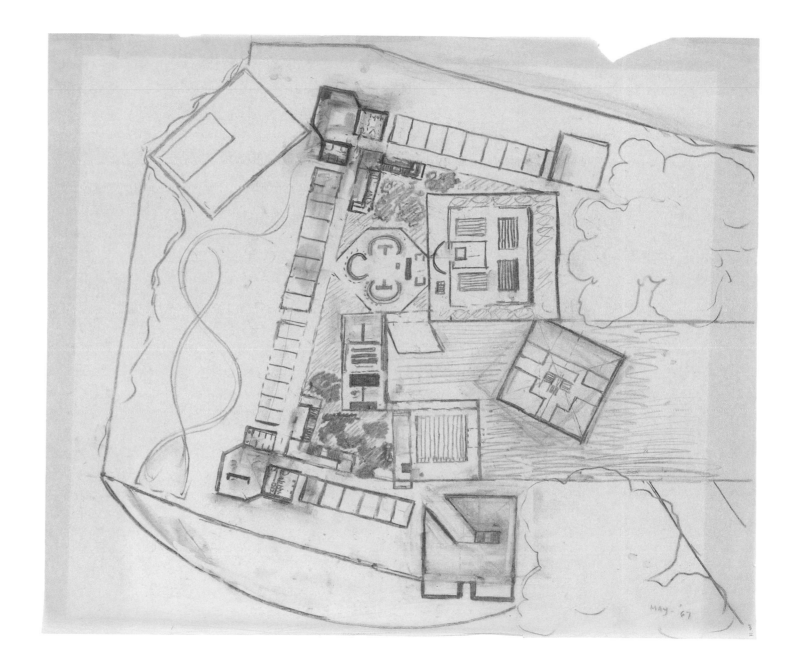

May-'67

115

98 Core: plan, for June 28, 1967, Louis Kahn
99 Core: plan, for June 28, 1967, Louis Kahn

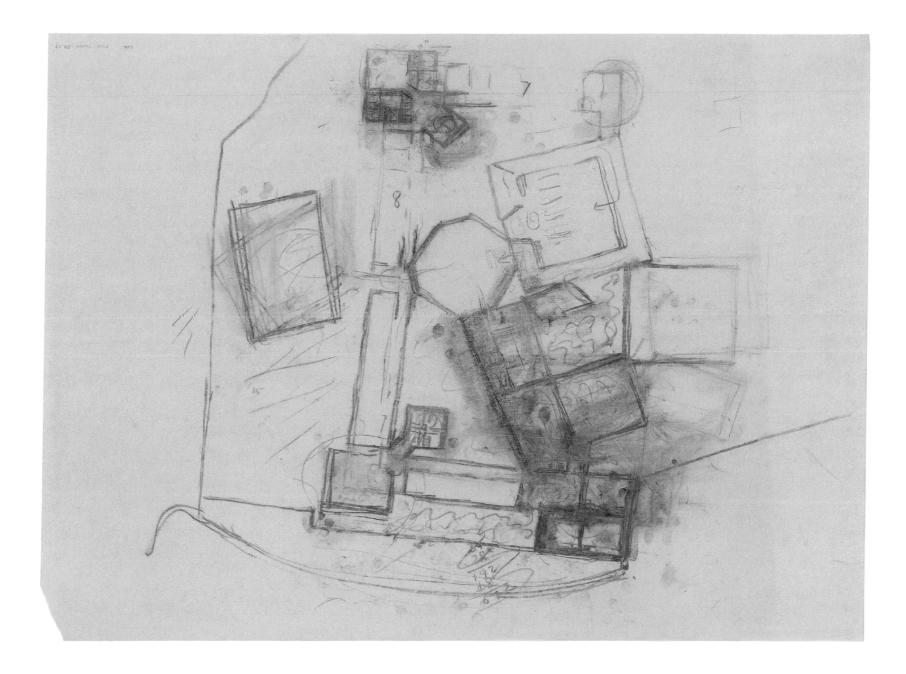

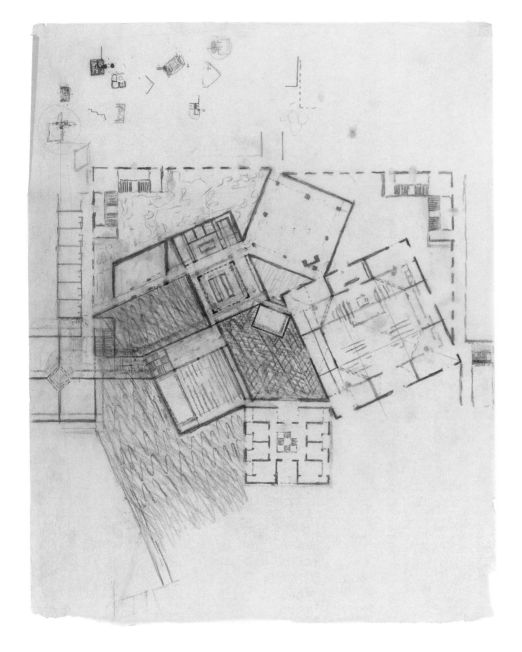

100 Plan fragment, for June 28, 1967, Louis Kahn (attributed)
101 First floor: plan, June 28, 1967

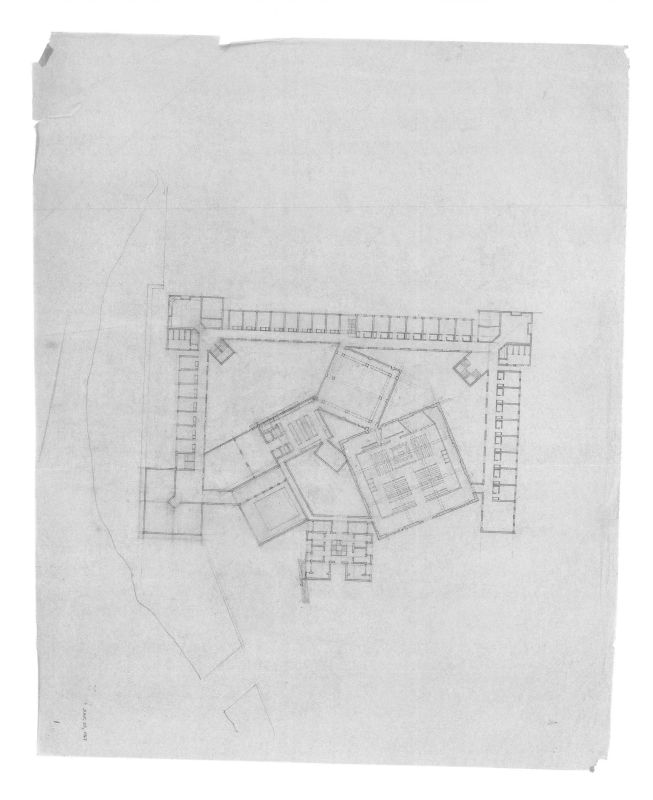

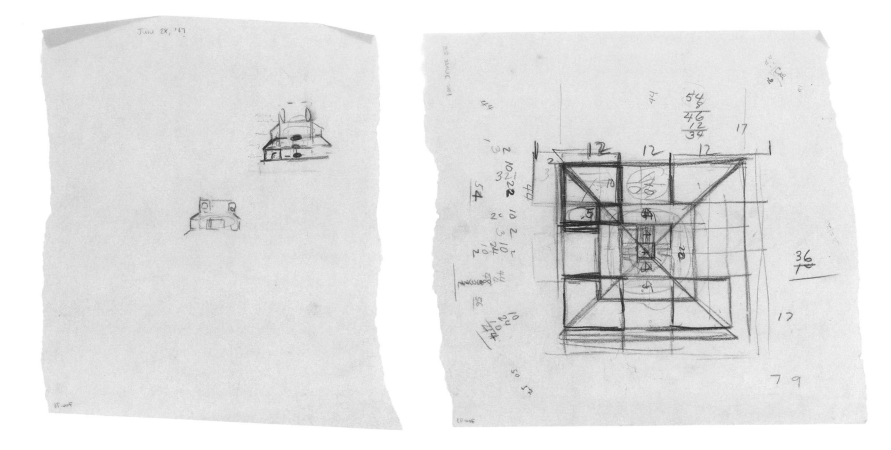

"The monastery which I am doing has an entrance place which happens to be a gate. It is decorated in the invitation of all religions, something which is now being started. But they are given a place only at the gate, because the sanctity of the monastery must be kept." Louis I. Kahn, "White Light, Black Shadow," 1969

102 Entry tower, for June 28, 1967, Louis Kahn
103 Tower: plan, for June 28, 1967, Louis Kahn
104 Tower: elevations, for June 28, 1967, Louis Kahn

JUNE 2?, 1767

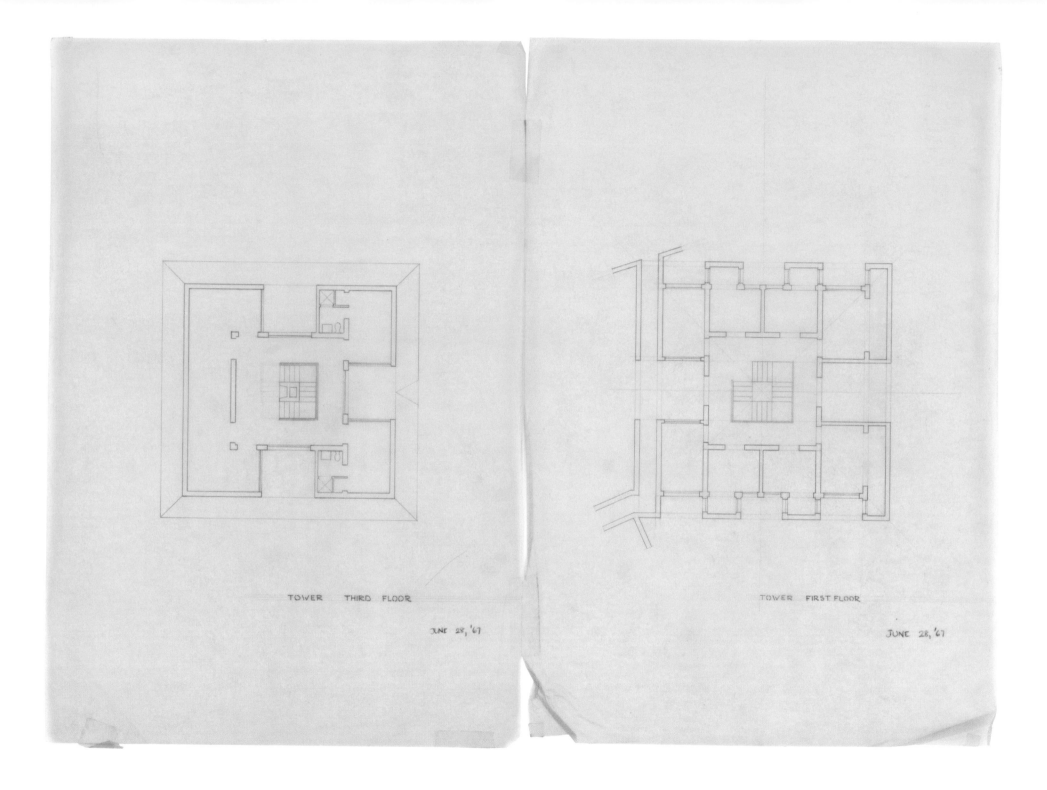

TOWER   THIRD FLOOR

JUNE 28, '67

TOWER   FIRST FLOOR

JUNE 28, '67

105 Tower: plans, June 28, 1967

106 Tower: elevation, section, June 28, 1967

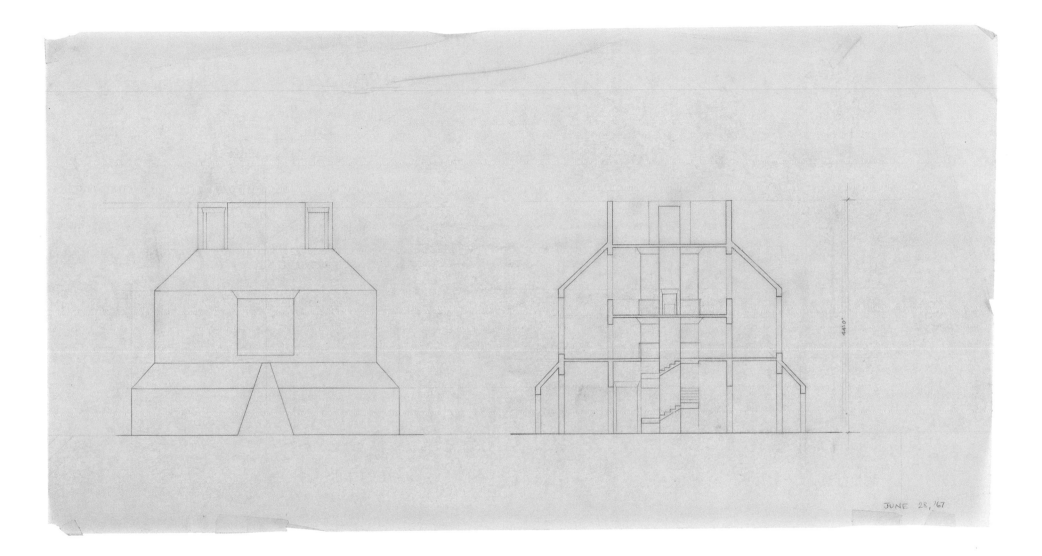

JUNE 28, '67

A COMPREHENSIVE SCHEME AND ITS PRESENTATION

A drawing from June 28, 1967 Fig. 101, based on a sketch from Kahn Fig. 100, is the first large-scale drafted floor plan of any scheme (¹⁄₁₆ in. = 1ft., approx. 1:200). This plan is further elaborated in a large site plan and elevations for presentation to the sisters and Father Phelen in Media on August 7. Fig. 107 The tightly drawn, pencil-on-vellum plans are, for the first time, a commitment to investigate a scheme in detail, intimating particulars of construction, consequences of collisions, and intricacies of scale. The disposition of the parts is largely the same as in May, with a few small but decisive changes. The auditorium has drifted to meet the tower, making space for a small service court and its entry. Freed of its service function, the central court is again a small garden around which the plan unfolds. Just as important, the new disposition of core spaces—for the first time linked together in a "continuous collision"—allows for an uninterrupted and non-hierarchical network of paths through the house. The most sensitive of these spaces—the chapel and the refectory—are double-layered, each with an ambulatory that is at once room and hallway. The tower has turned parallel to the cells, staking out a reference frame within which the core spaces rotate. Again, the plan seems to gain tension with its increasing geometric rigor.

With Kahn's ample and atmospheric charcoal sketches Figs.108–9 showing the way, the floor plan is accompanied for the first time by elevations from all sides. Figs.110–13 While the expressive "ziggurat" tower has remained, the other elements have cooled down. Gone are the multiple gables and circular arches, replaced by a more reticent and tectonically precise "brick order" of flat-roofed volumes, tapered pilasters, and jack arches. The contemporary Phillips Exeter Library (1965–72) is a close relative. Although these abbreviations may have originated in the architects' search for economy, it is not difficult to sense in the more subdued prisms a response to the Dominicans' vow of poverty, to the delicate scale of the landscape, and to the complex floor plan, which causes considerable visual excitement in itself; to sense, in short, a search for appropriateness.

107 Plan with site, August 1967

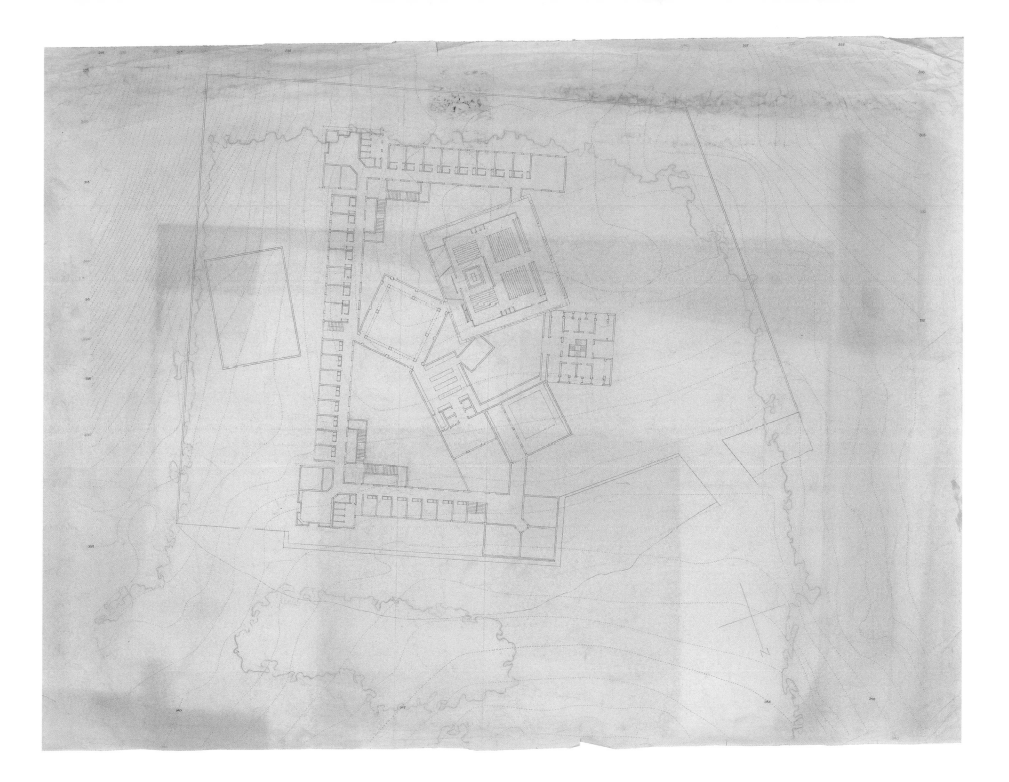

108 South elevation, August 7, 1967, Louis Kahn

LIK AUG 7, '67

109 East elevation, August 7, 1967, Louis Kahn

MOTHERHOUSE   LIK, AUG

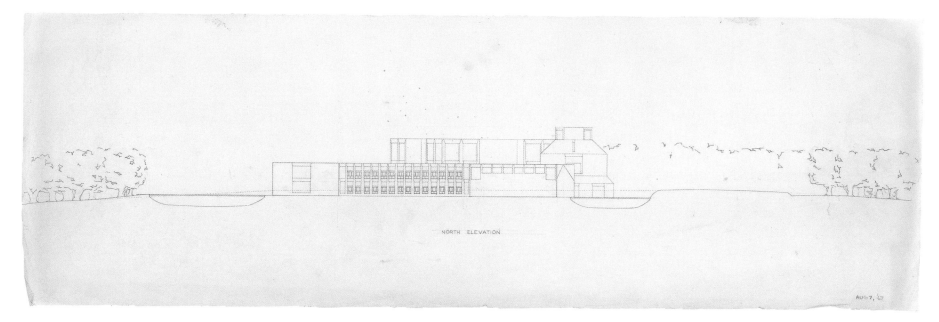

NORTH ELEVATION

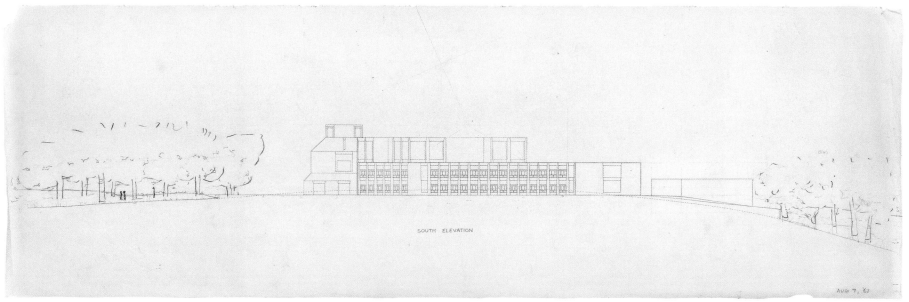

SOUTH ELEVATION

110 North elevation, August 7, 1967
111 South elevation, August 7, 1967
112 East elevation, August 7, 1967
113 West elevation, August 7, 1967

EAST ELEVATION

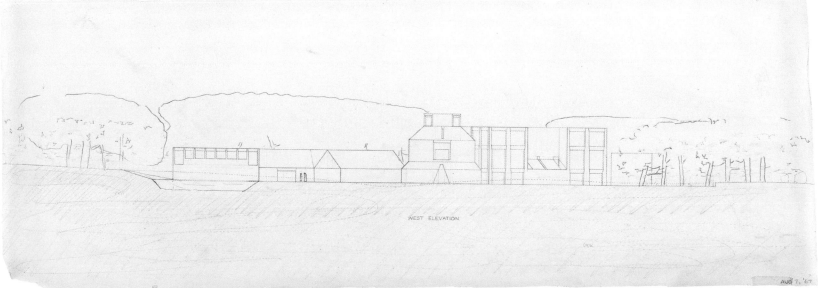

WEST ELEVATION

PRESENTATION AND SIGNS OF COMMITMENT

According to the minutes from the meeting and presentation on August 7, the sisters again accepted the premises of the plan and, together with the architects, set a number of refinements for the next stage of designing. The school was to be combined with the auditorium by placing the auditorium on the upper floor; the library—until now, either a discrete element or included in the school or auditorium building—was to be moved to the second floor of the tower. Additional sitting rooms—now totaling eight—were to be added to the west end of the cells. The liturgy and furnishing of the chapel were discussed with Father Phelan. For intimate worship, a small chapel ("a religious place in the religious place") for thirty persons was to be added to the east of the sacristy; a confessional room, "an agreeable room for two people to converse," would replace the confessional booths. A private room for the priest was to be located above the sacristy. In accordance with the Dominican ideal of an "action religion," Father Phelan suggested that chairs would be more appropriate than pews, which would allow alternate seating arrangements and even other non-liturgical uses.

Records from these weeks reflect the sisters' commitment. On August 7, 1967, almost a year and a half after their first meeting (!), Kahn and Mother Emmanuel signed an AIA contract for architectural services. Figs. 115–16 On August 24, 1967, Kahn wrote to the sisters, recommending four general contractors who might bid on the project. In November, the office of Vinokur-Pace, a frequent consultant to Kahn, was officially contracted for structural and mechanical engineering.[56] The project, having barely survived the winter, was now gaining momentum.

56 Letter, Kahn to Mother Mary Emmanuel, August 24, 1967, Box LIK 10, Kahn Collection.

"The client asks for areas, the architect must give him spaces; the client has in mind corridors, the architect finds reasons for galleries; the client gives the architect a budget, the architect must think in terms of economy; the client speaks of a lobby, the architect brings it to the dignity of a place of entrance."

Louis I. Kahn, 1973

114 Meeting notes, August 7, 1967, David Slovik
115–16 Contract, August 7, 1967, Louis Kahn/Mother Mary Emmanuel

CHANGES IN CONVENT PROGRAM ~~AGREED UPON AUG. 7, 1967~~
AFTER MEETING AUG. 7, 1967

SCHOOL TO BE COMBINED WITH AUDITORIUM.
    SERVING AREA OF AUDITORIUM MAY BE OMITTED
    AUDITORIUM TO BE ABOVE SCHOOL TO FREE GROUND

LIBRARY TO BE INCLUDED IN TOWER
    LIBRARY SHOULD BE ON SECOND FLOOR (I.E. ON FLOOR IMMEDIATELY
    ABOVE RECEPTION ROOM) ARCHIVES MAY BECOME PART OF THIS.
    CENTRAL STAIR SHOULD SERVE LIBRARY ONLY ADDITIONAL STAIRS
    TO SERVE GUEST ROOMS ABOVE
    TOWER MAY GROW TO ACCOMMODATE LIBRARY.

CHAPEL
    SMALL CHAPEL FOR 30 TO BE ADDED TO THE EAST OF
    THE SACRISTY SO THAT SACRISTY COMMUNICATES
    WITH BOTH LARGE CHAPEL AND SMALL ONE.
    NUNS QUARTERS TO BE OVER SACRISTY
    SEPARATE CHAIRS TO BE USED IN PLACE OF PEWS
    TO ALLOW USE OF CHAPEL FOR SPECIAL OCCASIONS
    CONFESSIONAL ROOM INSTEAD OF BOOTHS' AN AGREEABLE ROOM
    FOR TWO PERSONS TO CONVERSE, CONVENIENT TO THE SACRISTY

CELLS
    ADDITIONAL SITTING ROOMS (6) TO BE ADDED AT WEST
    ENDS OF CELLS. (TOTAL OF 6 RMS)

REFECTORY
    CAFETERIA FACILITIES TO REPLACE COURTYARD
    CENTRAL LAUNDRY ROOM

THE AMERICAN INSTITUTE OF ARCHITECTS

AIA Document B131

Standard Form of Agreement Between Owner and Architect

on a basis of a
PERCENTAGE OF CONSTRUCTION COST

AGREEMENT

made this seventh (7th) day of August in the year of Nineteen Hundred and Sixty-seven

BETWEEN The Corporation "DOMINICAN HOUSE OF RETREATS AND CATHOLIC GUILD"

the Owner, and

Louis I. Kahn

the Architect.

It is the intention of the Owner to construct a Motherhouse for a religious congregation.

hereinafter referred to as the Project.

The Owner and the Architect agree as set forth below.

This Agreement executed the day and year first written above.

OWNER _Mother Mary Louise Scheuer O.P._   ARCHITECT _Louis Kahn_

Architect's Registration No. AA - 014650

PARTS TOWARD WHOLE

Encouraging each part of the monastery to become what it "wants to be" results in a project that resembles as much several buildings as a single building. Given reason by the signing of the contract in August, by mid-October the architects had drawn each of the core spaces at larger scale. Figs. 117–125 The walls—until now drawn as simple lines—have "grown" a tectonic framework of pilasters, columns, and beams appropriate to their volumes and to the loads in play. Columns and frame are used in turn to articulate use-space: defining galleries or rooms-in-rooms, establishing concave or convex thresholds at the collisions of the volumes. (A comparison with the schematic transitions of earlier plans shows how significant is this enrichment.) Chapel, tower, and refectory all profit from this tectonic fleshing-out, with such small spatial gems as the tower's third-floor, cross-in-square room-fugue or the refectory's overlap with the kitchen. Only the school/auditorium lags behind: the attempt to combine the two uses is as yet unsuccessful (the circulation leading through a classroom!) and the construction still rather schematic.

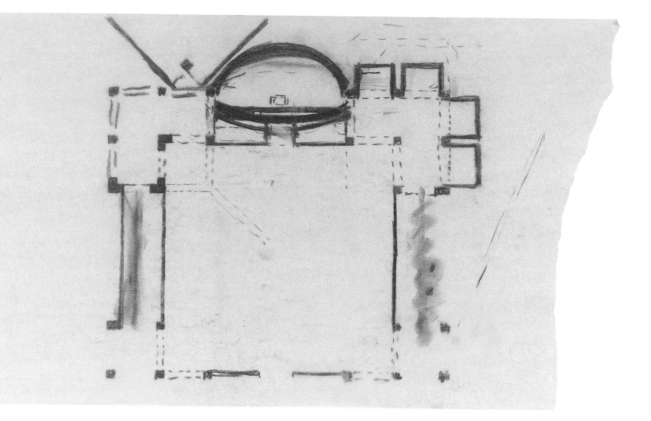

117 Chapel: plan, September–October 1967, Louis Kahn
118 Chapel: plan, September–October 1967, Louis Kahn

FROM FLATLAND TO SPACE: THE PLAN AS GENERATOR

By this stage, at the latest, it is abundantly clear that the architects have used orthographic plan drawings as their primary means of thinking spaces, with sections and elevations, perspectives and models used only sparingly. (This is true not only of this project, but, with the notable exception of the section-driven Kimbell Art Museum, of virtually all of Kahn's works.) If Kahn's priority lies, as claimed, in the development of an institution's "Form," it follows that the plan will tend to become the generator, laying out the parti in respect to the way that humans are likely to move and relate to each other—on a horizontal plane. But beyond its role as a socio-spatial diagram are other dimensions of plan drawing that demand our attention. In addition to its use as an agent for orchestrating mass and void (Kahn: "the rhythm of light—no light—light..."), plan notation—not unlike musical notation—is an instrument to both express and generate tension or repose, to describe phases of movement, pause, and rest. Alan Colquhoun has depicted, in his essay "The Beaux-Arts Plan," an experience of plan-as-partita that well fits Kahn's mature plans, the Dominican Motherhouse included: "When we 'read' a Beaux-Arts plan, we seem to be carrying out three operations at the same time, or at any rate in quick succession. First, we interpret the marks on the page as a Gestalt pattern. Second, we translate this into an imagined two-dimensional space which we experience sequentially—following the direction of narrow, bounded spaces, halting at square spaces, interpreting rhythmically arranged points as transparent boundaries, and so on. Finally, we translate this into three-dimensional volumes. From these interpretive steps we arrive at a coherent organization which does not gain its meaning from any but the most generalized functional attributions. It is in this generalized 'program' that one of the most striking analogies between the Beaux-Arts plan and the symphony lies."[57]

Colqhoun's passage is compelling for several reasons, one of which is the "impulse" of horizontal dimensions to unfold into three-dimensional space. From the Renaissance to the Ecole des Beaux-Arts, there existed wide consensus, either tacit or explicit, that a well-conceived plan is the seed of its own vertical dimensions: "Every three-dimensional form is born from its plan as a tree is born from its roots."[58] With the advent of slab-and-frame construction and with the resulting emphasis on the horizontal plane, modern architecture no longer upheld such a binding horizontal-vertical correspondence. Reflecting on this horizontal-vertical link it has been pointed out, "Not all drawings take advantage of this capacity. Compare, for example, the plan of a building such as the Villa Madama and Mies' project for a brick villa. The understanding that the plan notation presumes volumetric control seems to be extant in the former, while missing from the latter. Though some would have difficulty with the assumption of the plan as the primary organizational device, and would choose an alternate point of departure, such as the section, there is still the potential to express the essence of volume in the two-dimensional drawing. The issue is that the drawing that depicts only two dimensions is capable of expressing the essence of volume and surface—indeed, the aesthetic intent."[59]

But how exactly? A nagging question at this point—for Kahn's plans do not simply "extrude" into three dimensions—is just how and to what degree are volumes "inherent" in these plans, and how do Kahn and his associates go about "growing" those volumes/spaces out of two dimensions? (Questions that further beg the question of the relevance of Kahn's plan-based method in the face of digital 3D-modeling capacities.) It is important to note that along with the positions and "spacings" which the rooms have "found" in plan, it is precisely this articulation of their vertical dimensions that establishes their relative significance within the whole. Having broached this question, we must admit that the drawings seen to this point shed only dim light on the architects' means of developing spaces from their plans. This remains a point to dwell on as the schemes unfold.

57 Alan Colquhoun, "The Beaux-Arts Plan," *Architectural Design Profiles* 17, vol. 48, nos. 11–12 (1978), pp. 50–65.

58 Daniele Barbaro, *La Practica della Perpettia* [1568], facsimile ed., Bologna, 1977.

59 Michael Graves, "The Necessity of Drawing: Tangible Speculation," in Brian M. Ambroziak and Michael Graves, *Images of a Grand Tour*, New York, 2005, pp. 235–45. Originally published in 1977.

119 Chapel: plan, September/October 1967, Louis Kahn
120 Chapel: plan, October 12, 1967

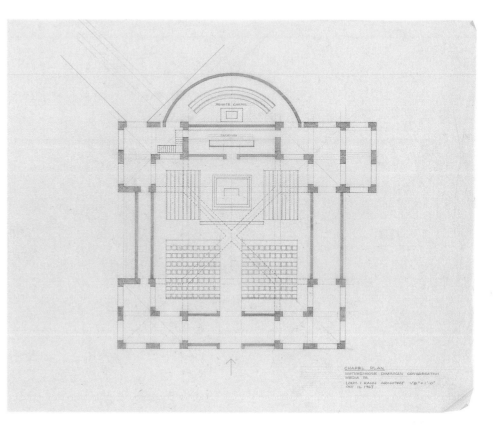

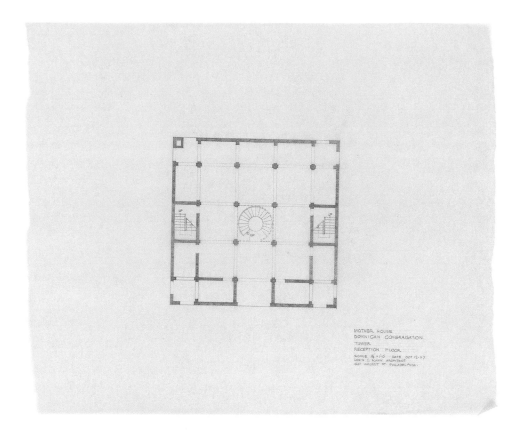

"The room is the beginning of architecture. It is the place of the mind. You in the room with its dimensions, its structure, its light respond to its character, its spiritual aura, recognizing that whatever the human proposes and makes becomes a life." Louis I. Kahn, "The Room, the Street, and Human Agreement," 1971

121–23 Entry tower: plan, October 12, 1967

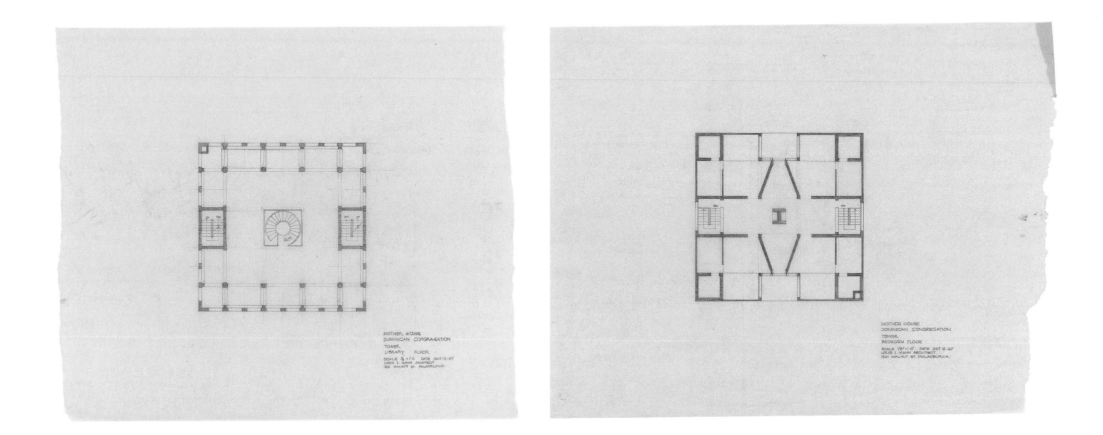

MOTHER HOUSE
DOMINICAN CONGREGATION
TOWER
LIBRARY FLOOR

SCALE ⅛" = 1'-0"   DATE OCT 12-67
LOUIS I. KAHN ARCHITECT
1501 WALNUT ST. PHILADELPHIA.

MOTHER HOUSE
DOMINICAN CONGREGATION
TOWER
BEDROOM FLOOR

SCALE ⅛" = 1'-0"   DATE OCT 12-67
LOUIS I. KAHN ARCHITECT
1501 WALNUT ST. PHILADELPHIA.

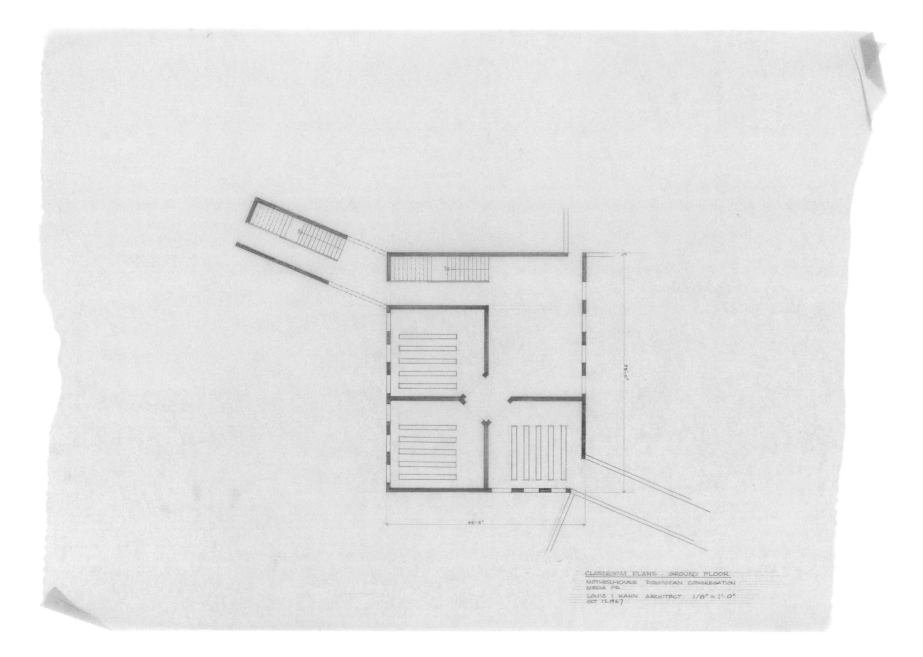

CLASSROOM PLANS : GROUND FLOOR
MOTHERHOUSE DOMINICAN CONGREGATION
MEDIA PA.
LOUIS I KAHN ARCHITECT 1/8" = 1'·0"
OCT 12·1967

124 Classroom: plan, October 12, 1967

125 Refectory: plan, October 12, 1967

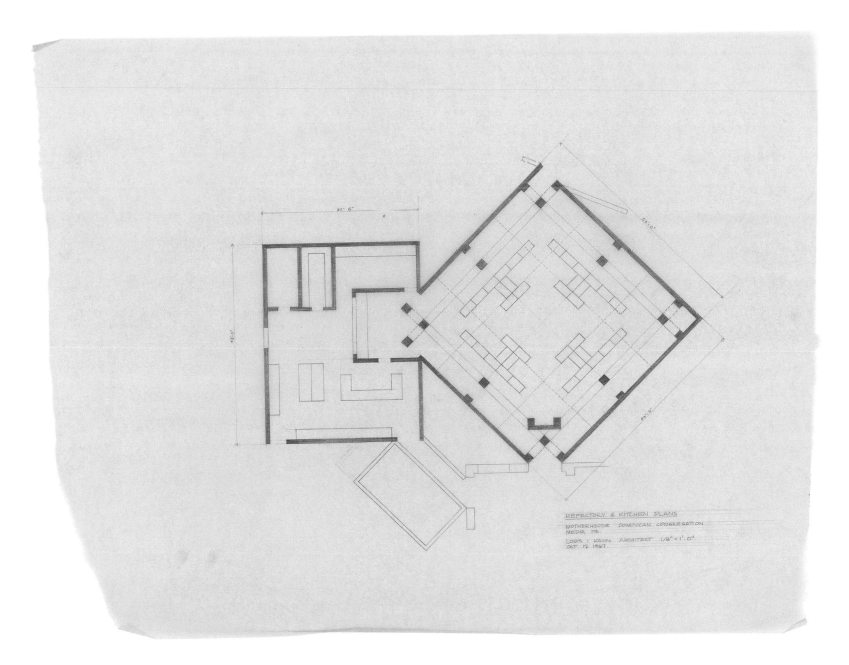

REFECTORY & KITCHEN PLANS

MOTHERHOUSE DOMINICAN CONGREGATION
MEDIA PA.

LOUIS I KAHN ARCHITECT 1/8"=1'.0"
OCT 12 1967

THE ELEMENTS COMPOSED

The autumn's detailed studies of the core spaces now coalesce into a comprehensive plan with Kahn's spacious charcoal drawing from February/March 1968. Fig. 126 With its extra-large scale (⅛ in. = 1 ft.) and its fuzzy texture of living and movable things, this evocative plan—perhaps more than any thus far—invites the viewer to inhabit its spaces and to mentally take part in the collage of activities unfolding within.

The plan has begun to exude a sense of dynamic and gregarious inhabitance, of proximities and distances, of expansion and contraction. Leaving the calm of their cells, the sisters are taken up in an ordered labyrinth, with multiple routes, possibilities of serendipitous meetings, and engaging detours. While each part of the monastery may indeed be an "entity in itself," the individual parts may only be fully understood through the synergies, both strong and fragile, they create with their neighbors. The layered ambulatory of the chapel (and, to a lesser degree, of the refectory) are intended to allow both nearness *and* separation—Kahn's "wink at the chapel" without going in: "First you have a sanctuary, and the sanctuary is for those who want to kneel. Around this sanctuary is an ambulatory for those who are not sure but want to be near. Outside is a court for those who want to feel the presence of the chapel. And the court has a wall. Those who pass the wall can just wink at it."[60]

Regardless of scale, this ordering of spaces as a sympathetic foil to the patterns of human interaction was for Kahn one of the prime purposes of architecture. An ordering, like the patterns of use for which it is thought, which is neither absolute nor predictable. (But—paradox of the indefinite—which requires absolute precision in planning!) By now, at the latest, we can begin to sense in the Motherhouse Kahn's ideal Albertian world, at once behaving like a very large house or a very small city.

60 Louis I. Kahn, "Form and Design," *Architectural Design* 31 (April 1961), p. 116.

"I think that architects should be composers and not designers. They should be composers of elements. The elements are things that are entities in themselves."

Louis I. Kahn, "Space and the Inspirations," 1967

126 First floor: plan, February/March 1968, Louis Kahn

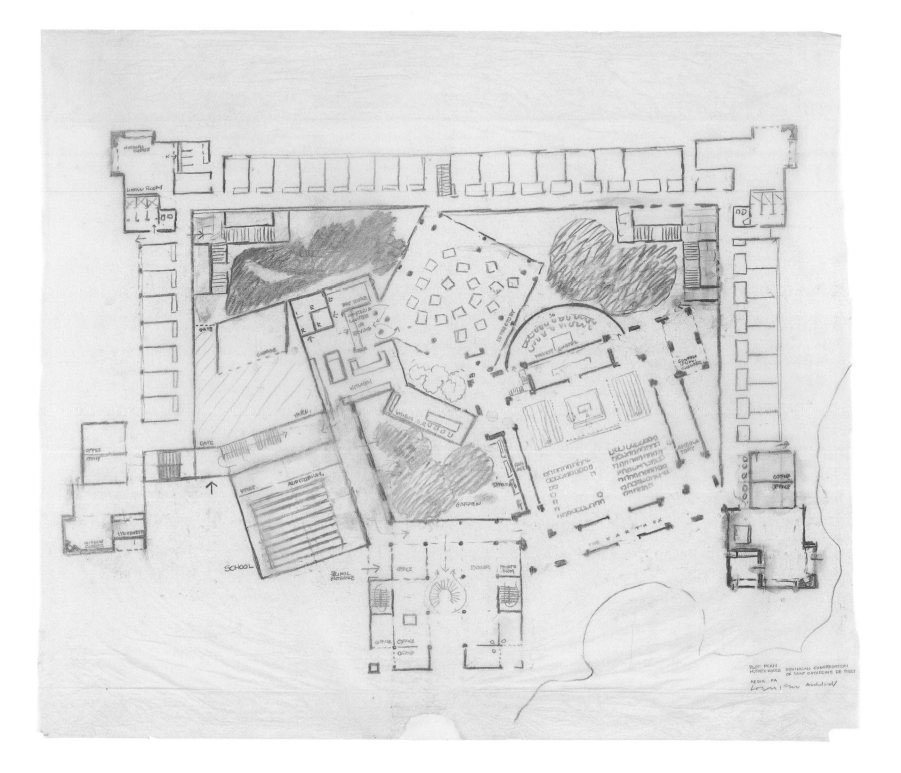

PLOT PLAN
MOTHER HOUSE   DOMINICAN CONGREGATION
OF SAINT CATHERINE DE RICCI

MEDIA PA

Louis I. Kahn   Architect

AN ICONIC PLAN

With a number of adjustments, Kahn's sketch is tautened in the associates' plan of April 22, 1968. Fig. 127 Although this plan still belongs to the intermediate steps, it has been by far the most frequently published of the Motherhouse variations to date, often presented as the "final design."[61]

A comparison of Kahn's sketch and the plan of April 22 validates the sisters' suggestion of placing the auditorium above the school. This simply makes functional sense, with the oft-frequented classrooms at ground level and the larger auditorium under the big roof upstairs. What is more generally demonstrated by this move is how, in a configurative craft such as architecture, the modification of a single element may significantly affect the rest. The subtraction of one element from the plan's equation relaxes the whole, ridding it of its formally and functionally most uncomfortable moments (the unresolved school, the kinks and conflicts in the circulation, etc.). All communal rooms have now found their place in the core, resulting—for the first time since June 1966—in a clear spatial order. What is convincing is the apparent ease with which the core spaces "casually" connect. The resulting circulation ring formed by the linked spaces echoes the outer ring of the cells' galleries, increasing the possibilities for traversing the plan. The tower now hosts three stairs: a central stair leading directly to the library in the second and third floors, and two additional stairs to the offices and guest rooms above. The new private chapel forms an apse-like appendage to the main chapel. The desired confessional room—present in Kahn's sketch—has been left out of April's plan.

The "inhabited wall" of cells is given living rooms at each of its corners, with four chimneys signaling its domestic use, anchoring the horizontal wings and staking the limits of the building. Although included in Kahn's February sketch, missing in April's plan are the stairs to the cells—only one has been drawn in the north wing. The draftsman has also taken Kahn's shorthand literally and filled in the windows of the cloister, drawing an unbroken wall to the courtyard. (Or have the windows moved above head level? A hall without natural light being unthinkable with Kahn.) Ironically, these two solutions—obviously never intended as being final—have belonged through their repeated publication to the plan's more "permanent" and enigmatic features.

61 An incomplete list of publications that have presented the plan of April 22, 1968, as the "final design," include Gast, Giurgola, McCarter, Saito, and *Monografías de Arquitectura & Vivienda,* special Kahn issue (2001). The reproduction used for these publications is based on an extremely large (⅛ in. = 1 ft.) first-floor plan. The other levels, though never published, had indeed been drawn in this scale.

127 First floor: plan, April 22, 1968

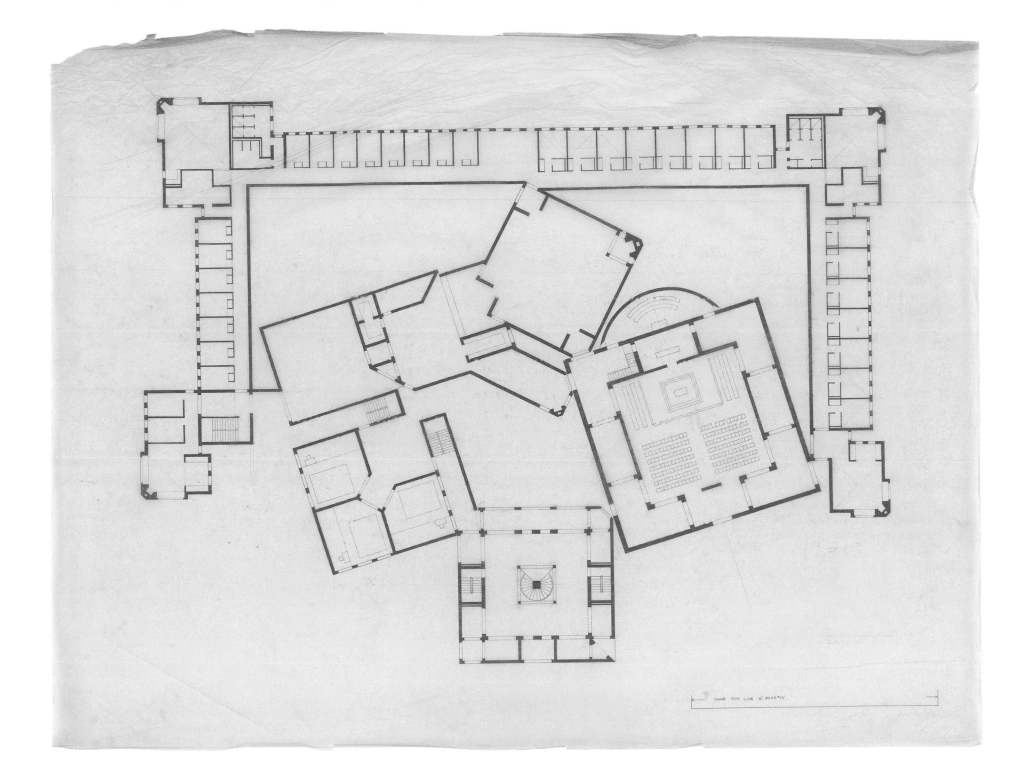

MAKE THIS LINE 6" EXACTLY.

"Each space must be defined by its structure and
the character of its natural light.... An architectural space
must reveal the evidence of its making by the space
itself." Louis I. Kahn, "Form and Design," 1960

128 Parti, March 7, 1968, Louis Kahn
129 Chapel, school: elevations, Spring 1968, Louis Kahn

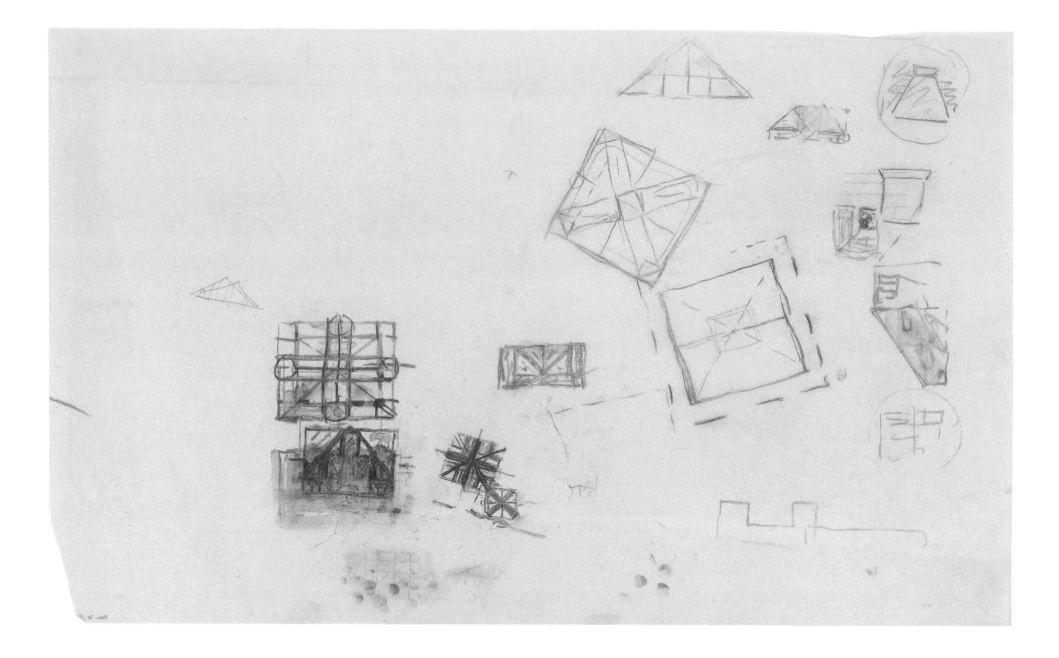

130–131 Chapel: roof study, Spring 1968, Louis Kahn

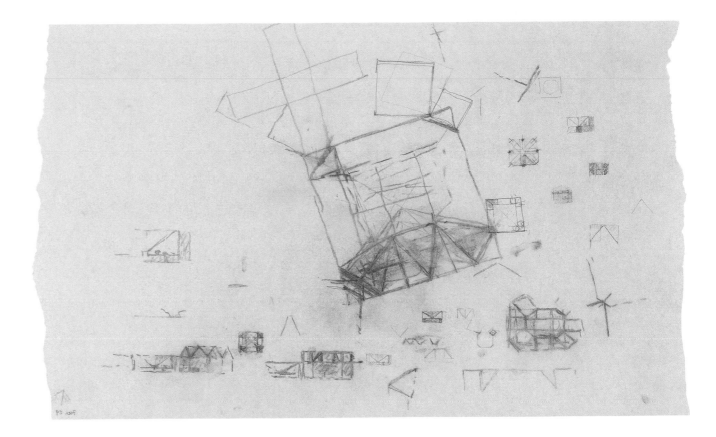

"The space induces the project.
If you have a space, something happens, the program
then starts. It doesn't start before you make
the space." Louis I. Kahn, Comments on the Exeter Library, 1972

132 Chapel, school: roof study, Spring 1968, Louis Kahn

COMPOSING THE VERTICAL DIMENSION

The studies for the elevations and sections from this phase attest to the continued infighting between expression and reticence. Figs. 129–38 The "ziggurat" tower has now become a carved cubic block, appendaged with what seems to be an outrigger belfry. Continuing to develop the "house" theme, chapel, school, and refectory are topped by giant fragments of hipped roofs—the school's roof chopped off dramatically on the courtyard sides, the chapel's roof clamped between giant hollow corner lanterns, which bring light rebounding into its interior. (The lanterns echo both the skylight monitors of the First Unitarian Church and the "hollow columns" of the mosque at Dhaka.) The façades are at once plastic and austere, the west entry somewhat sternly greeting the visitor with its prisms all but closed on their lower levels. Turning the corner toward the forest, the building transforms from a closed bearing-wall structure to an open masonry frame. Accompanying the elevations, two sections through the monastery—astonishingly, the first to be drawn since November 1966 and the very first to be drafted of *any* scheme—intimate the fall of natural light and the vertical modulation of space. Figs. 137–38

133 Chapel: section, Spring 1968
134 Chapel, refectory: section, Spring 1968

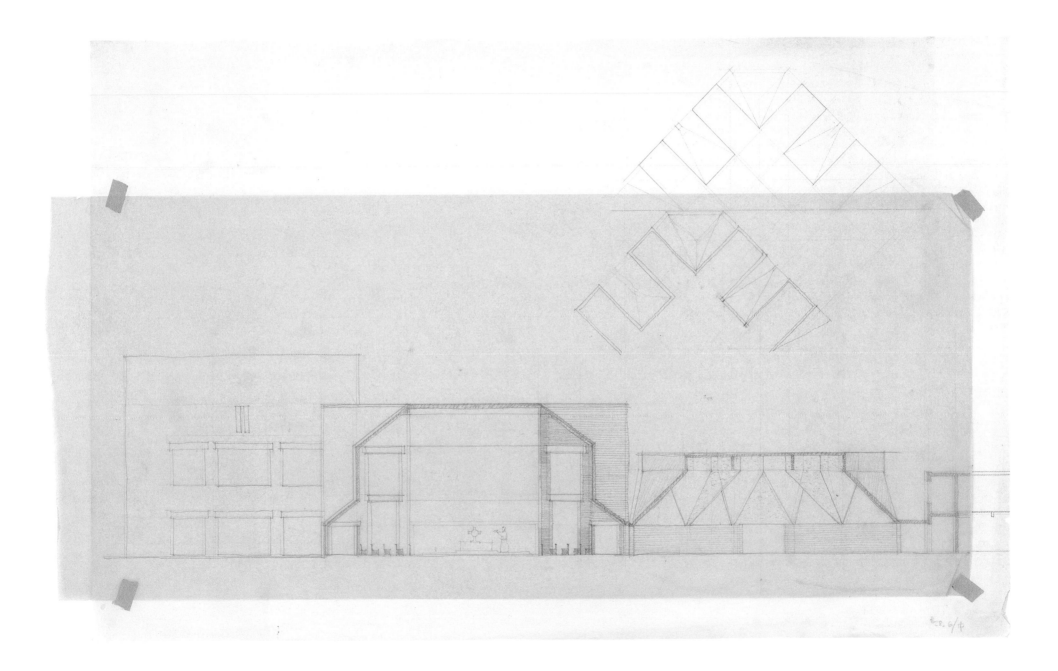

135 West elevation, April 22, 1968
136 East elevation, April 22, 1968

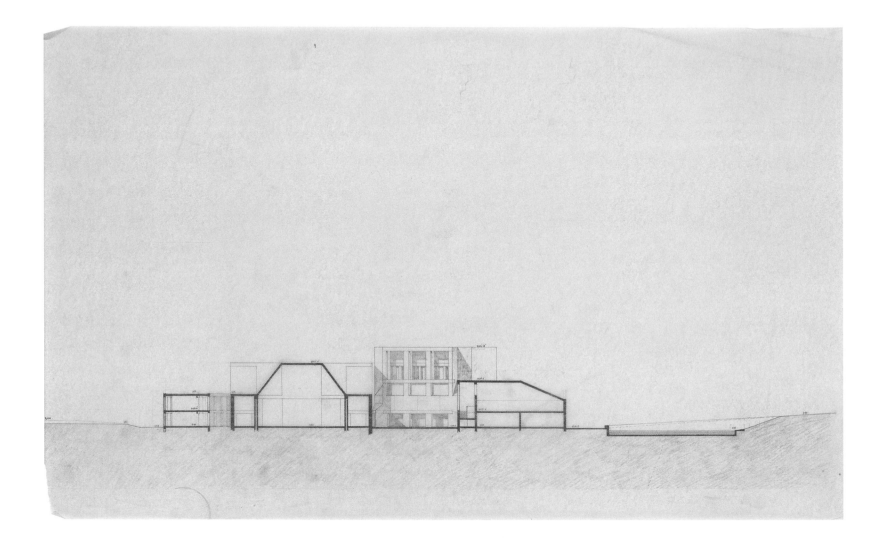

137 Section looking west, April 22, 1968
138 Section looking south, April 22, 1968

THE PLAN AS GESTALT

By late spring 1968, with the disposition of the parts apparently no longer in question, the architects turned now to the refinement of those parts and to the plan's context. Kahn's archive is rich with plans and prints from these weeks, for rather than working out minor changes by using tracing-paper overlays (which would have been the likely, economical method), entire plans have been redrawn to change a few details. Studying the different variations—which due to their minute differences are often difficult to order—one might conclude that one reason for this considerable extra work lies in the architects' regard for the plan as an organic structure or Gestalt pattern, that changes in one part of the field call for counter-changes elsewhere in order to maintain equilibrium and a common syntax.

In what is likely the first plan after April 22 Fig. 140—courtyard stairs and windows are still missing—two living rooms are removed; the small chapel has now taken on a triangular shape and the pool has returned, accompanied by a garden wall that seems to have as its main function the intertwining of building and surroundings. In a later plan Fig. 141 the stairs have returned to the cell tracts, the small chapel is now a more usable diamond shape, and the pool has again disappeared. A plan dated May 20, 1968, which continues to refine the previous steps, is evidence of the architects' constant battle with the budget. Fig. 142 In light of the tight budget almost every new plan is accompanied by a calculation of its area. Here, the consequences of shrinking the core spaces by approximately 10 percent are tested by pasting a reduced print of those rooms onto an existing plan.

139 Plan footprint, Spring 1968, Louis Kahn
140 Plan with site, Spring 1968

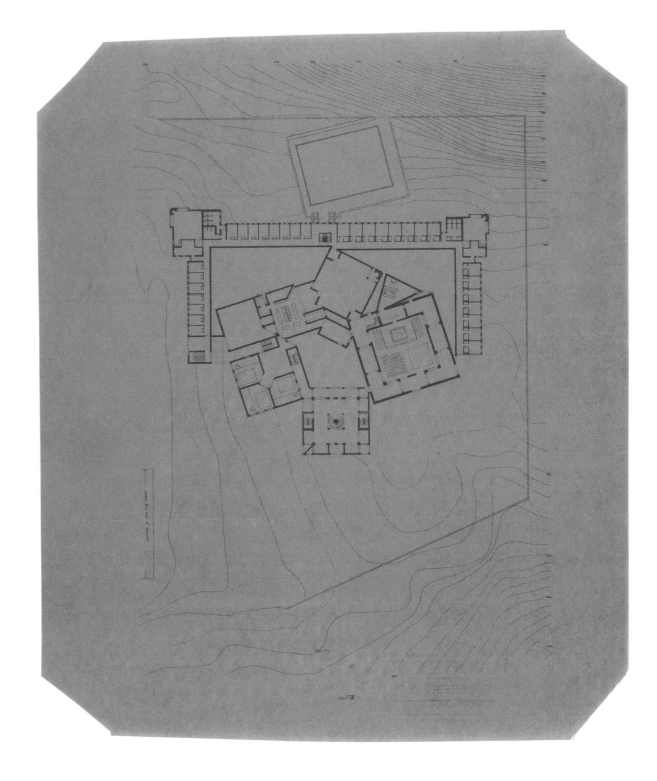

"Open before us is the architect's plan. Next to it a sheet of
music. The architect fleetingly reads his composition as
a structure of elements and spaces in their light. The musician
reads with the same overallness." Louis I. Kahn, "The Room, the Street, and Human Agreement," 1971

141 Plan with site, April 17, 1968

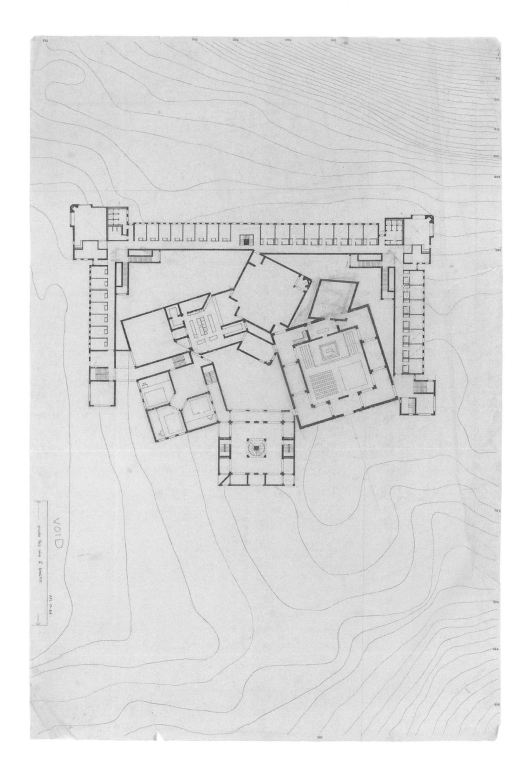

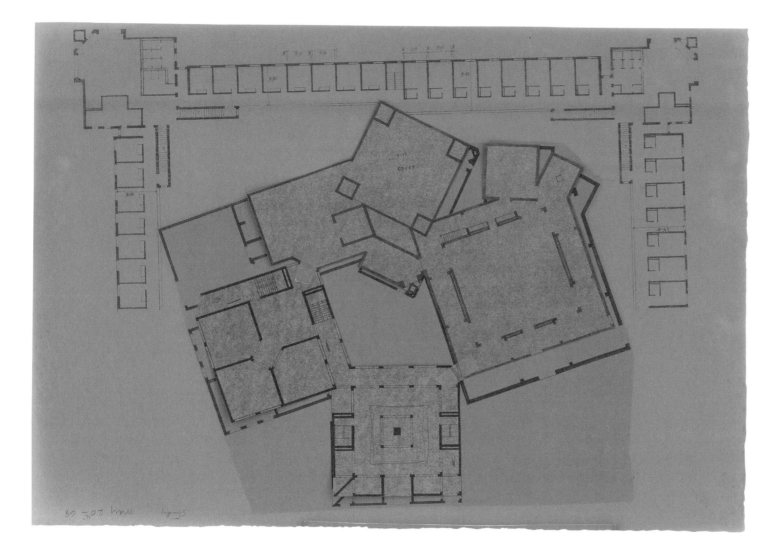

142 Plan with overlay, May 20, 1968

143 Plan with overlay, May 1968

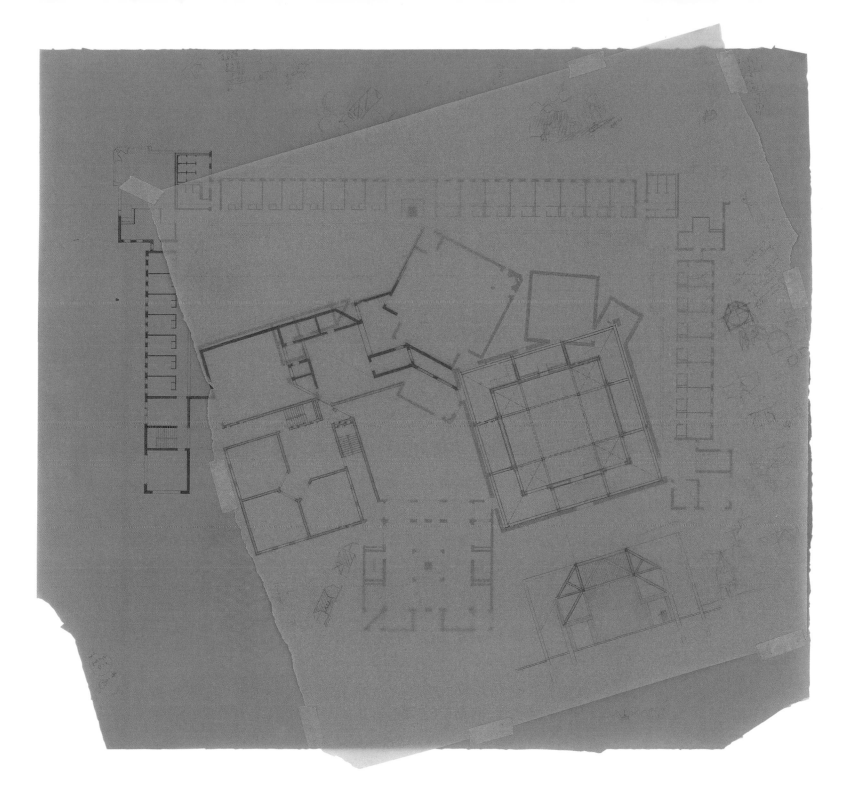

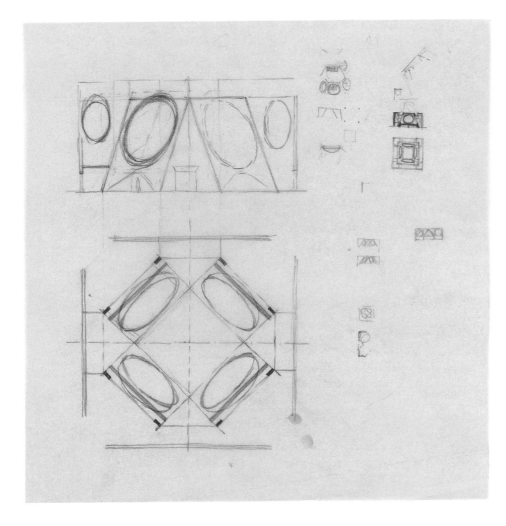

144 Chapel: plan, section, Spring 1968 (est.)
145 Chapel: study, Spring 1968, Louis Kahn

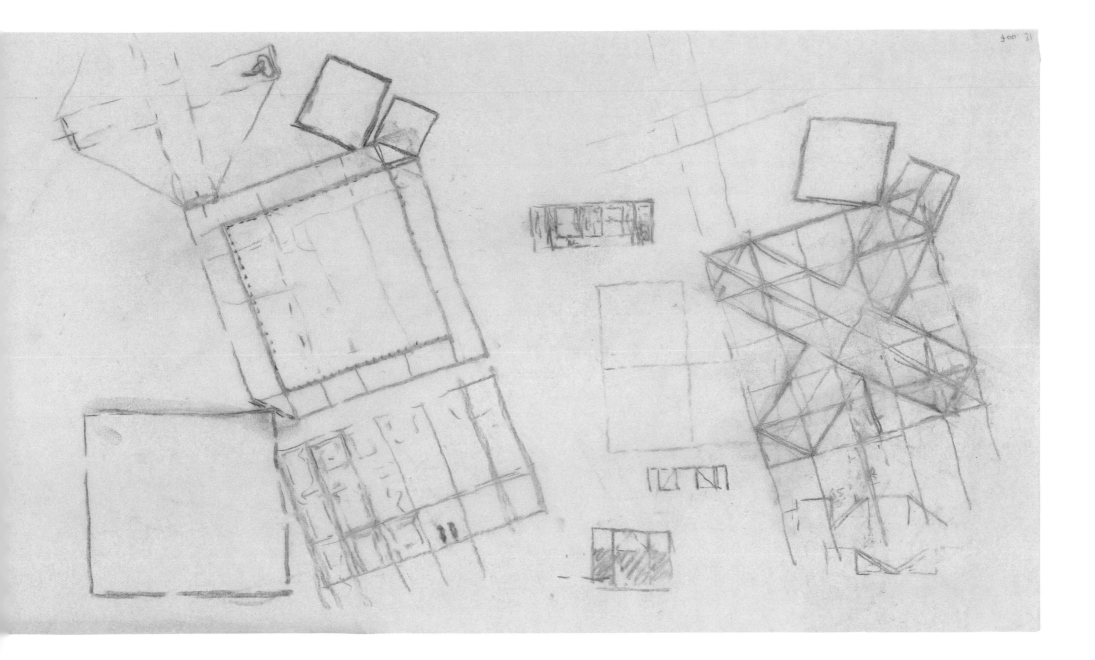

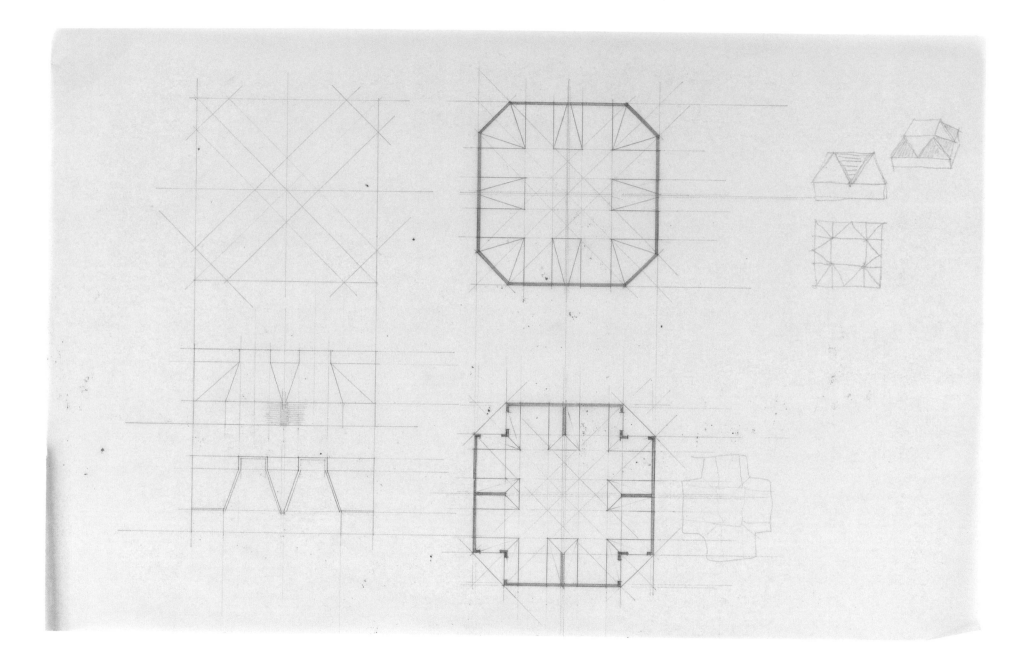

146 Refectory: plan, section, roof, Spring 1968
147 Refectory, chapel: plan, Spring 1968

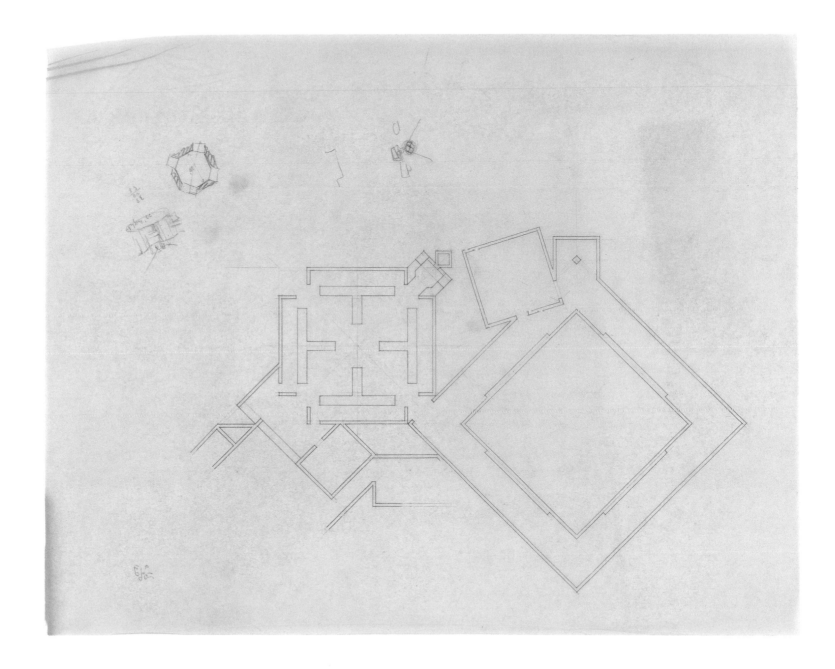

FINALLY, A COMPREHENSIVE PLAN

The overlay of May 20 is based on a fully developed set of floor plans in which virtually all questions of form and use have been addressed. Figs. 148–51 A banquet for floor plan devotees, all parts and all levels have now been thought through and drawn and we are finally shown the consequences of this extended, rigorous shifting and articulation of elementary plan shapes. The placement of library and auditorium in this "society of rooms" is now evident: their presence on the second level, their spacings to the ground floor. The multiple possibilities for traversing the plan are now apparent, with twelve different stairs exponentially deepening the plan's labyrinthine character. One might well imagine an inhabitant, setting out from her second-floor cell toward the chapel, to alternately choose a route over the library, the school, or the kitchen. (How much more *domestic* these possibilities make the convent than the earliest schemes!)

Even without the use of sections, a filigree fugue of tectonics, light, and space is revealed to the experienced plan-reader as the layered set of drawings unfolds vertically, making the comparison between plan notation and musical notation much less far-fetched than it tends to be. The tower's ground-floor office spaces become on the next floors the library's double-height, top-lit book niches, and further upward, the loggias of the guest rooms; the wall-folding superpositions of cross and square in chapel and refectory now become apparent in the upper levels. (The chapel admitting light over its corners, the refectory over the center of its gables, the thin, folded, light-reflecting planes, etc.) A spatial richness only hinted at in the published plan of April 22—conceived, but not yet shown—becomes undeniably manifest in these four plans. Here, at least in partial answer to the question of some pages back, is Kahn indeed "thinking" his extraordinarily three-dimensional spaces in a two-dimensional plan-partita.

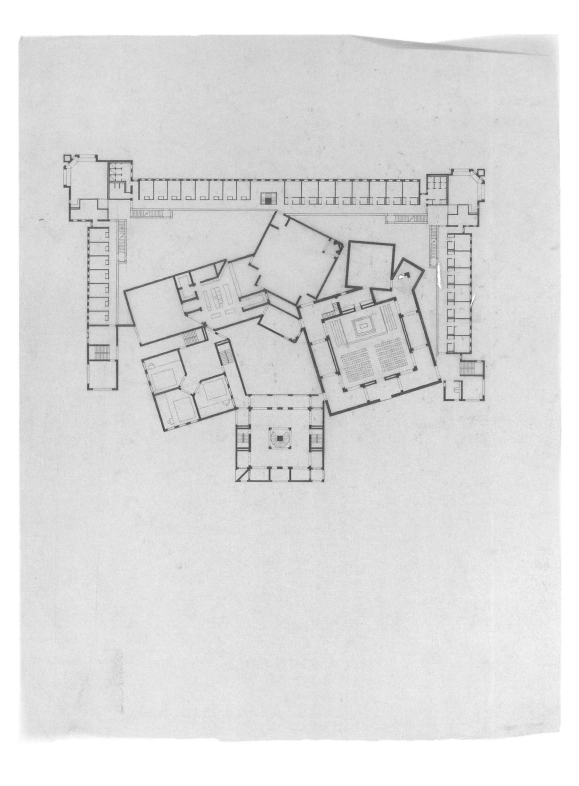

148 First floor: plan, May 20, 1968
149 Second floor: plan, May 20, 1968

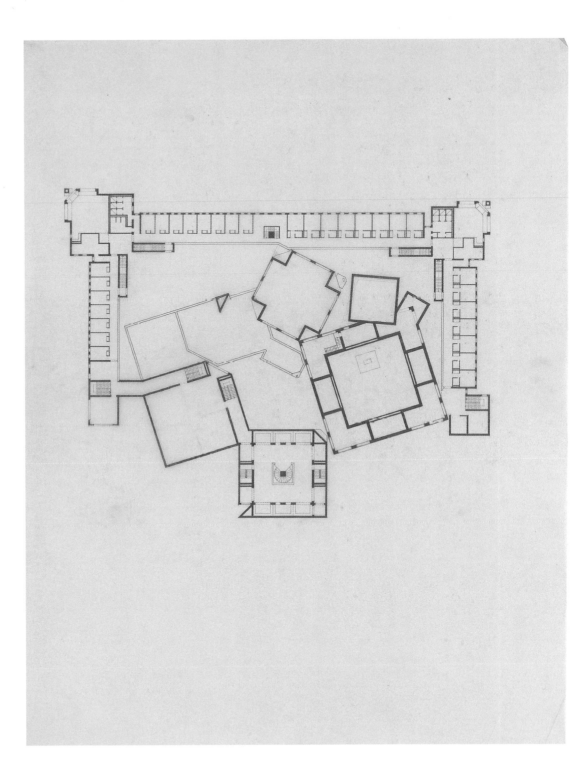

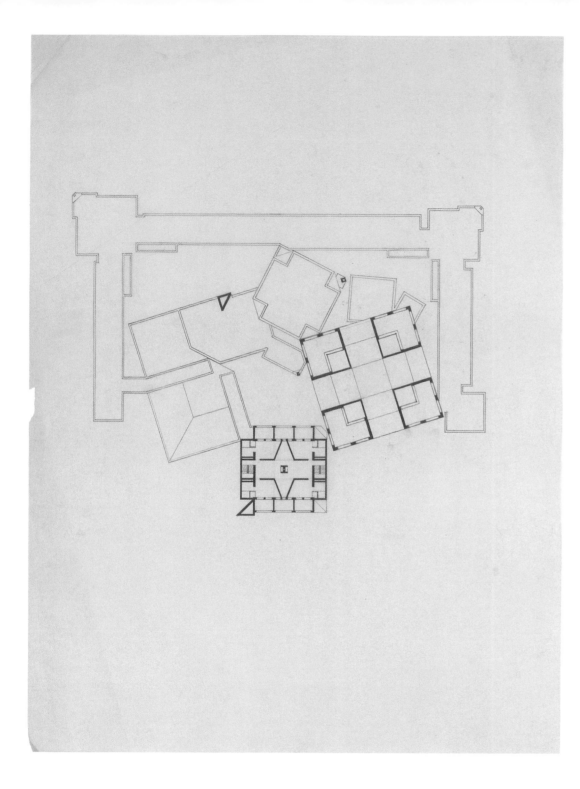

150 Third floor: plan, May 20, 1968
151 Roof: plan, May 20, 1968

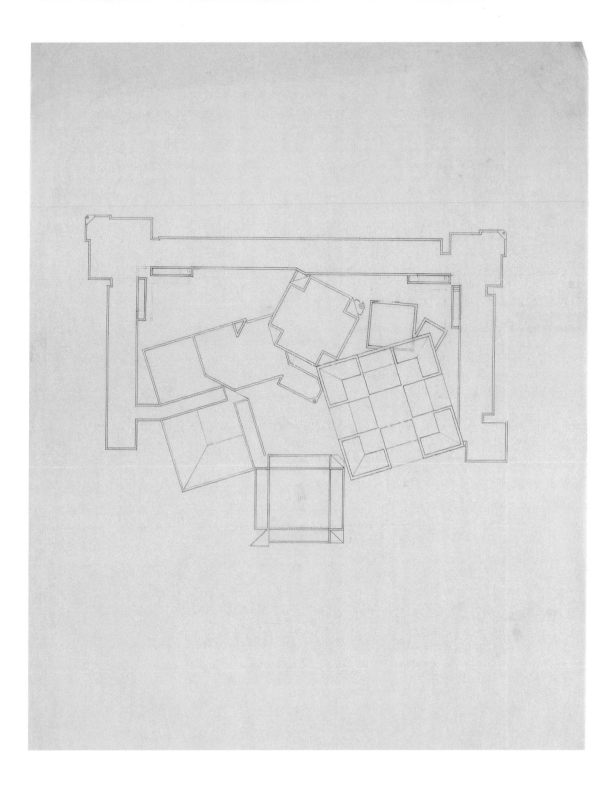

OUTSIDE IS ALSO INSIDE: THE RECIPROCAL SPACE
OF THE PLAN

Not only have the internal spaces of the monastery been large-ly resolved, but for the first time in several months the floor plan is also drawn in a comprehensive site plan, showing forest, topography, and approach. Fig. 152 If, in following the architects' taxing struggle with the plan, one has understandably lost sight of its context, it is once again apparent just how integral the surrounding landscape is to the interior life of that plan. As the core spaces rotate within the frame of the cells, so rotates the entire monastery within the forest clearing. As if caught in the same centrifugal pull, forest and pieces of monastery have become separate parts of a single, turning movement. The space between the forest's edge and the building's volumes becomes almost palpable through this rotation, with each ir-regular piece of in-between charged by the movement. Forest and architecture at once reinforce and contradict each other, describing at the same time the stasis of a forest clearing and some kind of movement away from that center.

If we approach the monastery along the entry drive—which echoes the angle of chapel and school, geometrically anchor-ing the rotating composition to its site—it becomes apparent that the complex resists any attempt at experiencing it frontally. (The elevations we have seen until now tend to let us forget this.) We slip into the forest clearing obliquely, being allowed only partial views of our goal, as if our own movement toward the building sets it rotating away from us. Any symmetry which the plan suggests is relativized by its siting. Frontal views of one volume are accompanied by diagonal views of others, the unseen rest receding against the edge of the forest. The pris-matic effect which we've encountered inside applies to the whole in its setting. Forest and architecture are thus conjoined, the whole experienced as if from the "inside"—even when out-doors. The explicitly "two" of interior and exterior are indeed implicitly "one."

"The plan does not begin nor end with the space he [the architect] has enveloped, but from the adjoining delicate ground sculpture it stretches beyond to the rolling contours and vegetation of the surrounding land and continues farther out to the distant hills." Louis I. Kahn, "Monumentality," 1944

152 Site plan, Spring 1968

$1'' = 50' - 0''$

REDUCTIONS AND REFINEMENTS

In spite of all efforts to the contrary, the budget continued to hover like Damocles' sword over the project. As the prospect of realization drew nearer, cost estimates increased in frequency and detail. In June, the plan is again distilled to reduce its area. Fig. 153 The frame of cells telescopes together at the central stair to reduce the circumference of the whole; the core volumes are reduced accordingly to fit the smaller space formed by the cells. With these adjustments, an additional 1,539 square feet (143 m²) could be wrung out of the plan. In July, the plan is again refined: one stair in the tower is eliminated, the stairs in the school tract are changed to straight-run, the north wing is adequately terminated, and an intermediate circulation space adjacent to the kitchen is added. Figs. 154–55 While these adjustments bring increased elegance, the architects' economizing has not taken place without loss; the tower in particular suffers from the loss of its outer spatial layer when compared to the plan of May.

153 First floor: plan, June 17, 1968

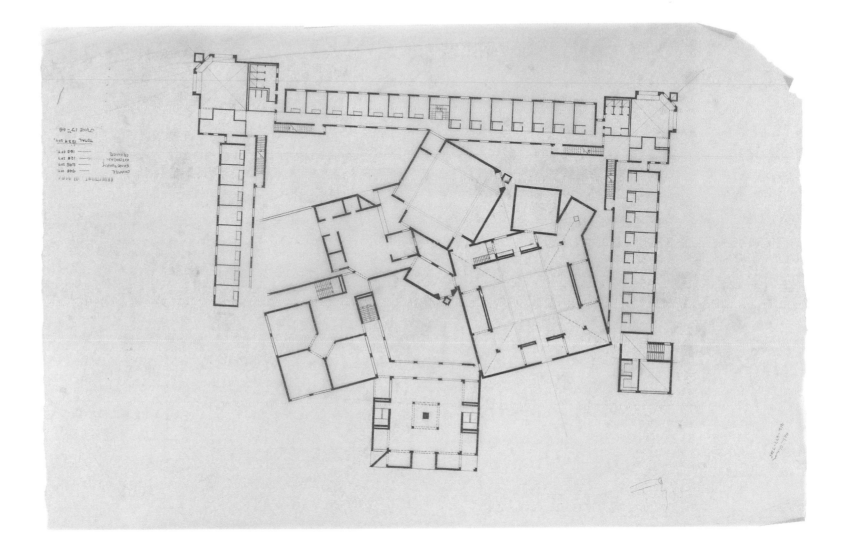

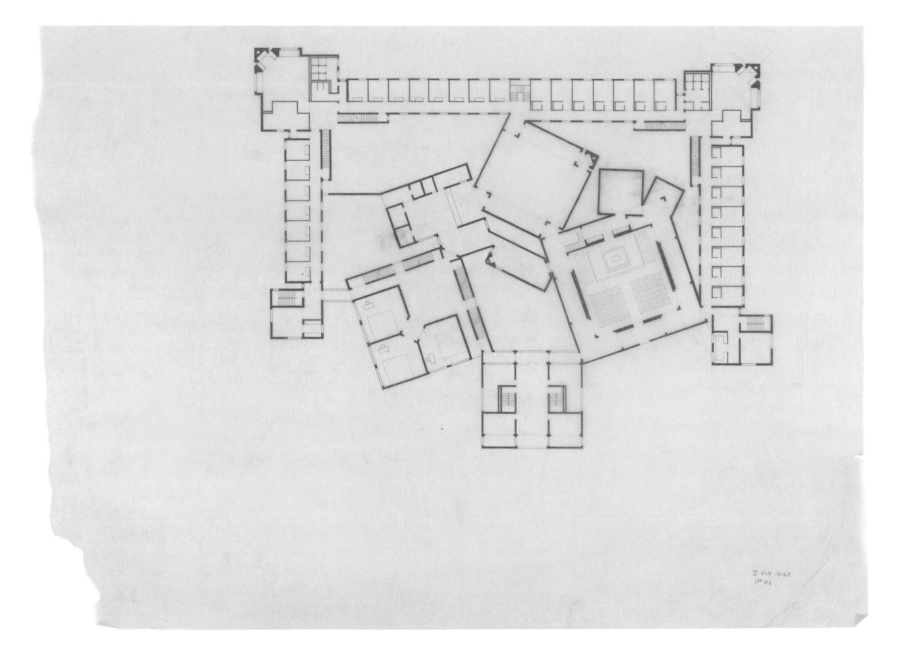

154 First floor: plan, July 10, 1968
155 Second floor: plan, July 10, 1968

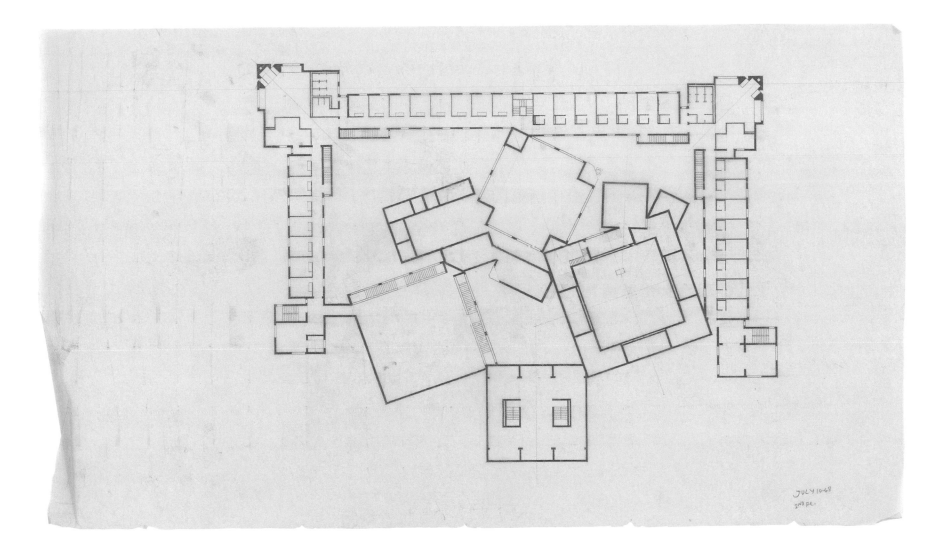

JULY 10-68
2ND pt.

"Each space must be defined by its structure and the character of its natural light.... An architectural space must reveal the evidence of its making by the space itself."

Louis I. Kahn, "Form and Design," 1960

156 Section through chapel, Summer 1968
157 Section looking north, Summer 1968
158 Section looking south, Summer 1968

159 West elevation, Spring/Summer 1968
160 East elevation, Spring/Summer 1968

180

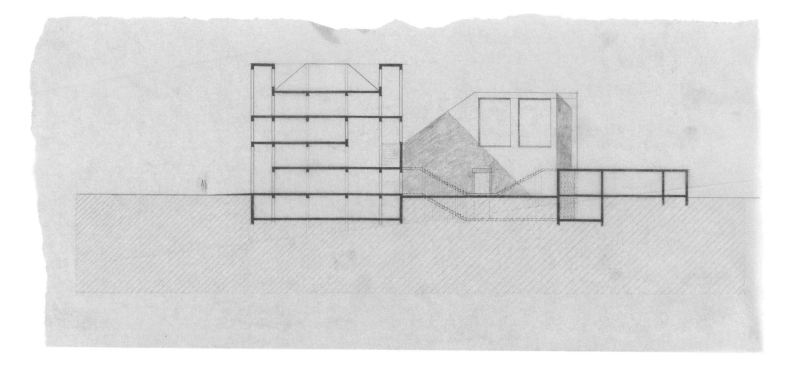

161 Entry tower: section, Summer 1968
162 Entry tower: section, Summer 1968

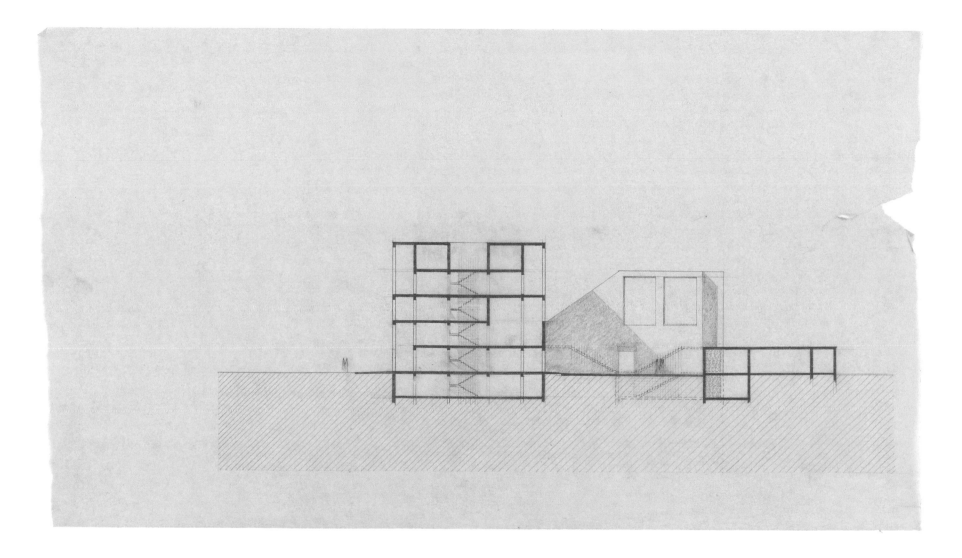

THE PLAN IN ITS FINAL STATE

By August, virtually each superfluous square foot had been wrung out of the plan, a schematic means of construction had been proposed, and the latest cost estimates were promising; the sisters were in accord and the architects were finally on the threshold of the construction drawing phase. A new set of plans—the last to be drawn as a set—shows the results of the previous weeks' distillation process. Figs. 164–67 The most obvious changes are the "hollow columns," which, in addition to adding visual weight to chapel, tower, and school, are "servant spaces": ductwork for air conditioning and heating. These tectonic/technical elaborations are used to spatially enrich the core: the outer corners of chapel and refectory are now supplemented by a re-entrant, inward-pointing movement. Thus turned back upon themselves, the stasis of the squares is challenged. Now, transitions between spaces are considerably more complex than in the roughshod collisions of earlier versions: thresholds are established, ceiling heights varied, spaces inflected both inwardly and outwardly, concaves answered by convexes. If the plan's juxtaposition of uses is its most bold hypothesis, it is the masterful resolution of these connections that makes that hypothesis plausible.

The myriad decisions, large and small, the multitude of adjustments, rough and fine, are testimony to a paradox in this Kahnian paradigm of order. This at first glace "spontaneous" composition—in order to reach a level of coherence and elegance above that of a banal conglomeration of parts—has required the greatest discipline in planning, a precision at least equal to that of Kahn's classical compositions. The months spent manipulating the plan are testimony to this fact. The parts, apparently tossed into place like so many dice, with resulting angles both acute and obtuse, are in fact precisely and subtly intertwined: in terms of geometry, constructive module, spatial sequences, and function. At this stage any attempt to move or even slightly re-dimension a relevant room would set off a chain reaction throughout the whole, disrupting its formal structure and making its multiple internal dependencies visible. The transitions that have been so laboriously constructed to appear incidental are anything but. To have captured the energy and tension of that first collage drawing in a formally resolved and completely functional plan is anything but trivial. It would at this point be worthwhile for the reader to linger in the spaces of this plan, to review the many steps taken, great and small, in order to reflect on the distance traveled.

"The plan is a society of rooms. The plan is one in which the rooms have talked to each other. The plan is the structure of the spaces in their light." Louis I. Kahn, "The Invisible City," June 19, 1972

163 Plan variation, August 1968

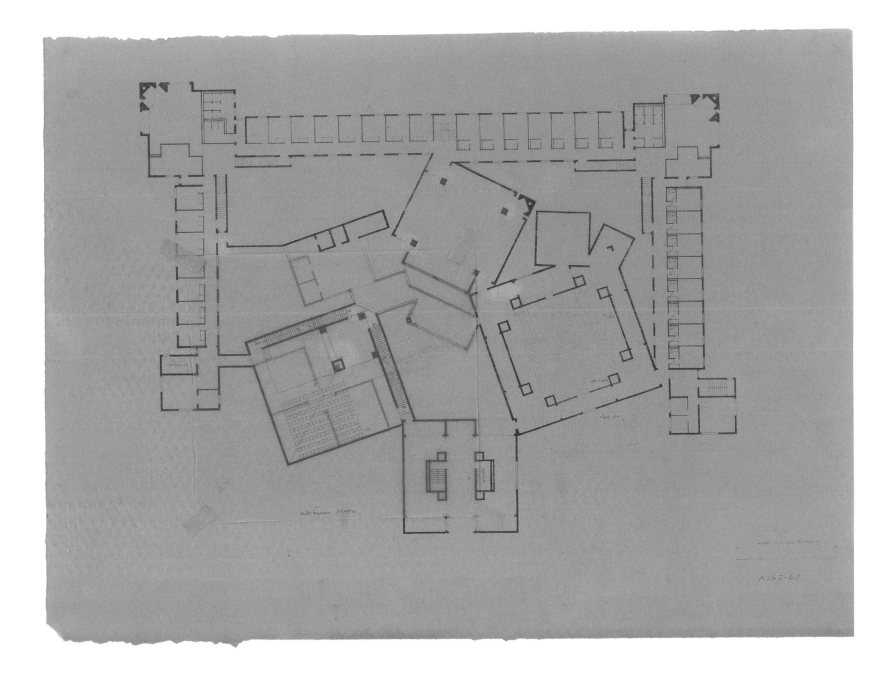

auditorium floor

AUG 5-68

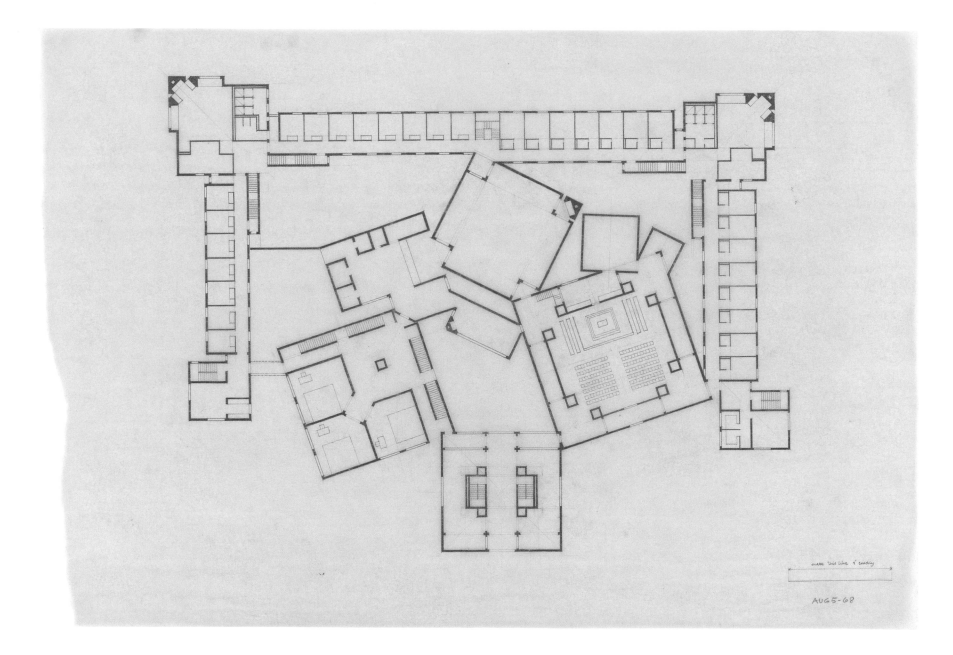

164 First floor: plan, August 5, 1968
165 Second floor: plan, August 5, 1968

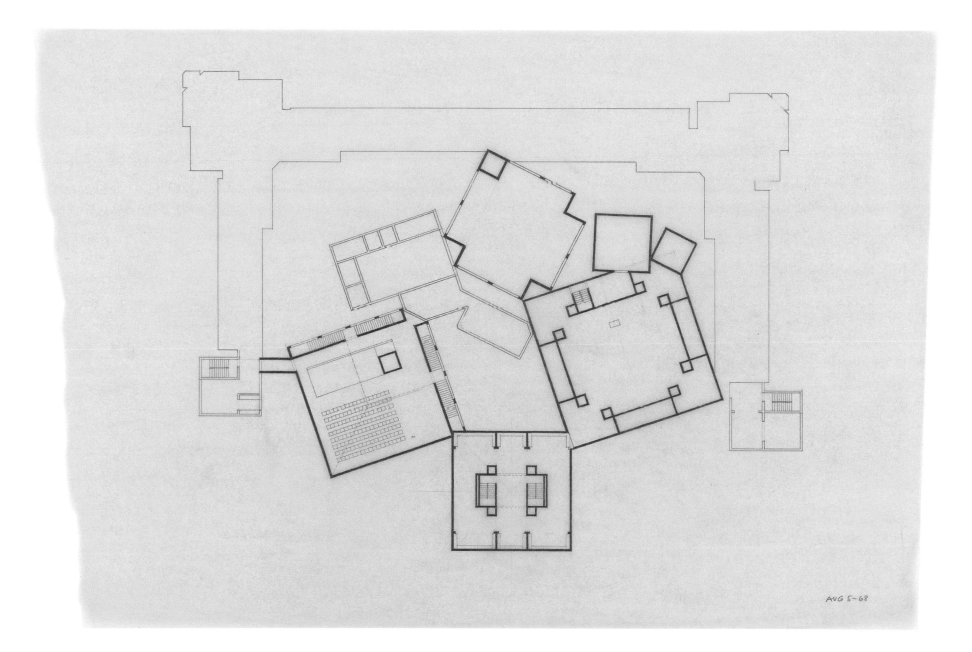

AUG 5-68

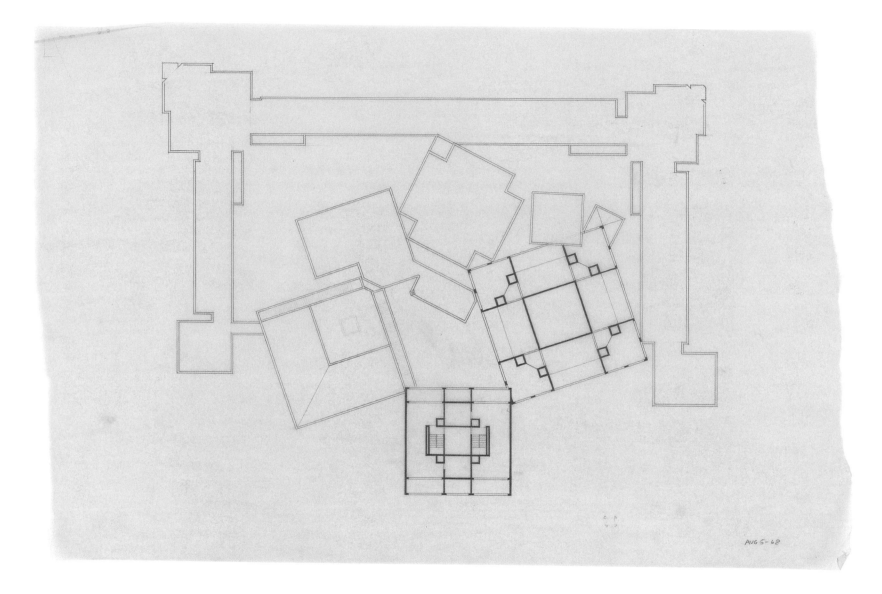

166 Third floor: plan, August 5, 1968
167 Basement: plan, August 5, 1968

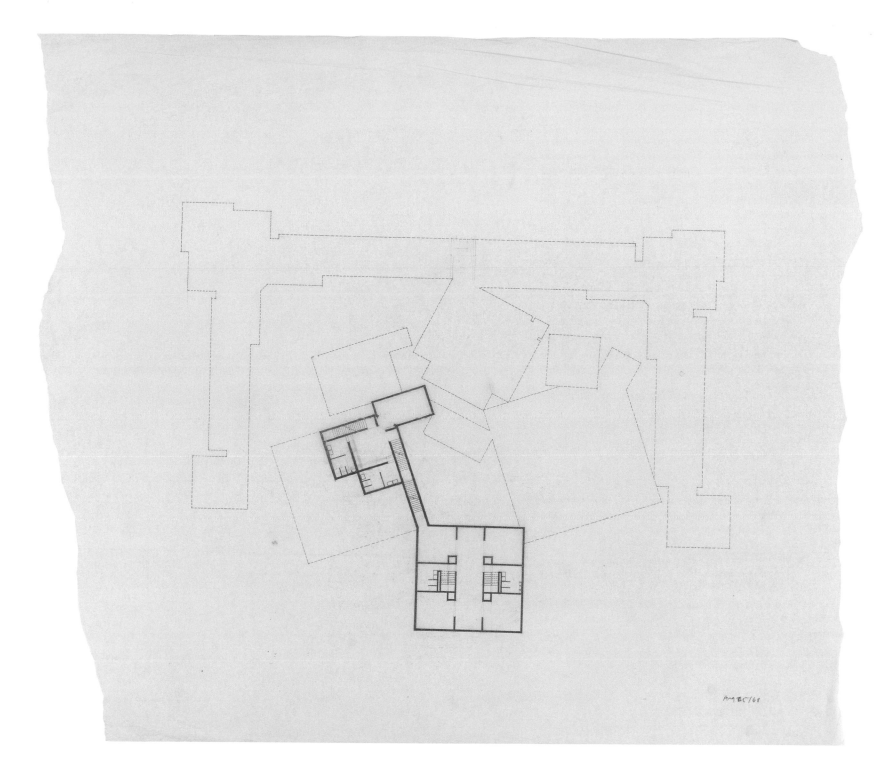

MATERIAL CONSEQUENCES

Over the length of the project, the architects' main effort has been directed toward the *configuration* of the spaces rather than at their *construction.* We recall that although the cells had been studied in detail quite early Figs. 68–73, it was not until the plans and elevations of August 1967 and the plan studies of October 1967 that the architects' pencils first began to linger at corners and connections and an appropriate tectonics for the core buildings begin to unfold. Figs. 107–25 This relatively late addressing of material and structure was not unique to the Dominican Motherhouse. While the Kahn of the fifties tended to begin his projects with a search for an all-enveloping structural system (the project for the Trenton Jewish Community Center, Adath Jeshurun Synagogue, Washington University Library, Clever House, etc.), Kahn of the sixties and seventies, while still seeking an architecture as a constructive art, recognized that its form must not necessarily be the result of rationalist structural determinism, but rather that its tectonics was to stand in service of more primary goals: "Form," degree of enclosure, configuration, relationship to context, etc. Thus, the mature Kahn said, "I never thought of the material first."[62]

An itemized cost estimate based on the latest scheme was prepared by Kahn's consultant Bill Gennetti on August 13, 1968 Fig. 172, and used as the basis of a summary that was presented by Kahn to the sisters in November. Figs. 168–71 The architects now stated a total construction price of $1,572,036, including landscaping, paving, and mechanical services for a convent that now measured 52,902 square feet (4,915 m²).

The cost estimates of August 1968 begin to give us a compact and spartan palette of materials with which to fill out the plans: concrete block (at $442,000 less than brick, Kahn's only real alternative), concrete or wooden floors, slate roofs, wooden windows, etc.

62 Louis I. Kahn, quoted in *Daidolos*, no. 43–46 (1992), p. 69.

168–71 Cost estimate, August 13, 1968
172 Cost estimate, August 13, 1968, Bill Gennetti

CONVENT FOR DOMINICAN SISTERS
FLOOR AREAS AS PER PLANS AND ESTIMATES
DATED AUGUST 13, 1968

Chapel.................................. 6300 sq. ft.
(Inclusive of small chapel and Confession Chambers)

Cells.................................. 25600 sq. ft.

Dining................................. 2926 sq. ft.

Kitchen................................ 1664 sq. ft.

School & Auditorium.................... 5424 sq. ft.

Library, Offices, Parking etc......... 10304 sq. ft.

Guest Dining........................... 684 sq. ft.

.... 52902 sq. ft.
Area of walls.......... 2900 sq. ft.

TOTAL.......... 55800 sq. ft.

Date: August 15, 1968

NOV 18 1968

CONVENT FOR DOMINICAN SISTERS
PRINCIPAL MATERIALS CONSIDERED
In The
COST ESTIMATE DATED AUGUST 13, 1968

NAMES OF BUILDING	WALLS	FLOORS	ROOF
Chapel	Concrete Block	Concrete	Concrete with Slate Shingles
Small Chapel	Concrete Block	Concrete	Concrete with Slate Shingles
Confession Chambers	Concrete Block	Concrete	Concrete with Slate Shingles
Cells	Concrete Block	Wood	Concrete with Slate Shingles
Dining	Concrete Block	Concrete	Concrete with Slate Shingles
Kitchen	Concrete Block	Concrete	Concrete with Slate Shingles
School & Auditorium	Concrete Block	Concrete	Concrete with Slate Shingles
Library	Concrete Block	Concrete	Concrete with Slate Shingles
Guest Dining	Concrete Block	Concrete	Concrete with Slate Shingles

Date: August 15, 1968

NOV 18 1968

CONVENT FOR DOMINICAN SISTERS

Estimated cost of General Construction using
Cement Concrete Block for walls

$1,050,036.00   (Date August 13, 1968)

The Total Estimated Cost of Mechanical from
the last Estimates.

$ 492,000.00

The Total Estimated Cost of Kitchen Equipment

$ 30,000.00

TOTAL...............$1,572,036.00

BUDGET.............$1,500,000.00

EXCESS .... $ 72,036.00

Date: August 15, 1968

CONVENT FOR DOMINICAN SISTERS

Estimated Cost of General Construction using
Cement Concrete Block for Walls.

$1,050,036.00   (Date August 13, 1968)

If brick instead of concrete block is used
for wall construction then the total increase
would be

$1,050,036.00
$ 442,000.00
        TOTAL.............$1,492,036.00

The total estimated cost of Mechanical from
the last estimates ....$ 492,000.00

The total estimated cost of Kitchen equipment
                                $ 30,000.00

TOTAL...... $2,014,036.00

BUDGET..... $1,500,000.00

EXCESS $ 514,036.00

DATE: August 15, 1968

DOMINICAN CONVENT NEAR MEDIA, PA.
W.L.G. ESTE.   Louis I. Kahn Architect
SHEET #1 OF 1   DATE: 9-13-68

PRELIMINARY BUDGET ESTIMATE
Cost of General Construction Summary

No.	Item	Quantity	Material Cost	Labor Cost	Total Cost
1	Excavation & Backfill	6850 c.y.	24970	—	24970
2	Conc. Work Incl. Stairs	1690 c.y.	118000	—	118000
3	Rein. Stl. & Mesh		24950	10250	35200
4	Masonry C.M.U. Ext. Int.		178000	—	178000
5	Built-Up Roof	21900 s.f.	22300	—	22300
6	Slate Roofing	10500 s.f.	19500	—	19500
7	Misc. Iron & Steel	lump sum	10440	—	10440
8	W.I. Railing for Stairs	900 l.f.	13400	—	13400
9	Wood Windows Frs. etc	191 ea.	19500	7500	37000
10	Folding Partitions-Screens	500 s.f.	6000	—	6000
11	Wd. Flooring Joists etc	68000 b.f.	9850	6400	15250
12	Hardwood Floor 7/8 sq. (net)	20600 s.f.	18300	—	18300
13	Carpentry & Lumber	various	1600	2000	3600
14	Millwork & Labor		6500	3500	10000
15	Bookcases-Desks-Chairs	each 60	18200	—	18200
16	Chest of Drawers	units 30	7500	—	7500
17	Wardrobes	ea. 30	6000	—	6000
18	Wd. Drs. & Frs. Int. & Ext.		12700	5100	17800
19	Finished Hardware	est. allowance	15500	—	15500
20	Rough Hardware	lump sum	3500	—	3500
21	Fireplace Brick & Jambs	11 M	4150	—	4150
22	Ceramic Tile Work Flr. & Walls	11900 s.f.	14600	—	14600
23	Metal Toilet Partitions	compl. 6	900	—	900
24	Toilet Room Accessories	pcs. 60	790	350	1140
25	Chalk & Cork Boards-Classrooms	500 s.f.	2500	—	2500
26	Bulletin Boards & Directory	ea. 60	1500	—	1500
27	Kitchenette-Dumbe Unit	units 4	4000	—	4000
28	Fire Extinguishers	units 60	2500	—	2500
29	Glass & Glazing-Windows	6490 s.f.	15600	—	15600
30	Marble Shower Partitions	2160 s.f.	15000	—	15000
31	Concrete Steps-Incl. Drink		13450	—	13450
					643800
32	Concrete Paving For Courts etc	10200 s.f.	9165	—	9165
	Allow For Site Work-Grading				
33	Walls-Ret.-Exp. Mac. Paving etc	various	125000	—	125000
	1/2 the amount of cost as before				
			748565	84400	777965
34	Field Operation Cost	estimated	61744	72300	134044
			805314	106700	912014
	Builders Profit	7.5%			68401
					980415
	Contingencies & Price Escalation	5%			49021
	Beyond Jan 1st 1970-Pro-rated				1029436
	Contract Bond-Pro-rated				8000
				TOTAL	$1,037,436
	Add Printing-of all Waterwork	lump sum			12600
					$1,050,036

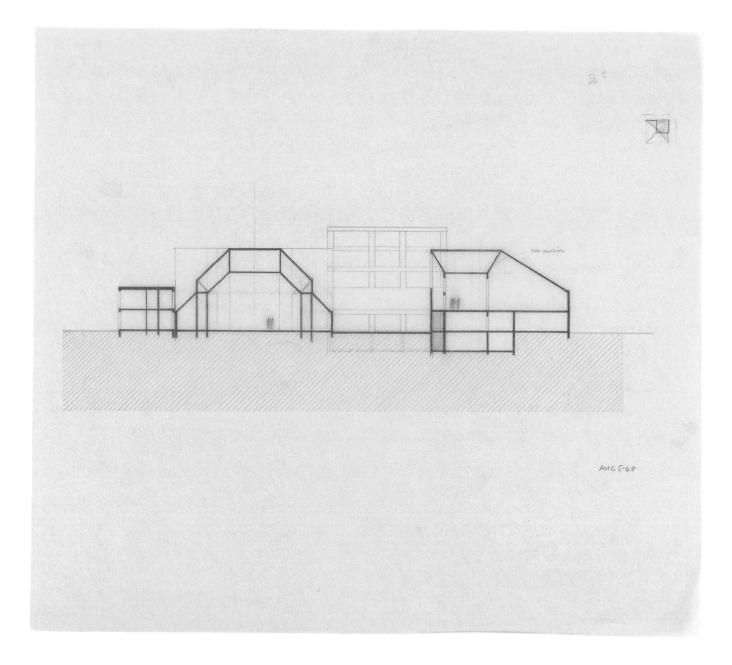

173 Core: section, August 5, 1968
174 Core: section, August 5, 1968

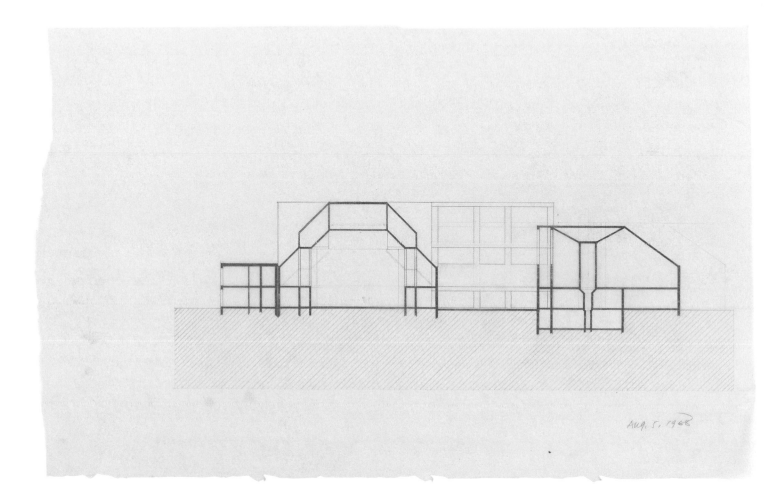

"The room is so marvelous that its size, its dimensions, its walls, its windows, its light—*its light,* not just light—have an effect on what you say and what you do." Louis I. Kahn, Third World Congress, Association of Architects and Engineers in Israel, December 1973

175 Cells: partial elevation, Summer 1968
176 Core: section, August 5, 1968

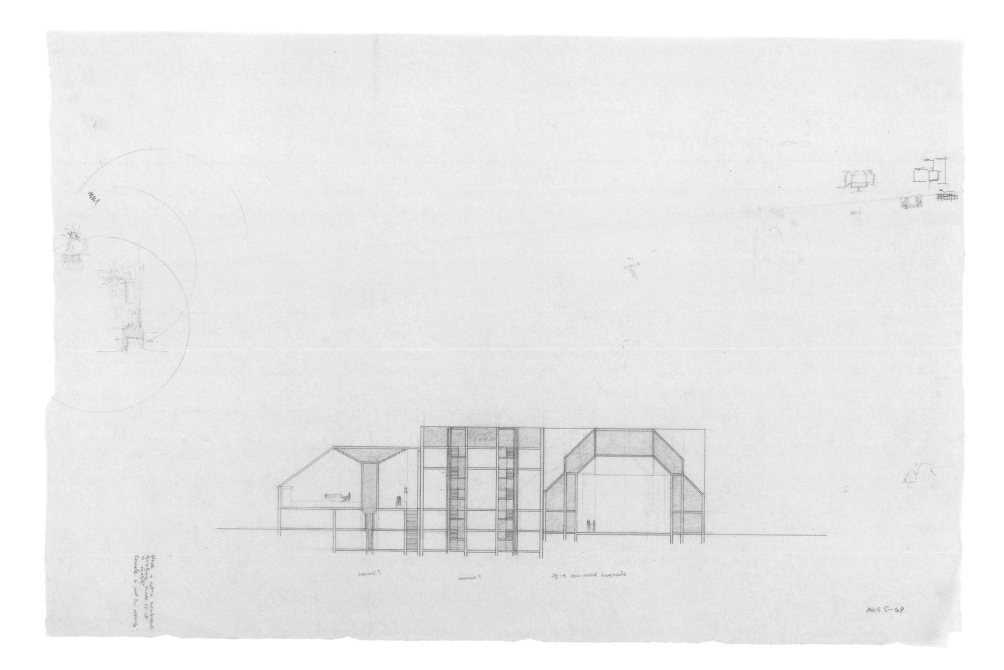

basement ?   basement ?   If we can avoid basements

AUG 5-68.

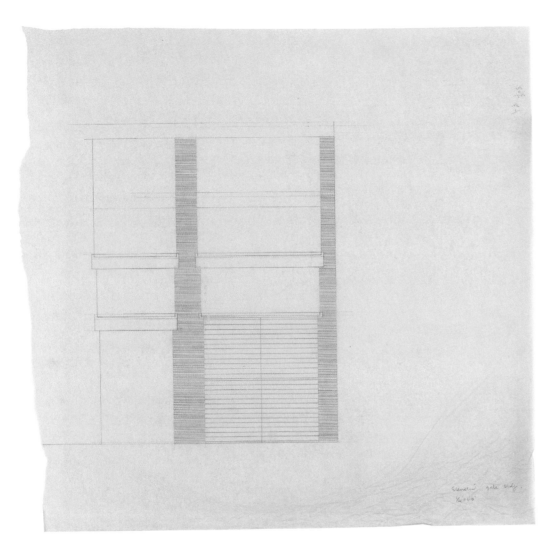

"Structure is the giver of light. When you decide on structure, you're deciding on light." Louis I. Kahn, "Silence and Light," 1969

177 Tower: wall detail, August 1968
178 West elevation, August 5, 1968

WEST ELEVATION
AUG-5-68

179 South elevation, August 5, 1968
180 East elevation, August 5, 1968

EAST ELEVATION
AUG 5-67

DRAWING TOWARD REALIZATION: THE DETAILS

Now, in fall and winter, the details of construction are explored, and always in regard to the sisters' austere budget. Kahn regularly used concrete block—that poor modern cousin of brick—in his budget-bound projects, and had gradually developed a hand for the material (DeVore House, Trenton Bath House, interiors of the Yale University Art Gallery and the First Unitarian Church, etc.). The true antecedent to the masonry work drawn for the Motherhouse is Kahn's small masterwork of thrift and elegance: the Tribune Review Building (1958–61). As in that building, here pilasters of brick-sized concrete masonry alternate with fields of standard-sized concrete block; the pilasters and their fillings telling of the walls' tectonics (Kahn: "A beam needs a column, a column needs a beam. There is no such thing as a beam on a wall."), while scoring a delicate gray-in-gray rhythm across the façade. ("The joint is the beginning of ornament.")

The elevations and details from this final phase intimate what had become the convent's rough and reticent austerity—a far cry from the exuberant baroqueness of the earliest scheme! Figs. 41–45 The details, though, hint at how these "Dominican poor" concrete-block walls, defining all spaces interior and exterior, are transformed by the architects' thought into something almost luxuriously ascetic. Figs. 177–93 Knowledge of Kahn's other masonry buildings helps us imagine how—through craftsman's jointing and the juxtaposition of elements from a limited palette of natural materials: lead, slate, cypress, or oak—the otherwise dull and grainy concrete blocks were to come alive in the natural light which they were to catch and reflect. This frugal meting out of costly materials and techniques in order to ennoble a budget-bound whole had been an effective tactic at the Tribune Review Building and would become a major strategy for the National Assembly at Dhaka, which Kahn later described: "The concrete is made like rotten stone. The marble inset mixes the fine with the rough and the fine takes over." [63]

63 Louis I. Kahn, in *What Will Be Has Always Been: The Words of Louis I. Kahn,* ed. Richard Saul Wurman, New York, 1986, p. 232.

"Block is not a membrane. Anything made of it is inert. Concrete is just the opposite." Louis I. Kahn, August 5, 1968

181 Wall section, Summer/Fall 1968

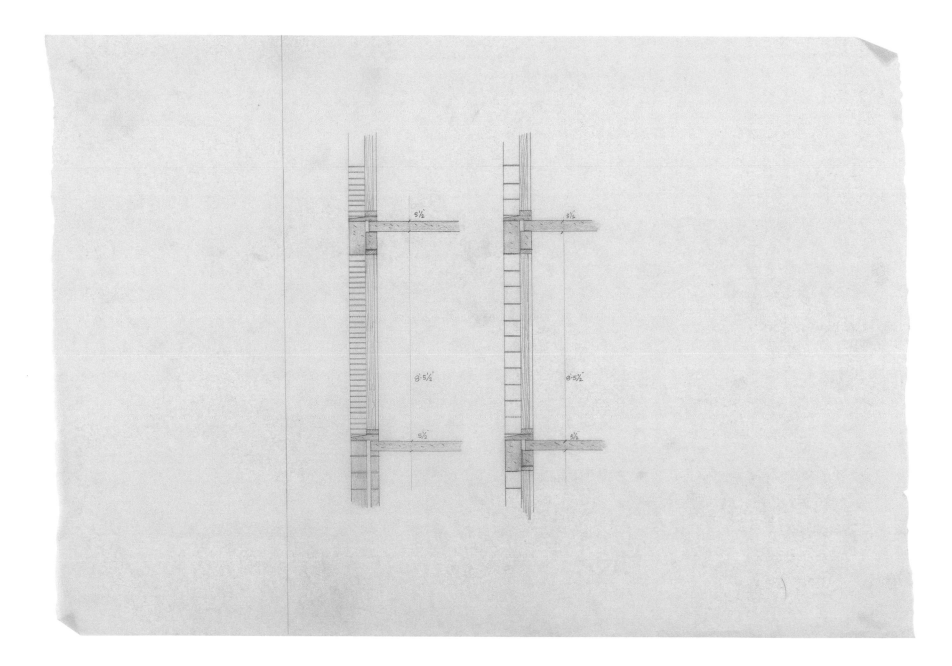

CONSTRUCTING THE CELLS

The last detailed studies of the cells Figs. 182–89 show how the spatial complexity of the earlier versions has fallen victim to the hard reality of the budget. As late as May 1968, the architects had drawn an open, frame-like exterior wall with two window openings per cell. Fig. 136 Now sections of closed wall and window alternate with nearly equal surface given to each. Long gone is the original façade-thickening built-in furniture, to be replaced by simple recessed window elements. The exterior wall has been drawn as a double-layered concrete block wall (from outside to inside: 8-in.-thick [20 cm] block, 2-in. [5 cm] of air space, 4-in.-thick [10 cm] block) while the walls between cells are a single 8-in. block width. Toilet rooms and closets are treated as wooden cabinets, with floor and ceiling also of wood. (Changed from the earlier concrete to a basic wooden plank-and-beam construction.) Although the wooden floor gives a warmer, more domestic atmosphere than concrete, in reading the drawings we can almost hear the sound of the sisters' shoes on this quite rudimentary construction— free from any acoustic dampening—demanding of them an almost tiptoe tread in their cells. This final version makes the concession of concrete floors in the hall.

As so often with Kahn, the wooden window frames are recessed to disappear behind the block when viewed from outside, suppressing detail at the middle scale and underscoring the primacy of the walls. Conversely, from the inside the frames act as picture frames to the view. Single courses of smaller concrete brick trace the datum of the floor levels around the entire monastery, visually binding cells and core buildings together like threads. Fig. 189

182 Small cell: section, October 23, 1968
183 Small cell: plan, October 23, 1968
184 Large cell: section, October 23, 1968
185 Large cell: plan, October 23, 1968

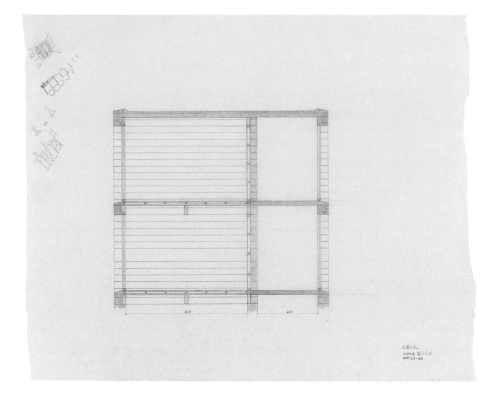

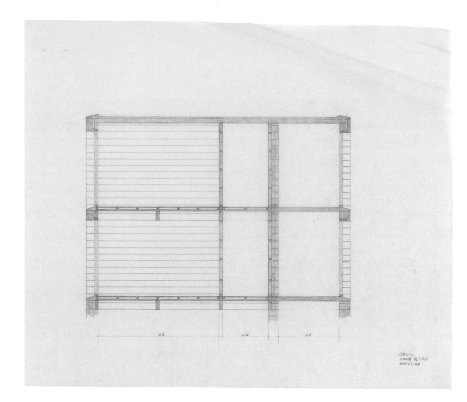

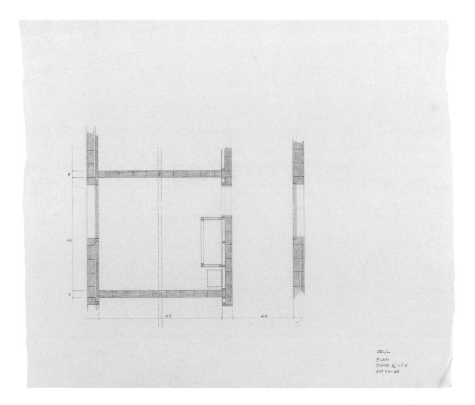

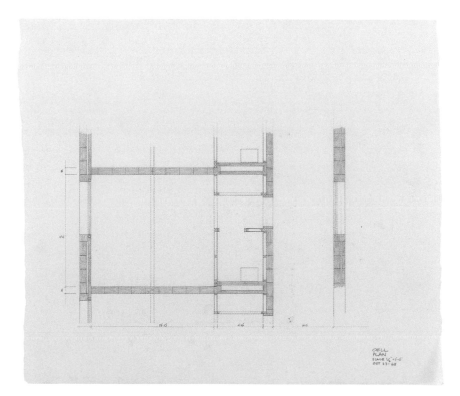

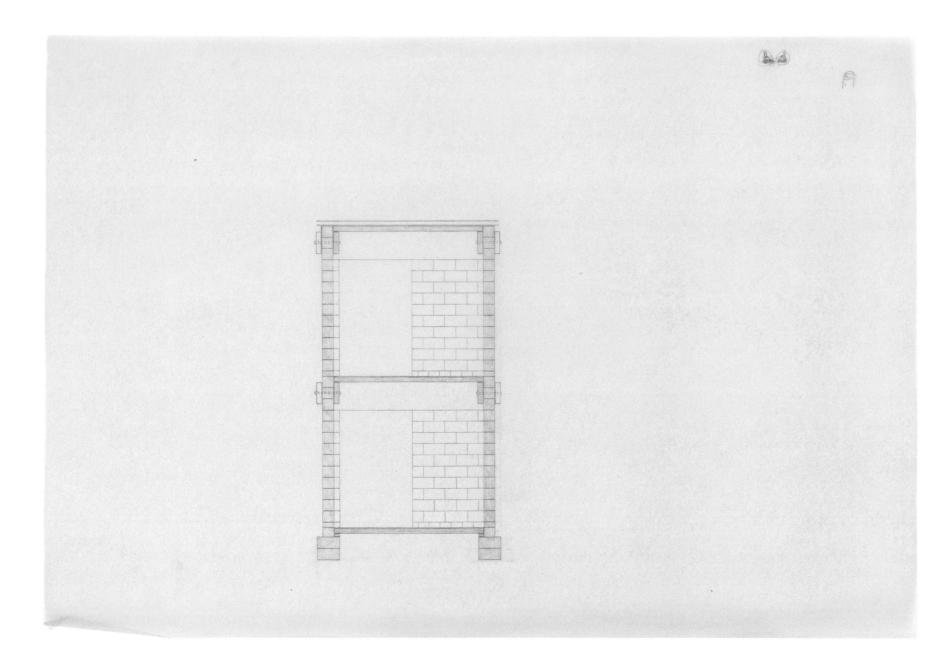

186 Cell: section, Summer/Fall 1968
187 Cells: horizontal sections, Summer/Fall 1968

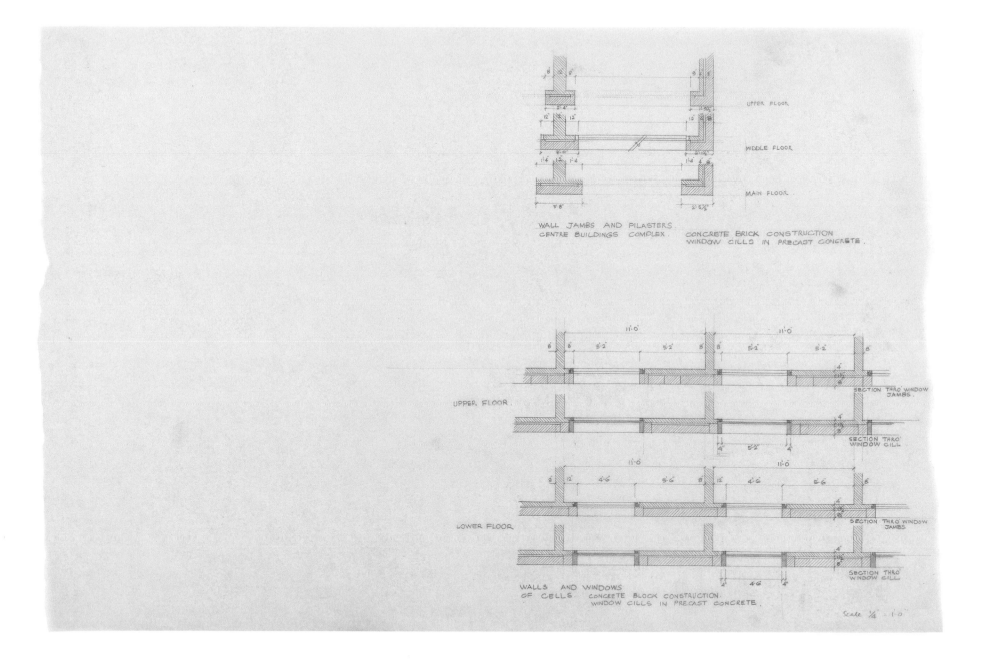

WALL JAMBS AND PILASTERS.
CENTRE BUILDINGS COMPLEX.   CONCRETE BRICK CONSTRUCTION
WINDOW CILLS IN PRECAST CONCRETE.

UPPER FLOOR

MIDDLE FLOOR

MAIN FLOOR.

UPPER FLOOR.

SECTION THRO' WINDOW JAMBS.

SECTION THRO' WINDOW CILL

LOWER FLOOR

SECTION THRO' WINDOW JAMBS

SECTION THRO' WINDOW CILL

WALLS AND WINDOWS
OF CELLS. CONCRETE BLOCK CONSTRUCTION.
WINDOW CILLS IN PRECAST CONCRETE.

Scale ¼ = 1'-0"

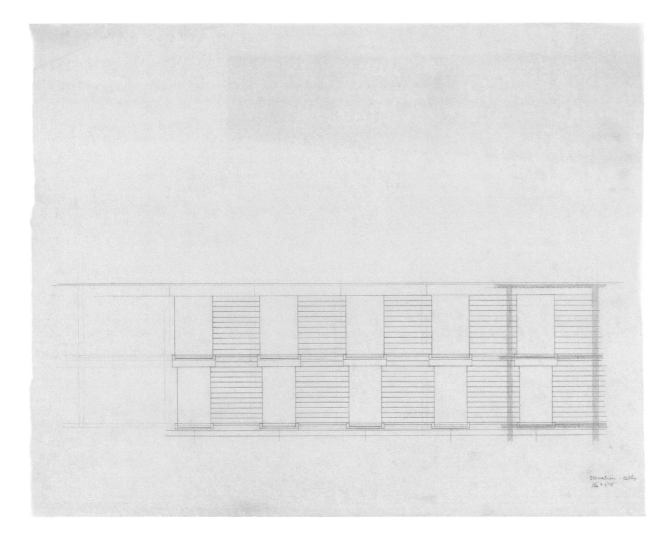

"The ornament is the recognition that a joint is ceremonious.
The joint implies ornament." Louis I. Kahn, Phillips Exeter Academy, 1972

188 Cell: elevation, section, Summer/Fall 1968
189 Cell: elevation, Summer/Fall 1968

elevation cells
1/2"=1'0"

CONSTRUCTING THE CORE SPACES

The core buildings are drawn with a 14-in.-thick (36 cm) exterior cavity wall consisting of an outer layer of 8-x-16-in. (20 × 40 cm) concrete blocks, 2 in. (5 cm) of rigid insulation, and an inner layer of 4-x-16-in. (10 × 40 cm) blocks. Pilasters bearing the greatest loads from beams are articulated using 4-x-12-in. (10 × 30 cm) brick-sized concrete masonry. Inside, walls and partitions are of concrete masonry, either standard 8-in. (20 cm) blocks or oversized 14-in. (36 cm) blocks for taller walls and columns. Lintels, windowsills, and copings are of rigorously proportioned precast concrete elements, and form an integral ornament adding long horizontal *legatos* to the repetitive *staccato* of the masonry. Figs. 190–95

These long-held-back construction details, together with those of the cells, are among the most fascinating drawings in the project's portfolios, for through them we may finally begin to visualize the texture, light, and feel of spaces which have, until now, remained generic, and to make the building more fully "our own." [63] The detailing of the walls is rigorously spare and eloquently communicative; nothing is superfluous, each decision giving subtle voice to the conditions of the wall's existence: the articulation of bearing and non-bearing components, of elements in tension and those in compression, of responses to weathering, etc. The floors of the core buildings were to be of poured-in-place concrete, meeting the walls in unmitigated, detail-free fashion. While the chapel is spanned by wooden trusses Fig. 190, the sloped roof of the school building was to be of folded plate concrete, creating an integral mechanical space; the hollow columns supporting the roof double as "servant" ducts. Fig. 194

63 On reading architects' construction drawings, see Martin Steinmann, "Techne: zur Arbeit von Peter Zumthor, in *Partituren und Bilder*, Lucerne, 1989, pp. 6–8.

"A beam needs a column, a column needs a beam.
There is no such thing as a beam on a wall."

Louis I. Kahn, "Silence and Light," 1969

190 Chapel: section, Summer/Fall 1968

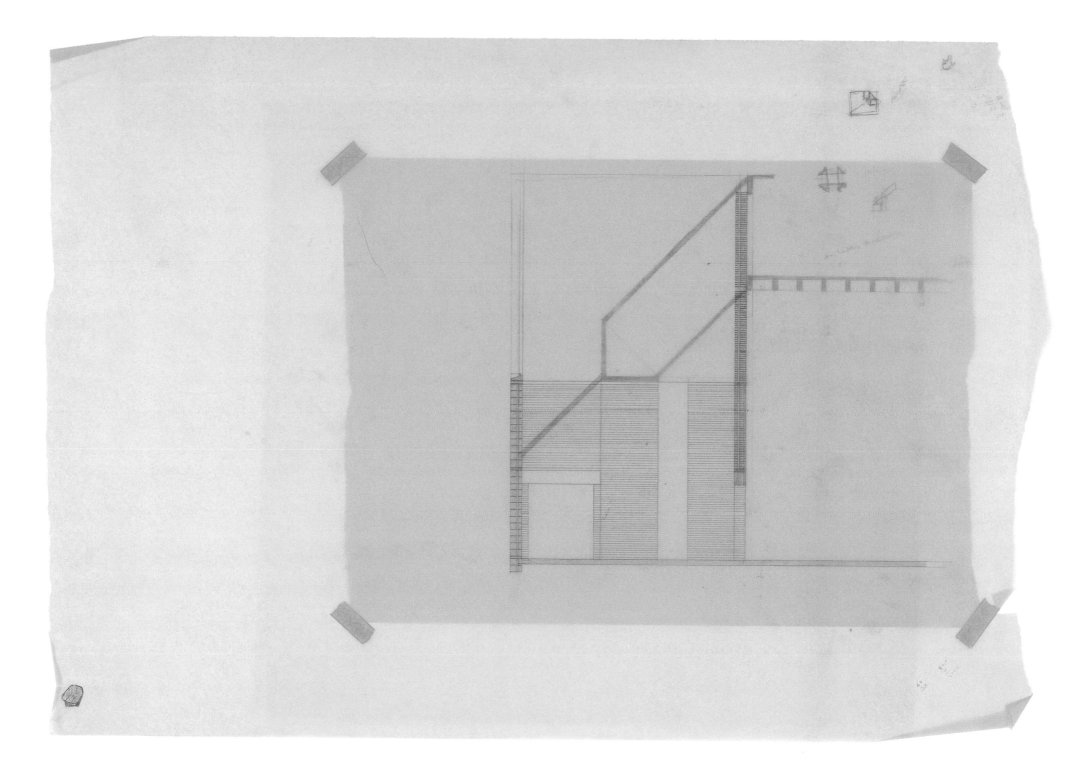

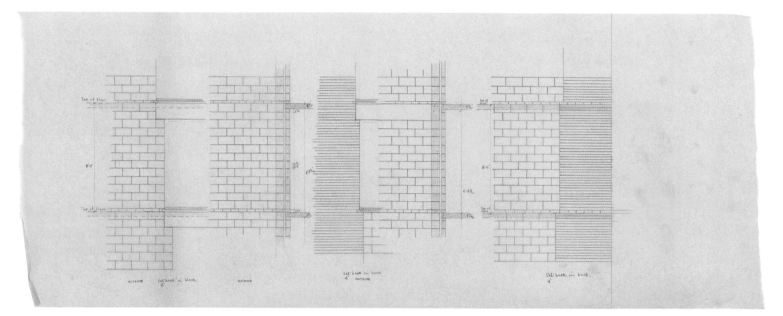

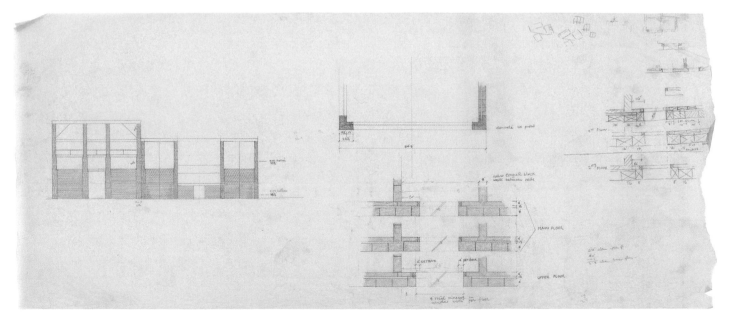

191–93 Core buildings: wall details, Summer/Fall 1968

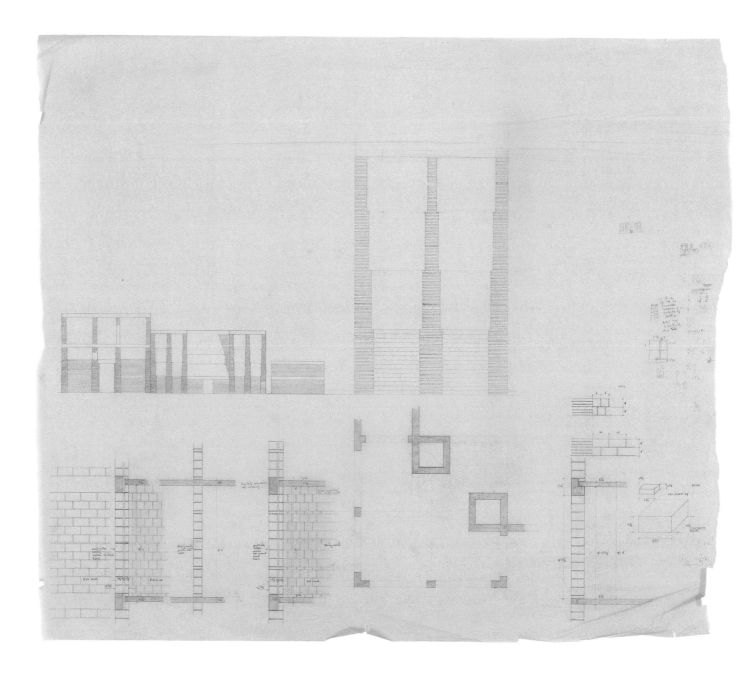

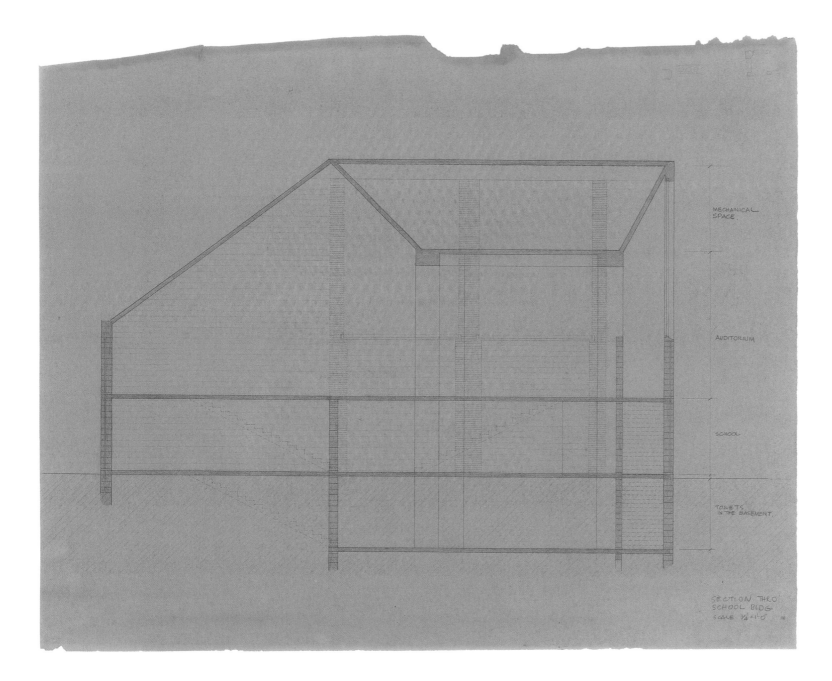

MECHANICAL
SPACE

AUDITORIUM

SCHOOL

TOILETS
IN THE BASEMENT.

SECTION THRO'
SCHOOL BLDG
SCALE ⅛"=1'-0"

194 School/auditorium: section, Summer/Fall 1968

195 School/auditorium: elevation, Summer/Fall 1968

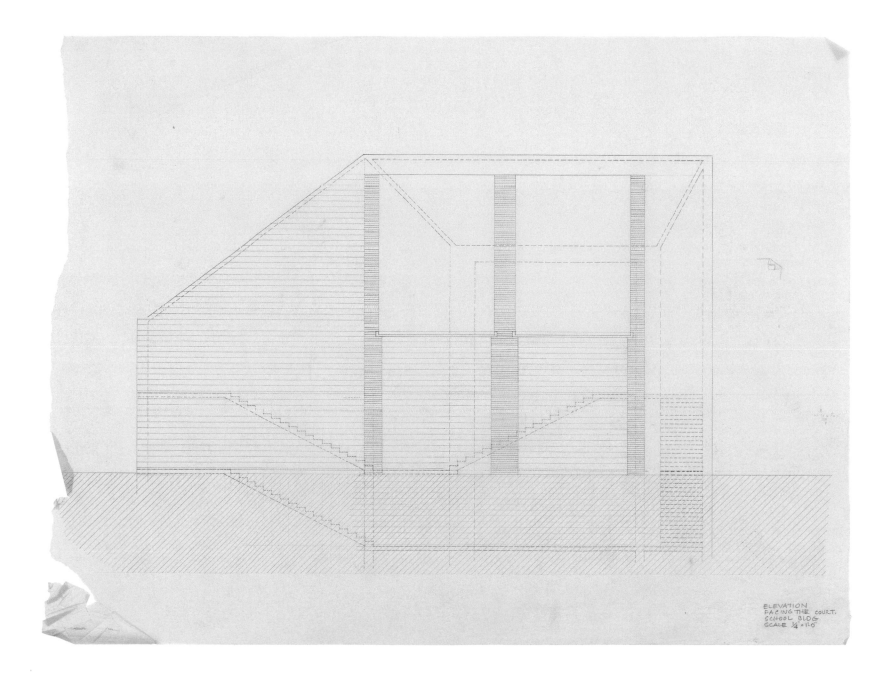

ELEVATION
FACING THE COURT.
SCHOOL BLDG
SCALE 1/4"=1'0"

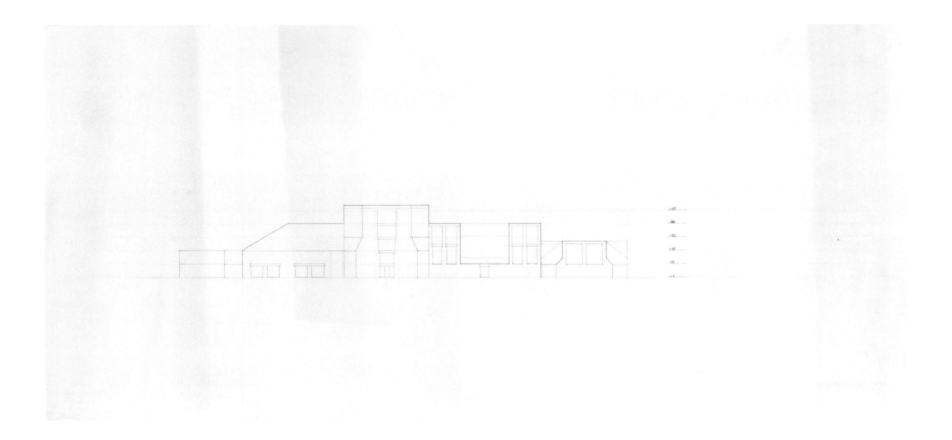

196 Core buildings: elevation, Fall/Winter 1968
197 First floor: plan, Summer/Fall 1968

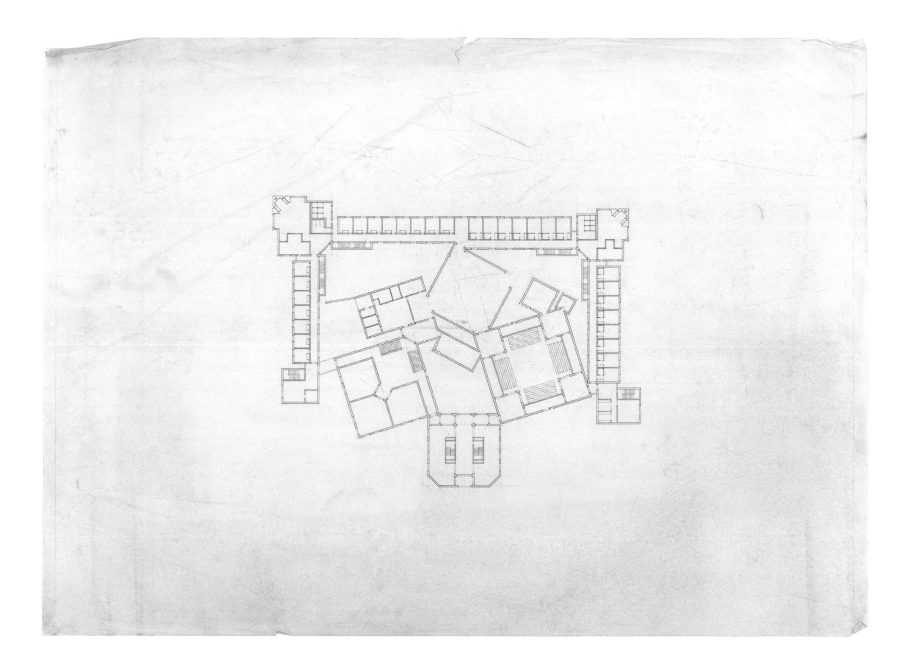

PREPARING THE WAY FOR CONSTRUCTION

A call for bidders was placed in fall and Kahn's office sent drawings to selected contractors for preliminary estimates. In fall and winter meetings, details were discussed with the clients: the merits of wood windows versus stainless steel, lead-coated copper versus slate, types of wood, kitchen equipment, seating arrangements in the chapel, final dimensions of classrooms, etc. On November 13, Kahn presented the projected costs in Media Figs. 168–71, and promised the sisters to complete design development preliminaries by mid-December; with an additional six-month head start for working drawings, and one and a half years for construction, they could move into their new convent within two years! Figs. 198–99 The project, after almost three years of intermittent planning, was finally on the verge of realization.

198–99 Meeting notes, November 12, 1968
200 Entry tower: floor plans, October 5, 1968

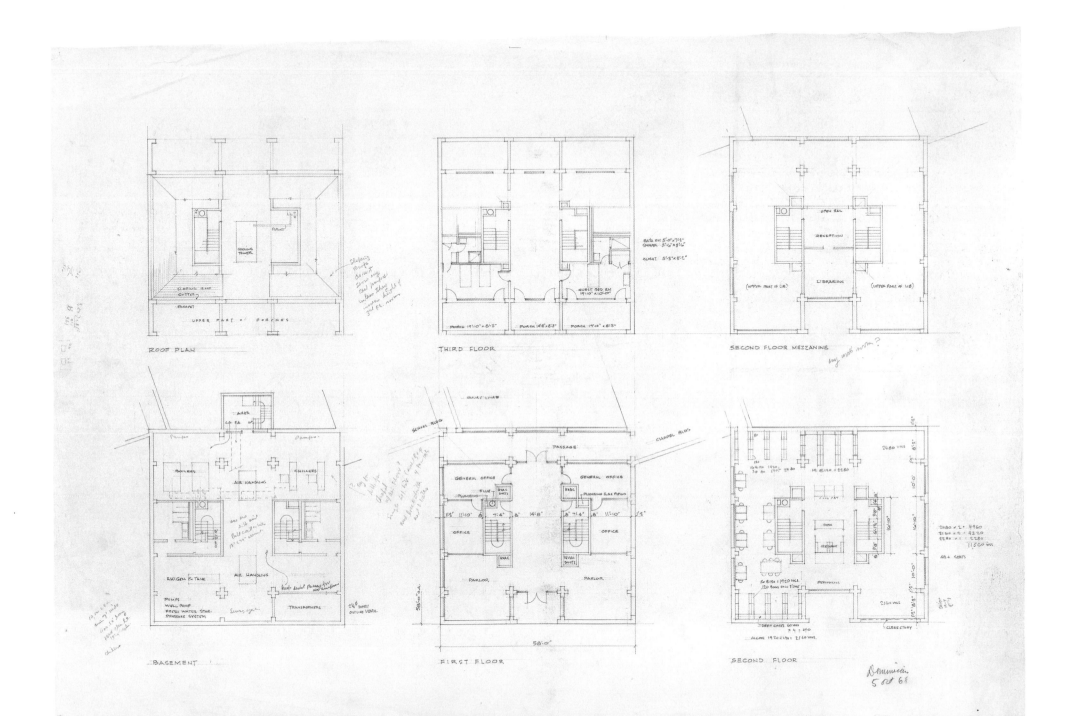

ROOF PLAN

THIRD FLOOR

SECOND FLOOR MEZZANINE

BASEMENT

FIRST FLOOR

SECOND FLOOR

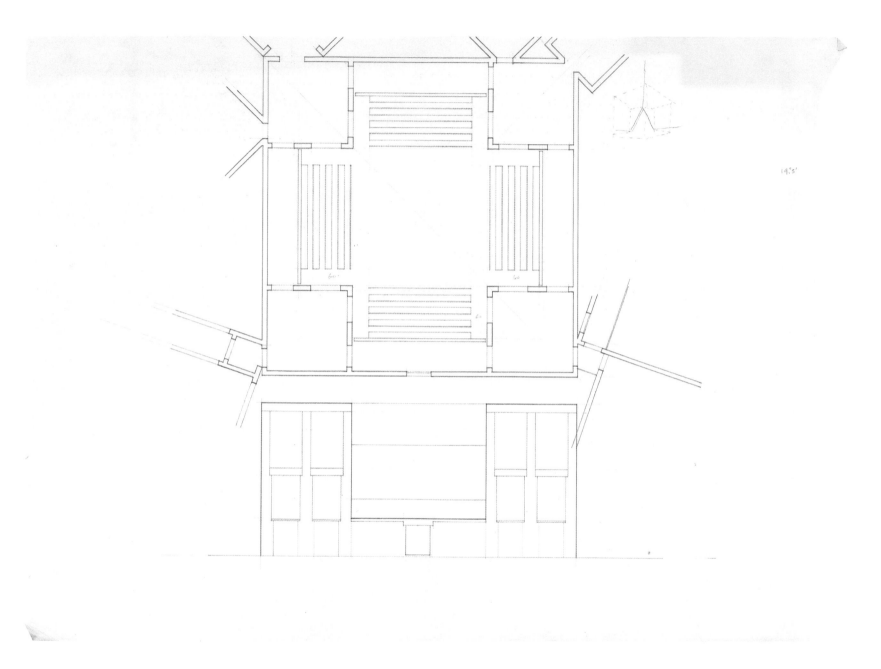

201 Chapel: plan, elevation, Fall/Winter 1968
202–3 Meeting notes (Dominican Motherhouse), March 10, 1969

MEETING OF GENERAL COUNCILLORS AND BUILDING COMMITTEE WITH
MOTHER MARY BERNADETTE

DATE: Monday, March 10, 1969.

TIME: 11 A M to 3 P M

PLACE: Motherhouse, Media, Pennsylvania.

TOPIC: The Proposed Motherhouse Building.

Having had time to study the Estimated Cost of General Construction which Mr. Louis I. Kahn submitted at our last meeting the
Committee Members and Councillors met with M.M.Bernadette to
discuss reactions,etc., as to whether or not to continue.The
following points were made after which a vote was taken as to
whether or not we would continue with the modified plan"as is" .
The vote was a unanimous "no".

1. Although we had asked Mr. Kahn to bring the
estimated cost to a $1,000,000.00 maximum it is
still close to $2,000,000.00. The Sisters pre-
sent felt that we could not burden the members
of the Congregation with such a big debt. It is
far more than we can afford.

2. Due to constatnly changing formation programs it
seems that candidates for religious life will be
spending more and more time away from the Motherhouse making it less and less necessary to build
the proposed classrooms and additional bedrooms
even though we have already cut down since we
we first began to plan it...it remains too large.

3. With fewer people here than we had planned for
and with receptions and professions taking place
in local convents, mission parishes, etc., putting
up a bigger chapel is no longer necessary.

4. The same holds true for building a bigger refectory.

5. Although we had planned to change to cement block
as it would be less expensive than brick we feel
that in the end it would not be a money-saving
scheme as the brick would far outlast the blocks.

6. Since we have an empty building...St Catherine's
Hall in Elkins Park...it was felt that we could
consider the possibility of using it in some way.

7/ The Baring Street mission situation was reviewed.
Mother Bernadette related how a number of ladies
have been assaulted in these last few months. The
Sisters feel that it is a very dangerous section
to have a residence for retired women. Also, it
was mentioned that the Sisters' quarters are in

very bad condition. Might not St Catherine's
Hall be extended and renovated for he use of our
older Sisters and also for the residents from
Baring Street.

There was much discussion after which the voting mentioned above
was-=== took place.

RESOLUTION: That Sister Mary James prepare a letter to Mr. Kahn
this week to inform him that we cannot possibly
continue with the original plan to build. Main
reasons being COST and the CONSTANT FLUX of our
way of life at this particular time.

More discussion followed on he need for extending and remodeling
the present Motherhouse building. It was agreed by the entire
group that this should also take place...and soon.

RESOLUTION: That Sister Mary Raphael make inquiries as to a
possible architect or architects from whom we might
get an estimate for such a job.

The extention would include:

1. 10 bedrooms

2. 1 Conference Room

3. 1 Classroom

4. New entranceway for retreatants

5. Dining hall

6. Meeting room

7. Cloak room

8. Lavatory for men

9. Lavatory for women

10. Kitchen and pantry space

11. Archives Room

12. Offices.

A SUDDEN END, A GREAT DISAPPOINTMENT

Now, on the threshold of attainment, the sisters would stop short. In spite of all successful measures to reduce costs, money had remained a dominant theme at their internal project meetings. The architects had squeezed and cut where they could and there were now no reserves should the inevitable happen and costs begin to slowly inch upward again. A more economical means of construction than the bare concrete-block walls was hardly conceivable, and the distilled plan could be reduced no further without compromising aesthetic integrity or use. The sisters, reluctant to burden their future generations with debt, were acutely aware of this.[65]

But budget problems, however real, were not the only or perhaps even the greatest threat to the project. Changes had been at work within the congregation and the society around it that would put an end to the work. On the one hand, the number of new postulants had dropped steadily in the four years since beginning the project, calling the sisters' need for more space seriously into question. Just as important were the Second Vatican Council's reforms to monastic life from 1965, the very year in which the sisters had initiated their project.[66] Their discussion and integration into the congregation had paralleled the long development of Kahn's design, which had ironically served as a catalyst for often heated debates on the virtues of traditional monastic life versus new opportunities for working in the world.[67] Eventually, the sisters began to see ever more of their seminary work and active religious life taking place outside of their convent—at churches, schools, community centers, universities—undermining their need for the proposed classrooms, the larger chapel, and thus the refectory and extra bedrooms. The vision of monastic life which had led the sisters to seek out Kahn in 1965 had by 1969 slowly but surely lost its consensus within the congregation. On March 10, 1969, the congregation's general councilors and building committee, faced with the decision of proceeding to build the final scheme, voted unanimously to stop all work on the project, giving their main reasons as "cost and the constant flux of our way of life at this particular time." Figs. 202–3 These were the late sixties, that volatile and expansive time in which, as Kahn himself had often repeated, "All of our institutions are on trial"—religious institutions as well. He could not have been anything

but extremely disappointed, though, when he received a letter, dated March 18, 1969, from Mother Emmanuel's successor as Prioress General, Mother Mary Bernadette. Fig. 204

65 Interview, author with Sisters Mary Irene Lolli, O.P., and Eileen Priscilla Primrose, O.P., Dominican Motherhouse, Elkins Park, PA, April 15, 2006.

66 For texts on Vatican II (1962–65), see the Vatican Archive, Documents of the II Vatican Council, http://www.vatican.va/archive/hist_councils/ii_vatican_council/ (accessed April 2006).

67 Interview, author with Sisters Mary Irene Lolli, O.P., and Eileen Priscilla Primrose, O.P.

204 Letter from Mother Mary Bernadette to Louis Kahn, March 18, 1969

mary, queen of all saints

motherhouse ~ dominican congregation of st. catherine de ricci

2850 NORTH PROVIDENCE ROAD
MEDIA, PENNSYLVANIA

Mr. Louis I. Kahn,
1501 Walnut Street,
Philadelphia, Pennsylvania. 19102.

MAR 20 1969

Dear Mr. Kahn,

It is my unpleasant duty to advise you that after much soul-searching and discussion we have decided to discontinue our plans for a new Motherhouse. The reasons are many and forceful. Aside from money which is, of course, a very real factor, we face at the moment constantly changing attitudes toward the manner and setting of religious life which opens up distinct forms this life is taking and will continue to take in the future.

In these days of re-evaluation, re-newal and re-study, we feel that the complex of buildings we originally envisioned would dictate decisions on our form of life rather than permit us to vary our life to fulfill our vocation amid the needs of today. We are in unanimous agreement that we cannot proceed with the original plans at this time.

For the present we have decided to provide for our aging Sisters at one of our other Convents. At Media we shall make some renovations to meet immediate needs.

I do not wish to imply that we are merely delaying our project for a year or two. For your sake as well as our own we feel it best to conclude our mutual agreement now. Will you please have sent to us a statement of fees we still owe? At the same time we would appreciate having whatever models or plans are available.

It has been an enriching experience and great pleasure to have been associated with you and your staff in this venture. We have all enjoyed and profited from it. Our sincere appreciation to you for your understanding, patience, and wisdom.

Sincerely,

Mother Mary Bernadette, O.P.,
Prioress General.

March 18, 1969.

LOOSE ENDS, AN OPEN WORK

Sadly, Mother Bernadette's letter would be the last official communiqué between the convent and Kahn. Sister Mary Irene Lolli, O.P., secretary of the building committee, and Sister Eileen Priscilla Primrose, O.P., member of the congregation's general councilors, vividly recalled years later how much the sisters regretted having to end their inspiring and friendly relationship with Kahn.[68] Aside from a minor remodeling of the existing house and the addition of a small chapel in order to adapt it to their own use, the sisters would never build at Media and the hillock they called Daffodil Hill would remain untouched over the next decades. The older sisters soon moved to the newly remodeled Saint Catherine's Hall, a former utility building at the second foundation's Elkins Park retreat, to be followed by the rest of the congregation in 1989, at which time house and property at Media were sold. In the turn-of-the-century real estate boom, both the hill and the rest of the property at Media were sold again, this time to be subdivided for high-end speculative houses, unceremoniously occupying the site and closing the door on a project which had been the source of so many rich thoughts.

If Kahn has led us over the past months on the long way from gesture to plan, through dissonance to resolution, it is a tenuous resolution he has found, spring-tight and seemingly waiting to further unfold. In spite of the "finished" design, it is impossible to say how the Dominican Motherhouse would have finally appeared and found its place in the lives of the sisters had it been built. Not everything had been decided; certainly there would have been late changes during the planning, there always were, sometimes decisive and indeed often welcomed by Kahn: "When you have all the answers to a building before you start building it, your answers are not true. The building gives you answers as it grows and becomes itself."[69] If the project remains one of Kahn's most enigmatic and compelling "uncompleted things," it is not only for its exemplary illustration of principle, but due to its combination of precise intention and loose ends which have been left to intertwine in our imaginations with so many different threads of reality.

68 Interview, author with Sisters Mary Irene Lolli, O.P., and Eileen Priscilla Primrose, O.P.

69 Louis I. Kahn, *Light is the Theme: Louis I. Kahn and the Kimbell Art Museum*, ed. Nell E. Johnson, Fort Worth, 1975. Among the more important "answers" which Kahn's buildings gave him during their construction include: the final state of the famous plaza at the Salk Institute, the last minute substitution of travertine for slate in that project, and the construction of the central roof of the National Assembly at Dhaka.

"The value of uncompleted things is very strong…. If the spirit is there and can be recorded, what is lost? The drawing is important, the incomplete scheme is important, if it has a central gravitational force which makes the arrangement not just an arrangement but something which gives a richness to the associations which are lost. Recording of that which has not been done must be made much of." Louis I. Kahn, 1973

APPENDIX

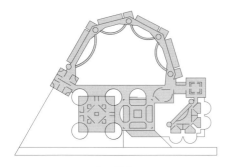

June 1966

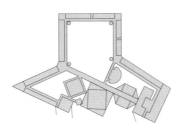

August–September 1966

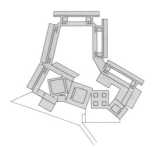

October–December 1966

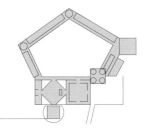

January–February 1967

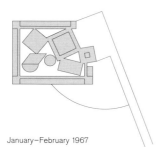

January–February 1967

March–April 1967

March–April 1967

March–April 1967

Evolution of the plan, 1966–68

January–February 1967

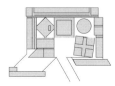

January–February 1967

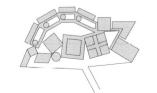

January–February 1967

January–February 1967

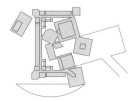

May 1967

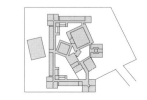

August 1967

April 1968

August 1968

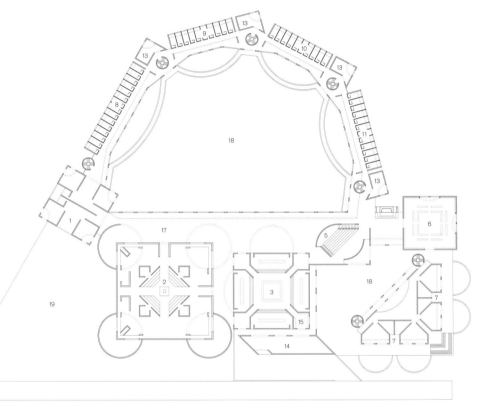

June 22, 1966

1 Tower/Entrance
2 Chapel
3 Refectory
4 Guest dining room
5 Auditorium
6 Library
7 School
8 Cells: postulants
9 Cells: novices
10 Cells: professed
11 Cells: older professed
12 Cells: guests
13 Living room
14 Kitchen
15 Service
16 Office
17 Cloister
18 Court
19 Entry court

Floor plans of June, September, and October 1966

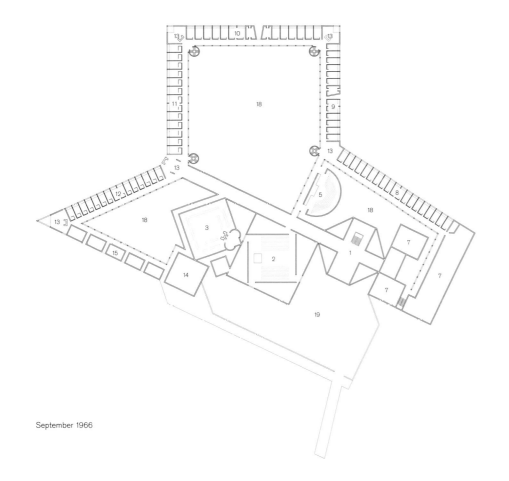

September 1966

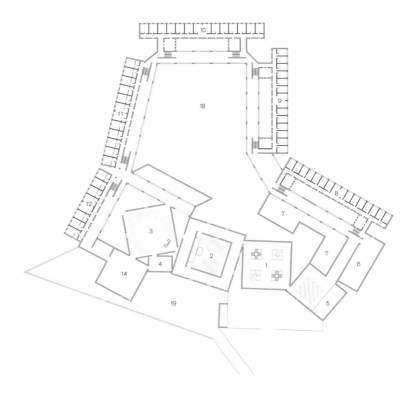

October 1966

m 5 10   20   50
ft 10   50   100   150
N

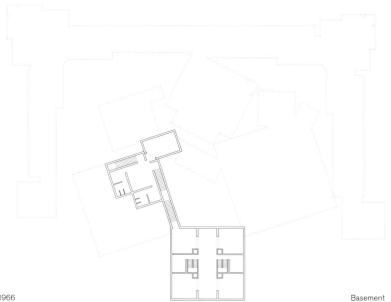

August 5, 1966   Basement

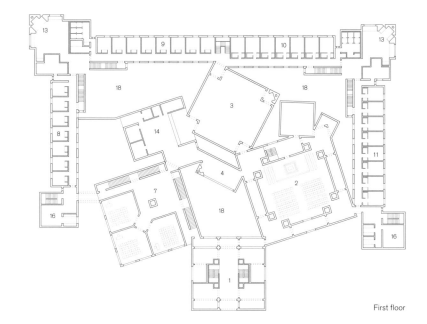

First floor

 1 Tower/Entrance
 2 Chapel
 3 Refectory
 4 Guest dining room
 5 Auditorium
 6 Library
 7 School
 8 Cells: postulants
 9 Cells: novices
10 Cells: professed
11 Cells: older professed
12 Cells: guests
13 Living room
14 Kitchen
15 Service
16 Office
17 Cloister
18 Court
19 Entry court

Floor plan of August 5, 1968 (similar to other plans after February 1967)

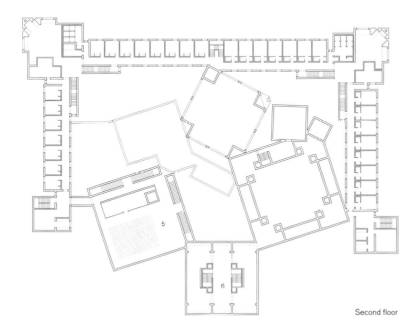

Second floor

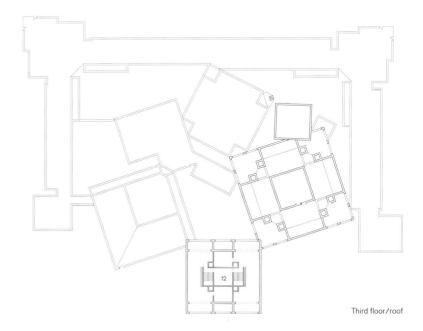

Third floor/roof

June 1966

September 1966

Evolution of site plan, 1966–68

October 1966

August 1968

LIST OF ILLUSTRATIONS

108 South elevation, August 7, 1967, Louis Kahn, diazo print, 30 ½ × 10 ½ in. (77.5 × 27 cm), ⅛ in. = 1 ft., 030.I.C.700.006
109 East elevation, August 7, 1967, Louis Kahn, charcoal on sketch paper, 44 ½ × 18 in. (113 × 45.5 cm), ⅛ in. = 1 ft., 030.I.A.700.4
110 North elevation, August 7, 1967, graphite pencil on vellum, 36 ¼ × 11 ¾ in. (92 × 30 cm), 1/16 in. = 1 ft., 030.I.C.700.001
111 South elevation, August 7, 1967, graphite pencil on vellum, 36 ¼ × 11 ¾ in. (92 × 30 cm), 1/16 in. = 1 ft., 030.I.C.700.001
112 East elevation, August 7, 1967, graphite pencil on vellum, 33 ½ × 11 ¾ in. (85 × 30 cm), 1/16 in. = 1 ft., 030.I.C.700.001
113 West elevation, August 7, 1967, graphite pencil on vellum, 33 ½ × 11 ¾ in. (85 × 30 cm), 1/16 in. = 1 ft., 030.I.C.700.001
114 Meeting notes, August 7, 1967, David Slovik, handwritten in graphite pencil, Box LIK 10
115–16 Contract, August 7, 1967, Louis Kahn/Mother Mary Emmanuel, offset print, 8 ½ × 11 in. (21.5 × 28 cm), Box LIK 10
117 Chapel: plan, September/October 1967, Louis Kahn, charcoal on sketch paper, 22 × 18 in. (56 × 45.5 cm), ⅛ in. = 1 ft., 030.I.A.700.2
118 Chapel: plan, September/October 1967, Louis Kahn, charcoal on sketch paper, 19 ½ × 11 ¾ in. (49.5 × 30 cm), ⅛ in. = 1 ft., 030.I.C.700.010
119 Chapel: plan, September/October 1967, Louis Kahn, charcoal on sketch paper, 18 ¼ × 18 in. (46.5 × 45.5 cm), ⅛ in. = 1 ft., 030.I.C.700.010
120 Chapel: plan, October 12, 1967, graphite pencil on sketch paper, 28 × 18 in. (71 × 45.5 cm), ⅛ in. = 1 ft., 030.I.C.700.001
121 Entry tower: plan, October 12, 1967, graphite pencil on sketch paper, 21 ½ × 18 in. (54.5 × 45.5 cm), ⅛ in. = 1 ft., 030.I.C.700.001
122 Entry tower: plan, October 12, 1967, graphite pencil on sketch paper, 21 × 18 in. (53.5 × 45.5 cm), ⅛ in. = 1 ft., 030.I.C.700.001
123 Entry tower: plan, October 12, 1967, graphite pencil on sketch paper, 24 ½ × 18 in. (62 × 45.5 cm), ⅛ in. = 1 ft., 030.I.C.700.001
124 Classroom: plan, October 12, 1967, graphite pencil on sketch paper, 25 × 18 in. (63.5 × 45.5 cm), ⅛ in. = 1 ft., 030.I.C.700.001
125 Refectory: plan, October 12, 1967, graphite pencil on sketch paper, 23 × 18 in. (58.5 × 45.5 cm), ⅛ in. = 1 ft., 030.I.C.700.001
126 First floor: plan, February/March 1968, Louis Kahn, charcoal on sketch paper, 41 ½ × 33 ½ in. (105 × 85 cm), ⅛ in. = 1 ft., 030.I.A.700.1
127 First floor: plan, April 22, 1968, graphite pencil on sketch paper, 45 ¾ × 35 ¼ in. (116 × 89.5 cm), ⅛ in. = 1 ft., 030.I.C.700.010
128 Parti, March 7, 1968, Louis Kahn, charcoal on sketch paper, 22 × 18 in. (56 × 45.5 cm), 030.I.A.700.2
129 Chapel, school: elevations, Spring 1968, Louis Kahn, charcoal on sketch paper, 22 ¼ × 11 ¾ in. (56.5 × 30 cm), 030.I.A.700.4
130 Chapel: roof study, Spring 1968, Louis Kahn, charcoal on sketch paper, 31 × 17 ½ in. (79 × 44.5 cm), 030.I.A.700.2
131 Chapel: roof study, Spring 1968, Louis Kahn, charcoal on sketch paper, 20 × 11 ¾ in. (51 × 30 cm), 030.I.A.700.2
132 Chapel, school: roof study, Spring 1968, Louis Kahn, charcoal on sketch paper, 25 ½ × 11 ¾ in. (65 × 30 cm), 030.I.A.700.2
133 Chapel: section, Spring 1968, negro pencil on sketch paper, 17 ¾ × 14 ½ in. (45 × 37 cm), 1/16 in. = 1 ft., 030.I.C.700.007
134 Chapel, refectory: section, Spring 1968, graphite pencil on sketch paper, 28 ¼ × 11 ¾ in. (72 × 30 cm), ⅛ in. = 1 ft., 030.I.C.700.007
135 West elevation, April 22, 1968, graphite pencil on sketch paper, 32 ½ × 23 ½ in. (82.5 × 60 cm), 1/16 in. = 1 ft., 030.I.C.700.010
136 East elevation, April 22, 1968, graphite pencil on sketch paper, 30 × 23 ¾ in. (79 × 60.5 cm), 1/16 in. = 1 ft., 030.I.C.700.010
137 Section looking west, April 22, 1968, graphite pencil on sketch paper, 30 ½ × 18 in. (77.5 × 45.5 cm), 1/16 in. = 1 ft., 030.I.C.700.010
138 Section looking south, April 22, 1968, graphite pencil on sketch paper, 37 × 24 in. (94 × 61 cm), 1/16 in. = 1 ft., 030.I.C.700.010
139 Plan footprint, Spring 1968, Louis Kahn, charcoal on sketch paper, 29 × 23 ½ in. (74 × 60 cm), 1/16 in. = 1 ft., 030.I.A.700.1
140 Plan with site, Spring 1968, sepia diazo print, 13 × 11 in. (33 × 28 cm), 030.I.C.700.12
141 Plan with site, April 17, 1968, graphite pencil on sketch paper, 35 ½ × 23 ½ in. (90 × 59.5 cm), 1/16 in. = 1 ft., 030.I.C.700.001
142 Plan with overlay, May 20, 1968, diazo print/sepia diazo print, 21 × 15 in. (53 × 38 cm), 1/16 in. = 1 ft., 030.I.C.700.002
143 Plan with overlay, May 1968, graphite pencil on sketch paper/sepia diazo print, 22 ½ × 20 ½ in. (57 × 52 cm), 1/16 in. = 1 ft., 030.I.C.700.002
144 Chapel: plan, section, Spring 1968*, graphite pencil on sketch paper, 11 ¾ × 11 ½ in. (30 × 29 cm), 1/16 in. = 1 ft., 030.I.C.700.009
145 Chapel: study, Spring 1968, Louis Kahn, charcoal on sketch paper, 27 ½ × 11 ¾ in. (70 × 30 cm), 1/16 in. = 1 ft., 030.I.A.700.2
146 Refectory: plan, section, roof, Spring 1968, graphite and color pencil on sketch paper, 18 ¾ × 11 ¾ in. (47.5 × 30 cm), 1/16 in. = 1 ft., 030.I.C.700.007
147 Refectory, chapel: plan, Spring 1968, graphite pencil on sketch paper, 15 × 11 ¾ in. (38 × 30 cm), 1/16 in. = 1 ft., 030I.C.700.007
148 First floor: plan, May 20, 1968, graphite pencil on sketch paper, 31 × 23 ½ in. (79 × 59.5 cm), 1/16 in. = 1 ft., 030.I.C.700.010
149 Second floor: plan, May 20, 1968, graphite pencil on sketch paper, 32 ¾ × 23 ½ in. (83 × 59.5 cm), 1/16 in. = 1 ft., 030.I.C.700.010
150 Third floor: plan, May 20, 1968, graphite pencil on sketch paper, 34 × 23 ½ in. (86 × 59.5 cm), 1/16 in. = 1 ft., 030.I.C.700.010
151 Roof: plan, May 20, 1968, graphite pencil on sketch paper, 34 × 23 ½ in. (86 × 59.5 cm), 1/16 in. = 1 ft., 030.I.C.700.010
152 Site plan, Spring 1968, graphite pencil on sketch paper, 31 × 23 ¾ in. (79 × 60.5 cm), 1 in. = 50 ft., 030.I.C.700.010
153 First floor: plan, June 17, 1968, graphite pencil on sketch paper, 27 ¼ × 18 in. (69 × 45.5 cm), 1/16 in. = 1 ft., 030.I.C.700.001
154 First floor: plan, July 10, 1968, graphite pencil on sketch paper, 29 ½ × 24 in. (75 × 61 cm), 1/16 in. = 1 ft., 030.I.C.700.001
155 Second floor: plan, July 10, 1968, graphite pencil on sketch paper, 31 × 18 in. (79 × 45.5 cm), 1/16 in. = 1 ft., 030.I.C.700.001
156 Section through chapel, Summer 1968, graphite pencil on sketch paper, 18 × 13 ½ in. (44.5 × 34 cm), 1/16 in. = 1 ft., 030.I.C.700.007
157 Section looking north, Summer 1968, graphite pencil on sketch paper, 18 × 11 ½ in. (45.5 × 29 cm), 1/16 in. = 1 ft., 030.I.C.700.007
158 Section looking south, Summer 1968, graphite pencil on sketch paper, 30 ½ × 11 ¾ in. (77.5 × 30 cm), 1/16 in. = 1 ft., 030.I.C.700.007
159 West elevation, Spring/Summer 1968, graphite pencil on sketch paper, 23 ½ × 18 in. (60 × 45.5 cm), 1/16 in. = 1 ft., 030.I.C.700.010
160 East elevation, Spring/Summer 1968, graphite pencil on sketch paper, 26 ½ × 18 in. (67 × 45.5 cm), 1/16 in.1 ft., 030.I.C.700.010
161 Entry tower: section, Summer 1968, graphite pencil on sketch paper, 18 × 8 in. (44.5 × 20.5 cm), 1/16 in. = 1 ft., 030.I.C.700.010
162 Entry tower: section, Summer 1968, graphite pencil on sketch paper, 21 × 11 ¾ in. (53.5 × 30 cm), 1/16 in. = 1 ft., 030.I.C.700.010
163 Plan variation, August 1968, sketch paper/sepia diazo print, 25 ½ × 19 ¼ in. (65 × 49 cm), 1/16 in. = 1 ft., 030.I.C.700.002
164 First floor: plan, August 5, 1968, graphite pencil on sketch paper, 26 ¾ × 18 in. (68 × 45.5 cm), 1/16 in. = 1 ft., 030.I.C.700.001
165 Second floor: plan, August 5, 1968, graphite pencil on sketch paper, 27 × 18 in. (68.5 × 45.5 cm), 1/16 in. = 1 ft., 030.I.C.700.001
166 Third floor: plan, August 5, 1968, graphite pencil on sketch paper, 27 × 18 in. (68.5 × 45.5 cm), 1/16 in. = 1 ft., 030.I.C.700.001
167 Basement: plan, August 5, 1968, graphite pencil on sketch paper, 28 × 24 in. (71 × 61 cm), 1/16 in. = 1 ft., 030.I.C.700.001
168–71 Cost estimate, August 13, 1968, typewritten, Box LIK 10
172 Cost estimate, August 13, 1968, Bill Gennetti, handwritten, Box LIK 10
173 Core: section, August 5, 1968, graphite pencil on sketch paper, 20 × 18 in (51 × 45.59, 1/16 in. = 1 ft., 030.I.C.700.001
174 Core: section, August 5, 1968, graphite pencil on sketch paper, 21 ¼ × 13 ½ in. (54 × 34.5 cm), 1/16 in. = 1 ft., 030.I.C.700.001
175 Cells: partial elevation, Summer 1968, graphite pencil on sketch paper, 24 ½ × 11 ½ in. (62 × 29 cm), ⅛ in. = 1 ft., 030.I.C.700.010
176 Core: section, August 5, 1968, graphite pencil on sketch paper, 27 ½ × 18 ¾ in. (70 × 47.5 cm), 1/16 in. = 1 ft., 030.I.C.700.001
177 Tower: wall detail, August 1968, graphite pencil on sketch paper, 18 ¾ × 18 ¾ in. (47.5 × 47.5 cm), ¼ in. = 1 ft., 030.I.C.700.007
178 West elevation, August 5, 1968, graphite pencil on sketch paper, 21 ¾ × 11 ¾ in. (53.5 × 30 cm), 1/16 in. = 1 ft., 030.I.C.700.001
179 South elevation, August 5, 1968, graphite pencil on sketch paper, 27 ½ × 11 ¾ in. (70 × 30 cm), 1/16 in. = 1 ft., 030.I.C.700.001
180 East elevation, August 5, 1968, graphite pencil on sketch paper, 27 ½ × 11 ¾ in. (70 × 30 cm), 1/16 in. = 1 ft., 030.I.C.700.001
181 Wall section, Summer/Fall 1968, graphite pencil on sketch paper, 17 × 11 ¾ in. (43 × 30 cm), ½ in. = 1 ft., 030.I.C.700.007
182 Small cell: section, October 23, 1968, graphite pencil on sketch paper, 24 × 18 ½ in. (61 × 46.5 cm), ½ in. = 1 ft., 030.I.C.700.001
183 Small cell: plan, October 23, 1968, graphite pencil on sketch paper, 27 ½ × 11 ¾ in. (70 × 30 cm), ½ in. = 1 ft., 030.I.C.700.001
184 Large cell: section, October 23, 1968, graphite pencil on sketch paper, 24 × 18 ½ in. (61 × 46.5 cm), ½ in. = 1 ft., 030.I.C.700.001
185 Large cell: plan, October 23, 1968, graphite pencil on sketch paper, 20 ¼ × 18 ½ in. (51.5 × 46.5 cm), ½ in. = 1 ft., 030.I.C.700.001
186 Cell: section, Summer/Fall 1968, graphite and color pencil on sketch paper, 26 × 17 ¼ in. (66 × 44 cm), ½ in. = 1 ft., 030.I.C.700.007
187 Cells: horizontal sections, Summer/Fall 1968, graphite pencil on sketch paper, 18 × 11 ¾ in. (45.5 × 30 cm), ¼ in. = 1 ft., 030.I.C.700.007
188 Cell: elevation, section, Summer/Fall 1968, graphite pencil on sketch paper, 21 × 17 in. (53.5 × 43 cm), ¼ in. = 1 ft., 030.I.C.700.007
189 Cell: elevation, Summer/Fall 1968, graphite pencil on sketch paper, 24 ½ × 11 ¾ in. (62 × 30 cm), ¼ in. = 1 ft., 030.I.C.700.007
190 Chapel: section, Summer/Fall 1968, graphite pencil on sketch paper, 25 ½ × 18 ½ in. (65 × 46.5 cm), ⅛ in. = 1 ft., 030.I.C.700.007
191 Core buildings: wall details, Summer/Fall 1968, graphite pencil on sketch paper, 30 × 11 ¾ in. (76 × 30 cm), ¼ in. = 1 ft., 030.I.C.700.007
192 Core buildings: wall details, Summer/Fall 1968, graphite pencil on sketch paper, 28 ¼ × 11 ¾ in. (72 × 30 cm), various scales, 030.I.C.700.007
193 Core buildings: wall details, Summer/Fall 1968, graphite pencil on sketch paper, 26 ¾ × 24 in. (68 × 61 cm), various scales, 030.I.C.700.007
194 School/auditorium: section, Summer/Fall 1968, sepia diazo print, 22 ½ × 18 ½ in. (57 × 46.5 cm), ¼ in. = 1 ft., 030.I.C.700.005
195 School/auditorium: elevation, Summer/Fall 1968, graphite pencil on sketch paper, 24 × 18 ¾ in. (61 × 47.5 cm), ¼ in. = 1 ft., 030.I.C.700.007
196 Core buildings: elevation, Fall/Winter 1968, graphite pencil on vellum, 36 × 16 ½ (91.5 × 42 cm), 1/33 in. = 1 ft., 030.I.C.700.008
197 First floor: plan, Summer/Fall 1968, graphite pencil on vellum, 41 × 30 in. (104 × 76 cm), 1/16 in. = 1 ft., 030.I.C.700.008
198–99 Meeting notes, November 12, 1968, graphite pencil on paper, 8 ¾ × 11 (22 × 28 cm), Box LIK 10
200 Entry tower: floor plans, October 5, 1968, graphite pencil on vellum, 36 × 25 ½ in. (91.5 × 65 cm), 1/16 in. = 1 ft., 030.I.C.700.001
201 Chapel: plan, elevation, Fall/Winter 1968, graphite pencil on vellum, 24 × 18 in. (61 × 45.5 cm), ⅛ in. = 1 ft., 030.I.C.700.008
202–3 Meeting notes (Dominican Motherhouse), March 10, 1969, typewritten, Archive DMH
204 Letter from Mother Mary Bernadette to Louis Kahn, March 18, 1969, Box LIK 10
Back cover Louis I. Kahn in his office, undated, Kahn Collection (photo: George Pohl)

ACKNOWLEDGMENTS

Lou Kahn knew that "Nobody ever paid for the price of a book. They paid for the printing." This book was paid for with many forms of help given by many others. Not all of them can be listed here, nor are those mentioned responsible for any errors, omissions, or exaggerations, for which I alone am responsible. My warmest thanks go to:

In Philadelphia and the U.S.:
Bill Whitaker, Collections Manger of the University of Pennsylvania's Architectural Archives, for his generous support, good advice, and for being such an excellent and good-humored source on all things Kahn;
Nancy Thorne, for her great patience and beyond-the-call-of-duty help with my research;
Julia Moore Converse, former Director of Penn's Architectural Archives, for organizing such a wonderful place of research;
Harriet Pattison, for a long and memorable discussion on Kahn and landscape;
Amy Brown Polk for her kind hospitality during my meeting with her late husband David Polk;
Sister Mary Irene Lolli, O.P., and Sister Eileen Patricia Primrose, O.P., of the Dominican Motherhouse of St. Catherine De Ricci for opening their archive and sharing their experiences of working with Louis Kahn;
Michael J. Lewis for his repeated support and his kind appraisal of the rough text;
David van Zanten for sharing an excellent lecture on "Kahn and Composition" and for supplying me with the quote from Piet Mondrian that eventually became this book's title;
The many others who took their time to discuss this project with me, among them David DeLong, David B. Brownlee, Duncan Buell, and Jim Kise;
Carolyn Kelly of the Graham Foundation for helping me to get the most out of a generous grant;
Those who have backed up their enthusiasm for Louis Kahn's work and for this project with other forms of generous support: Nathanial Kahn, Larry Korman, Moshe Safdie, and Steven Holl.

In Karlsruhe:
Walter Nägeli, chairman of the Institute for Architectural Design, where I have taught for the past years, for his support and for the culture of critical inquiry and exploration within which this book—and the dissertation that preceded it—grew;
Dr. Hans J. Böker, for his expertise and advice on that dissertation;
All of my colleagues at our institute, for sharing in the adventure of this project, contributing to the discourse around it, and for taking up the slack created by my own involvement;
Especially to Gudrun Wiedemer, who in spite of her own workload, always took time for serious evaluation and encouragement;
Susanne Elisabeth Berger and Karin Bierlich for their skill and assistance with drawings and diagrams;
Werner Sewing, for helping out in a pinch;
Steffie Gawlik, for her generous support when it was needed;
Walter Kohne, for being a long-term sounding board on this subject and others around it;
The many students of my seminars who, with their own explorations helped sharpen my eyes and deepen my understanding of Kahn's work.

In Switzerland and Barcelona:
Lars Müller, for his enthusiasm, skill and commitment. With his eye for both the small detail and the big picture, I cannot imagine a better partner for this project;
Ellen Mey, for guiding this project surely forward from first contact to bound book;
Martina Mullis, for her skill and patience in laying out this book and its partner publication;
Jonathan Fox, for his sure hand and unerring eye in editing the text.

At Home:
Most of all, my thanks go to my partner Helena Hörig, for all of the patient and loving support which made this project possible.

This Publication was made possible with the generous support of the following organizations and persons:

The Graham Foundation for Advanced Studies in the Fine Arts

Deutsche Forschungsgemeinschaft (DFG)/German Research Foundation

Fachgebiet für Bauplanung und Entwerfen, Karlsruher Institut für Technologie/Institute for Architectural Design, Art and Theory, Karlsruhe Institute of Technology

Fakultät für Architektur, Karlsruher Institut für Technologie/Faculty of Architecture, Karlsruhe Institute of Technology

Karlsruher Universitätsgesellschaft

Larry Korman

Moshe Safdie

Steven Holl

Michael Merrill
LOUIS KAHN
DRAWING TO FIND OUT
The Dominican Motherhouse
and the Patient Search for Architecture

Design: Integral Lars Müller/Lars Müller and Martina Mullis
Copyediting: Jonathan Fox
Lithography: connova GmbH, Appenweier, Germany
Paper: Tatami white, 150 g/m², 1.3
Printing and Binding: Kösel, Altusried-Krugzell, Germany

Lars Müller Publishers
Baden, Switzerland
www.lars-muller-publishers.com

ISBN 978-3-03778-221-7

Printed in Germany

9 8 7 6 5 4 3 2 1

This book corresponds with the companion publication *Louis Kahn: On the Thoughtful Making of Spaces* (Lars Müller Publishers, 2010, ISBN 978-3-03778-220-0).

The research for both books originated with the doctoral dissertation "Louis Kahn and the Dominican Motherhouse: Problems of Space" (Universität Karlsruhe, 2008).